SMALL FIRMS
AND
LOCAL ECONOMIC NETWORKS

SMALL FIRMS
AND
LOCAL ECONOMIC NETWORKS:
THE DEATH OF THE LOCAL
ECONOMY?

James Curran
and
Robert Blackburn

P·C·P
Paul Chapman
Publishing Ltd

Copyright © 1994 J. Curran & R. A. Blackburn

Paul Chapman Publishing Ltd
144 Liverpool Road
London
N1 1LA

British Library Cataloguing in Publication Data

Curran, J.
  Small Firms and Local Economic Networks
  I. Title   II. Blackburn, Robert A.
  658.02

  ISBN 1 85396 209 0

Typeset by Dorwyn Ltd, Rowlands Castle, Hants
Printed and bound by
Athenaeum Press, Newcastle upon Tyne.

A B C D E F G H   9 8 7 6 5 4

James Curran is Midland Bank Professor and Director of the Small Business Research Centre at Kingston University. He is an internationally known, long-established researcher who has written extensively on a wide variety of aspects of the small business. From 1989–1992 he was Director of the Centre for Research on Small Service Sector Enterprises set up by the Economic and Social Research Council as part of its Small Business Research Initiative.

Robert A. Blackburn is Midland Bank Research Fellow and Senior Lecturer in Human Resource Management at Kingston University. He has been involved in a range of research on small businesses including their employment practices, the future of small-scale enterprise, ethnic businesses and a study of small service sector businesses. He has published extensively in the area and with James Curran was co-editor of *Paths of Enterprise: The Future of the Small Business* (Routledge, 1991).

CONTENTS

LIST OF FIGURES

LIST OF TABLES

PREFACE

Interest in the small enterprise and its role in the UK economy has increased enormously during the last 15 years. This increased attention reflects the recognition among politicians and academics that small-scale economic activities have had a remarkable resurgence since the 1960s. Over 10% of those in employment now work for themselves, mainly in one- or two-person enterprises. By 1991, businesses with less than 20 employees were responsible for over one-third of employment in the non-government sector: in 1979 this proportion was only just over 25%. Even in the 1989–1991 period, when recession was rapidly deepening, small businesses contributed disproportionately to the number of new jobs created, outperforming larger businesses and showing great resilience in coping with the difficult economic conditions.

The close links between the small firm and the local economy have often been stressed. The corner shop serving the needs of local consumers and the small engineering firm supplying parts and services to other local businesses – including large businesses – have been seen as typifying the involvement of small businesses in the local economy and community. Given the expansion in the numbers of small businesses in the 1980s, particularly in newer areas of the economy, and the other changes which have occurred in Britain's economy and local communities, the links between small businesses and local economies deserve a fresh look to assess how close these links remain.

The research upon which this book is based was also concerned with a wider range of issues including the connections between small and large businesses. Much of the previous research on this took the links between businesses, small and large, and their relations within local economies for granted or was unsystematic in the way it addressed these issues. Whatever the results of previous research, however, this also needed to be examined again if only to assess the results of the unprecedented changes which have produced the UK economy of the 1990s. These include the massive shift away from manufacturing to services, the radical changes in the management strategies of large firms which began in the 1980s such as the rationalisation of supplier chains, and the shift of focus to a concern with wider European Community and global markets.

As our title suggests, our findings lead us to argue that the links between small businesses and local economies are weakening and, indeed, that the idea of 'the local economy' itself may be losing salience as a useful way of conceptualising economic activities and the connections between economic and non-economic local activities. Similarly, the relations between small and large firms appear now not only to be less close geographically than many previous views have implied but may well be growing more distant. In turn, these findings have important implications for other issues such as policies for local economic regeneration and training.

The research for the book consisted of two main projects supported by different sponsors. We would like to acknowledge first of all the very generous support provided by the Midland Bank for one of the projects. This support was part of a larger, long-term programme of support by the bank of the work of the Small Business Research Centre at Kingston University. Since 1987 this support has enabled the centre to undertake research on topics as diverse as school students' attitudes to enterprise to assessing the effectiveness of soft loans as a way of reducing the 'finance gap' thought to inhibit the development of the small business in the UK. The particular project upon which this book draws investigated the links between small and large businesses in local economies.

The second project consisted of a set of studies supported by the Economic and Social Research Council and other sponsors as part of the council's major research initiative on the small business between 1989 and 1992. In addition to the council's own funding, the project also benefited from financial support provided by Barclays Bank, the Commission of the European Communities (DGXXIII), the Department of Employment and the Rural Development Commission. Naturally, the views expressed in the book do not necessarily reflect those of any of the sponsors.

The research projects involved a large number of other researchers and we would particularly like to mention: Brian Abbott, Sharon Black, Susan Gleave, Robin Jarvis, John Kitching, Valerie Mills, Louise Roberts-Reid, Gay Swirles and Adrian Woods. We would also like to acknowledge the contribution of Valerie Alsop to the preparation of the manuscript of the book. In addition, other members of the Centre's research staff, involved in other projects, have also contributed through their suggestions and help in tracking down source materials.

Neither project would have been possible without the generous participation of the 426 owner-managers and large organisation representatives who took part in face-to-face and later telephone interviews and the 175 employees of the small firms who were also interviewed face to face. Their willingness to answer questions, supply additional information and, in many instances, to allow the researchers to re-interview them a second, third, fourth and even fifth time, was more than we had any right to expect. Representatives of local authority planning and economic development units, chambers of commerce, enterprise agencies and TECs also gave us a great deal of information and help in understanding their roles and the changes in their localities. We are very grateful to all of these for their generosity in giving their time to the research.

James Curran and Robert A. Blackburn
Kingston University
March 1994

LOCAL ECONOMIES, LOCALITIES AND SMALL FIRMS

INTRODUCTION

The link between the small business and locality is embedded deeply in conventional views of both small-scale enterprise and, to a lesser extent, local economies. Depictions of the markets served by small businesses often stress their local character. While there are references to small firms with national, even international, markets for their products or services (Storey and Johnson, 1987:152–153), the emphasis is more commonly on small firms serving local markets and communities.

In fact, not a great deal is known about the character, size and shape of the markets served by small firms. For some types of business such as the corner shop the market is probably a limited geographical area, a few streets for those walking or a few minutes in a car (Kirby, 1986). But small businesses are present in almost every kind of economic activity and any notion that their markets are always 'local' in the corner shop sense is clearly untenable. Equally, given the heterogeneity of small-scale enterprise, generalisations about small businesses and their markets are difficult to substantiate except at a superficial level.

Nor is the notion of the 'local economy' itself very clearly understood. In analytical terms, it is not difficult to take some geographical area, for example, a 'travel-to-work area' or 'local labour market area' drawn from official statistics of one kind or another, and designate this a 'local economy'. Yet the extent to which businesses located within the boundaries of a 'local economy' defined in this way form some integrated set of economic activities is clearly an open question. 'Local economies', however defined, will have links, direct or indirect, material or cognitive, with a wider economy, regional or national or even international. To what extent do such links undermine (or conceivably reinforce) levels of economic integration within the designated geographical boundaries taken to constitute the 'local economy'? Moreover, the rapidity and depth of change of the economic structure in the last decade has rendered much previous analysis mere historical accounts. What are the trends over time: for instance, is what has been described as the 'globalisation of the economy' (Porter, 1990) robbing 'local economies' in the above sense of their significance as relevant units of analysis? Or to what extent is globalisation being achieved through localisation?

Economic activities are only part of the wider, social relations in which people engage. Typically, in the discussion of the small firm and local economic activities, the economic is over-emphasised at the expense of the social, the political and the non-economic generally. But economic relations in any geographically demarcated area comprise only one dimension of the relations which influence economic activities. In other words, non-economic social relations, from local sports clubs to local political party activities to religious groups, are also aspects of 'the local economy' in the sense that they offer potential vehicles for economic linkages. Economic activities, in their turn, may help promote and sustain non-economic activities. Large firms' social clubs, for instance, have often been much more than simply meeting places for their employees.

One notion sometimes used to integrate economic and non-economic activities in a locality is 'community'. Although difficult to define, broadly the idea frequently appears to refer to a geographical territory with associated social relations and culture within which a majority of the population experiences its main everyday social and economic relations.[1] The cultural dimension is developed sufficiently in a 'community' for its economic, social and political aspects to cohere into a focus of self-identification for those involved. They are willing to describe themselves as members of this 'community', signified by statements about 'belonging to' or being 'from Barnsley' or the like.

The phrase 'the local economic community' is sometimes used interchangeably with the 'local economy' but it might also be taken as hinting more or less explicitly at the idea of an economy comprising more than simply economic functions in a narrow sense. That is, it recognises that economic activities entail other kinds of non-economic activities which, in turn, influence, support and constrain the economic. For example, Bennett and McCoshan (1993:Ch. 9) discuss the importance of local networks as a means of strengthening the economic base of an area. However vague all these ideas are, they have links with the ways in which people make sense of social and economic experiences with others, otherwise they would not be so widely or commonly used in everyday discourse.

What is profoundly unsatisfactory about the above is the lack of clarity, the lack of rigour and, most importantly, the lack of well-founded data and analysis to support the assumptions about small firms and local economies, however the latter is defined. One suspicion is that much of this thinking and its persistence is linked to idealisations of localities and communities. This is shown in idealisations of rural living particularly among the urban middle class. This is echoed in many urban areas where the same people refer to their part of London or other heavily urbanised area, as 'the village' seeking apparently to create some parallel with a romanticised view of rural life. Interestingly, such idealisations give little attention to the ways in which 'the village' is sustained economically. In fact, current economic realities are often dismissed as barriers to the realisation of the social and community values of their ideal.

In this book, the initial concerns are to reconceptualise the 'local economy' and the role of small firms in such economies. Current debates on the significance of local economic activities and small firms, together with evidence offered by other researchers, are examined critically against data from an extensive study of small businesses in a range of localities collected since 1990. The result is an assessment of the links between small firms and local economies which has considerable implications for the overall view of the role of local economies and communities in Britain.

SMALL BUSINESSES, LOCAL ECONOMIES AND CONTEMPORARY DEBATES

A major reason why it is particularly apposite now to discuss relations between small firms and local economies and communities is the emergence of a powerful thesis and major debate centred precisely on these issues.[2] A convenient label for the above is the *industrial district thesis* which, in turn, is an important element in a wider debate on the extent and character of economic restructuring evident in advanced industrial societies, including Britain. One more general label offered for the new organisational-economic order is the Post-Fordist economy (Murray, 1989). Another, using the name of a widely cited concrete example is the Benetton economy (Murray, 1985). While the theorising on economic restructuring is now complex, one element which emerges prominently is the central role given to small firms (Curran, 1991). In the industrial district thesis, this role is especially central.[3]

The industrial district thesis may be summarised in a number of ways since there are several versions (Brusco, 1982; Piore and Sabel, 1984; Goodman et al., 1989; Hirst and Zeitlin, 1989; Pyke, Becattini and Sengenberger, 1990; Pyke, 1992). Essentially, the thesis argues that a major component of the wider radical economic restructuring occurring in Western Europe, North America, and Japan, as well as in several of the newly developing economies, is the emergence of powerful economic networks of mainly small enterprises spatially concentrated in specific geographical areas. The most famous of these 'industrial districts', in terms of the attention it has received, is in North Eastern Italy, the Emilia-Romagna district (Piore and Sabel, 1984; Pyke, Becattini and Sengenberger, 1990). Others have extended the notion to encompass 'districts' as far apart as Silicon Valley in California in the United States and Sakaki in Japan (Friedman, 1988).

One of the most recent and clearest ideal typical formulations of the industrial district is offered by Pyke (1992). He describes it as an:

industrial system . . . composed of (generally) independent small firms, organised on a local or regional basis, belonging to the same industrial sector (including all upstream and downstream activities), the individual firms tending to specialise in a particular production phase, organised together, and with local institutions, through relationships of both competition and co-operation.

(Pyke, 1992:2)

Each small firm tends to specialise in one or two stages of the production process. Firms often co-operate with each other sharing technical knowledge, tools and even personnel. They demonstrate the often remarked upon advantage of small firms, namely flexibility in response to the market, both by having highly responsive, highly entrepreneurial owner-managers and by adopting computer aided design (CAD) and computer-based flexible production systems. This networking and technological flexibility is perfectly in tune with recent developments in national and world markets, which have become fragmented and rapidly changing. Both undermine the advantages large-scale mass production firms previously enjoyed in the 1950s and 1960s in the so-called 'Fordist' economies of advanced industrial societies.

Co-operation and vigorous competition co-exist in the industrial district. Brusco (1992) delineates this as co-operation between firms up and down the production chain and competition between firms producing the same product or at the same point in the production chain. Other firms in the network may act as brokers, that is, perform tasks that ensure the smooth functioning of the network as a whole. Among the most important tasks are those associated with marketing, which enables the industrial district to be integrated effectively into the wider economy. In the ideal typical case, this integration is not just into the national economy but the global economy.

What is especially important to note about this conceptualisation is the implied linking of the economic and the non-economic. The latter has been brought out explicitly by others writing about industrial districts (eg Becattini, 1989). Here the emphasis has been on the key role played by the social and political infrastructures of the district. These are long established, close knit communities cemented together by strongly developed, stable common value systems. They promote economic co-operation and trust by embedding economic relations in a wider web of spatial relations, which clearly define and sanction acceptable and unacceptable forms of economic behaviour. In short, these produce a local economic community with high levels of trust. As others have pointed out (eg Batstone, 1991) *trust* is critical to maintaining high levels of ordered, stable economic relations especially where the economic units involved are small. Batstone goes so far as to label this 'social capital' as on a par with the more emphasised physical capital of classical economics.

Among the non-economic elements in the social and cultural infrastructure in Pyke's (1992) ideal type are local political parties, religion and a stable population linked through an intricate and extensive kinship order. In addition, other neo-economic structures are also powerful reinforcing elements which, in other circumstances and economic settings, would play a different, less integrative role. For instance, trade unions and small firm employers' associations do not simply represent members' interests in an antagonistic labour versus capital way, but are co-ordinating bodies between members and small firms. For example, employers' associations can act as important information gatherers and disseminators as well as provide collective services such as export market research and bulk purchasing for members. Trade unions can help create a smoothly functioning labour market where the majority of employers are small. For example, they can take on, or significantly participate in, the provision of employee training where small employers find this difficult because of their size.[4]

What is also crucial about the industrial district thesis is the way in which it is integral to debates on economic restructuring more generally. Proponents make a link between industrial districts and the newly emerging cross-national or world economy. The districts are seen as ways in which industrial societies can restructure and revitalise their economies (Hirst and Zeitlin, 1989). In place of the large old-style, vertically integrated businesses that are slow to respond to change and unresponsive to rapidly changing world markets, industrial districts emerge composed of networks of mainly small producers operating within a support infrastructure of social and political institutions. They can collectively realise the economies of scale and scope needed to cope effectively with rapidly changing international markets (Pyke, 1992:2–4).

INDUSTRIAL DISTRICTS AND BRITAIN

Leaving aside the burgeoning debate on the validity of the industrial district thesis as applied to its supposed geographical place of genesis (see eg Amin and Robins, 1990) to what extent can the ideal type be applied to Britain? How far do small firms and local economies approximate to the ideal type of Pyke (1992) and what is the likelihood of the survival or emergence of such districts in Britain's restructuring economy? More generally, how helpful is the thesis in clarifying some of the conceptual problems introduced earlier on the character of 'local economies' and 'communities' and the role of small firms?

Approximations to the industrial district have been common in Britain in the past. The key elements of this genre of production activities are pools of common factors of production which can collectively provide external economies of scale and encourage managers to put work out to suppliers rather than keep it in-house. In other words, the division of labour is at the level of the firm rather than at the level of separate functions within the firm. One of the best known examples was the Sheffield cutlery trade whose heyday passed earlier in the century (Marshall, 1932; 1987). Others included the

Black Country 'metal bashing' district on the edge of Birmingham (itself, an 'industrial district' by the 19th century) which in some ways incorporated the Black Country (Marshall, 1987; Massey et al., 1992:16). Other approximations of industrial districts were textile machinery manufacturing firms centred on Rochdale (Penn, 1992)[5] and textile related activities in the rest of Lancashire and the North West, and in Yorkshire (Marshall, 1987; Lazonick, 1981).

The decline of the Sheffield cutlery trade has been well documented as has the Black Country small firm engineering district (Marshall, 1987) and the Lancashire cotton industry (Lazonick, 1981). Penn (1992:223–225) concludes his recent examination of the Rochdale textile machine manufacturing 'industrial district' by arguing that while there remained inter-firm relations, there had been a 'progressive uncoupling of the constituent parts' of previous inter-firm networks (Penn, 1992:22). There remain large manufacturing firms who use local subcontractors but mainly only as a last resort. Inter-firm relations are determined by external market relations not informal or formal networks of inter-firm relations. In short, the local economy shows less and less resemblance to an 'industrial district'.

NEW INDUSTRIAL DISTRICTS IN THE UK

Some would argue that new industrial districts have emerged recently, anchored in the new economic sectors of the late 20th century and based heavily on small firms. For example, the so-called 'Cambridge Phenomenon' of high tech firms, many of which are small, is often regarded as an emerging 'high tech' industrial district. It is compared sometimes to Silicon Valley in California, also described as a high tech 'industrial district' (Saxenian, 1985; 1990).

The growth of high tech manufacturing and software firms in the Cambridge area from the early 1970s is well established (Keeble and Wever, 1986; Segal Quince and Partners, 1985; Oakey, 1984; Oakey, 1991). It has also been argued that this growth has led to inter-firm links or 'strategic alliances' (Cooke, 1988; Dickson et al., 1994) culminating in the region/locality becoming a major innovation area (Aydalot and Keeble, 1988).

Others, however, have cast doubt on the extent of inter-firm links in the Cambridge high tech area and especially on their character. For instance, it has been argued that many inter-firm relations are with businesses outside the locality, either elsewhere in the UK (Segal Quince and Partners, 1985) or outside the UK, especially as a result of ownership patterns (Oakey et al., 1988). The trend in Cambridge high tech firms has been for an increasing proportion of businesses to be either subsidiaries or branches of businesses whose headquarters are outside the UK (Segal Quince and Partners, 1985:565). In other words, the intensity of inter-firm relations is much lower than the ideal type industrial district suggests is needed. These linkages with the wider economy, especially the global economy, rob the locality of any ability to have much of an independent impact or to be a positive economic force beyond its geographical boundaries:

> The Cambridge area has moved from being a sleepy backwater (in investment terms) which participated hardly at all in previous major eras of manufacturing accumulation to being one of the key links (perhaps *the* key link) from the UK economy into the current era. Yet it is a second-rung link
>
> (Massey et al., 1992:183, emphasis in the original)[6]

For a high tech 'industrial district' to be accepted as existing anywhere, more is required than simply an examination of the numbers of firms and inter-firm relations in the locality. As Pyke's (1992) ideal type stresses, there are social, cultural and political dimensions to be considered. Yet, in the discussion of geographical concentrations of high tech small firms,[7] non-economic aspects are rarely mentioned. The extent of the 'embeddedness' of high tech firms in the Cambridge area, that is, the extent to which they are integrated into a social and normatively based micro-economy based on strong community institutions, including local government, is rarely examined. Without these non-economic elements, the required levels of co-operation, trust, common services such as training and labour market provisions, and politically driven local economic strategies cannot be achieved. But also, without these, the label 'industrial district' is not appropriate.[8]

Since the above issues are not often examined[9] it is difficult to be conclusive on whether high tech concentrations such as that located around Cambridge approximate to the ideal type industrial district. However, indirectly, the indications are that this is unlikely. The Cambridge concentration of high tech firms is often linked to the university's excellence in research. This provides a knowledge resource for many of the firms as well as some of the most skilled personnel employed. However, the university is a major international institution and this sits uncomfortably with the notion of strong, local integration. In fact, some accounts hint strongly at a division between the university on the one hand and the wider community and local government on the other hand in the formative period of local high tech small firm concentration (Massey et al., 1992:125–176).

Central to the emergence of new high tech industrial districts to replace those that have crumbled away as a result of economic decline, reconstruction and severe periodic recession, are professionally qualified people who are involved in high tech firms and their links with local communities. The people involved consist of high tech entrepreneurs (Lloyd, 1986), managers, a key group of graduate scientists and technologists, craft workers and semi- and unskilled workers.

Many of the people working, managing and starting high tech small firms and the key knowledge workers employed, such as the design and development engineers, research specialists and computing specialists, are unlikely to have close links with the local community. Many are mobile specialists willing to move from one firm to another, one region to another even one country to another, to further their careers (Malecki and Bradbury, 1992). While they may well find the Cambridge area pleasant in which to live and bring up their families, their integration into the community generally is unlikely to be deep. The chances of the firms and their workers becoming a part of close knit communities with common values are negligible.

The conclusion which might be drawn from this brief preliminary analysis is that the concept of 'industrial district' might be useful in examining historical instances of local concentrations of particular kinds of economic activities which flourished in the 19th century and the early decades of this century. Economic restructuring, community and social changes since the 1950s, however, seem to have brought about the demise of earlier examples in the UK. There may be new candidates for industrial district status growing out of the restructured economy and social order which has emerged in the last couple of decades. However, one of the most widely touted possible cases, the concentration of high tech small firms which has emerged around Cambridge, has been examined and the evidence, although incomplete, offers little support for a new high tech industrial district.[10]

More generally, the structural instabilities which have beset the UK economy since the early 1970s, the uneven integration into and impact of, the globalisation of economic activities on Britain and the social effects of two severe recessions, have not provided very fertile ground for the emergence of industrial districts. To these negative influences can be added massive urban redevelopment, population shifts from inner cities to the suburbs and smaller towns (Allen and Massey, 1988:186) and from urban to rural areas (Keeble et al., 1992:1). All these contribute to undermining existing community and social relations, the essential non-economic prerequisites for industrial districts.

An alternative recent argument suggests the industrial district as the basis for an economic revival strategy for Britain (see eg Hirst and Zeitlin, 1989). This sees the industrial district as a way of harnessing the dynamism of small firms and local economic strengths for Britain's economic future. It will be argued below that the case for industrial districts as a policy strategy is no more persuasive than those suggesting that the UK economy is producing them as a result of restructuring and technological change.

REGIONS AND LOCALITIES

One of the best and longest established developed specialisms in analysing the UK economy might be labelled 'regional studies'. In this multi-disciplinary arena, economists, geographers, sociologists and planners meet to analyse spatial variations in social and economic phenomena. This has traditionally been allied to policy formulation and evaluation as UK governments of all parties have long had policies for encouraging and shaping economic development in various parts of the UK since at least the 1930s. In the 1980s, the focus on regional economic activities and social patterns received renewed emphasis from those arguing that more attention should be given to spatial considerations in analysing contemporary Britain (see especially, Allen and Massey, 1988 and Massey and Allen, 1988).

The main analytical unit in this economic geography/policy approach is the 'region'. The conceptual basis of this as an analytical unit is difficult to trace and finding a suitable definition has been described as a 'nightmare' (Richardson, 1976:17). The practical basis of the notion in Britain stems from the interest in addressing the particularly severe slump in certain areas in the 1930s which was the prime concern of the Barlow Commission (Hall, 1992). These spatially uneven patterns of development metamorphosed into units for administrative convenience, particularly for central government, based on an amalgamation of counties. Since the drawing up of regional boundaries after World War Two, the collection of official statistics and much of the analysis by academics has been based on these definitions. What a 'region' refers to in relation to any notion of a local economy, however, is unclear. For example, the so-called standard regions including, for example, 'Northern England' or 'Wales' or the 'South East' are large geographical areas containing extensive variations in the levels and character of economic activities, the communities in which the population live and the patterns of symbolic identification that people develop about themselves and how they differ from people elsewhere in the UK.

Economic patterns in the region have changed considerably in recent decades, especially with the decline of manufacturing and the expansion of services (McDowell, 1989). This has been accompanied by a rapid expansion in the numbers of small businesses (Daly, 1990:559). But because so many of these newer activities are spatially non-specific, there is no particular reason for them to have any links to any locality within the region. *Some* services businesses may be lured by spatially specific attractions, for example, some may feel a need to be geographically proximate to the centre of government or to the higher educational/research institutions disproportionately found in the South East region. But these are not the kinds of links with the community and other businesses which produce a local economy in the conventional sense.[11]

The attachment of geographers and economists to the standard regions appears largely a matter of statistical convenience and a reluctance to address the underlying realities of substantive economic and social relations in contemporary Britain, that is, the actual relations in which people engage in pursuing economic and non-economic lives (Burrows and Curran, 1989). Official statistics, for instance, are produced for the standard regions on a wide variety of topics, ranging from official unemployment levels to Value Added Tax (VAT) registrations and deregistrations, to levels of earnings and expenditure. The temptation to number crunch this data to produce a large variety of 'regional analyses' sustains several journals and a steady flow of monographs and books.

Yet what such analyses can tell us about the UK economy and especially local economies in the substantive sense is limited. Clearly, they offer a broad brush comparison of different areas of the UK for the particular statistics considered with an additionally valuable time-series element added. They can also provoke discussions of issues which might not otherwise be so apparent, such as those under the heading of 'the North–South divide' (see eg, Martin, 1988; Martin and Tyler, 1992). The latter, however, as the discussion developed, also revealed the crudity of regional analyses. It was quickly pointed out that within several of the regions within the 'North' and the 'South', variations in levels of economic activities, income levels, the provision of public services etc were greater than the differences between the 'North' and 'South' aggregated (Champion and Green, 1987 and 1988; Savage, 1989:254).

The 'region' as a unit of analysis is also a prime focus of discussion of policy and policy-making. Debate and policies centred on the 'region' have been a major feature of UK economic strategies for well over half a century. The quantitative imbalances in economic activities, employment and infrastructural provision between regions has mainly been seen as a problem to be solved either by encouraging mobile resources such as labour to move from one region to another or by positive interventions, for example, in infrastructural provision and the promotion of economic activities in the so-called depressed regions (Hall, 1992; Martin and Tyler, 1992).

In the 1980s, the emphasis in regional policy shifted to supply-side policies and a contraction in the areas eligible for assistance.[12] For example, instead of encouraging labour to move from region to region, policy aimed to remove the rigidities of the labour market which prevented falls in labour costs in depressed regions (Bennett and McCoshan, 1993:Ch. 5). Enterprise, it was argued by government, should be encouraged through small-firm generation to raise levels of economic activity in all regions but especially in the depressed areas (Martin and Tyler, 1992:146–47). While a full assessment of this policy shift needs more time to permit the full impact to develop, present indications of success are not strong (Martin and Tyler, 1992:153–65).

The reasons for the difficulties in developing and implementing an effective set of regional policies are undoubtedly complex but one which can be suggested is that, by concentrating on 'region', an arbitrary geographical unit, they have failed to engage with economic relations, communities and change at the most appropriate level. The latter would be much closer to the ground level of substantive economic and social relations. The configurations of substantive relations are quite unrelated to the 'regions' in the conventional policy-makers' analyses.

INNER CITIES

There are, however, other approaches and units of analysis used by geographers and policy-makers, some of which might have claims to escape the limitations of regional analysis outlined above. One obvious example here comes from urban analyses. The 'inner city' and the 'new town' of the 1960s and the 1970s and their related policies, attracted considerable attention and government energy over the years. The new town developments are now largely historical. Government in the 1980s saw the new towns as having fulfilled their policy objectives and where the public presence remained, as in new town corporations, these were to be dissolved and their assets privatised wherever possible (Deakin and Edwards, 1993).

Inner cities and inner city policies, on the other hand, have remained very much in vogue. Attention to inner cities and urban issues generally was prompted by much the same stimulus as that which produced regional policies – economic and community decline (Moore, 1992). But the analysis devoted to inner cities has been much less narrowly economic than that devoted to the regions. For instance, the social consequences of economic decline in the form of political protest, levels of crime and housing provision with the effects on community integration, have all received considerable attention (eg Deakin and Edwards, 1993:Ch. 3). But in practice attention in policy terms concentrated on the analysis of the decline in manufacturing, the failure of the services sector to grow, the loss of labour (especially skilled labour) and growing unemployment among the remaining population.

Policies in the 1980s designed to solve inner city problems largely followed the supply-side emphasis of regional policies (Action for Cities, 1987) but with the difference of conceding that the market would need a powerful kick start. The latter was in the form of aid directed through Urban Development Corporations (UDCs), Urban Programmes, enterprise zones and other similar schemes involving grants and subsidies of one kind or another.[13] One characteristic that many of the schemes emphasised was small enterprise generation. The sums involved are difficult to estimate precisely. Moore (1992:126) suggests that government initiatives specific to inner cities were funded to about £900 million in 1990–1991 with other schemes which, though not inner city specific, still had a significant impact, adding about £400 million more.[14] Another estimate suggests a much higher expenditure on inner city schemes in 1988/89 from the three main participating departments: £1,130m from the Department of the Environment, £1,120m from the Department of Employment Group and £220m from the DTI (Deakin and Edwards, 1993:59, citing National Audit Office figures).

Given the complexities of the large number of initiatives, evaluation of their effectiveness is not easy, though attempts have been made both by independent researchers and on behalf of government departments (see eg, Audit Commission, 1989; Pickvance, 1990; Tym and Partners, 1984; P A Cambridge Economic Consultants, 1987). Most have concentrated on measuring aggregate economic effects, often employing very simple criteria such as the number of jobs created at what cost per job or, more generally, relatively simple accounting techniques adapted from private sector business practice. In other words, while the policies upon which initiatives were based often had stated social and community objectives, the assessment of their effectiveness generally reverted to the kinds of aggregate economic measures redolent of those deployed in assessing regional economic policies.

The criteria of assessment selected has often tended to pull policy implementation in directions likely to show the results in a good light. For instance, the redevelopment of London's docklands was measured in terms of the derelict land and docks which were cleared and built upon. Canary Wharf, the housing developments and associated infrastructure, were highlighted together with some, but less, attention to the numbers of jobs created. One result of a property-led development initiative was relatively few opportunities for small enterprises, especially those which might have been started by the existing local population, since the returns for providing premises and other support for small businesses were not sufficient to attract commercial developers and the public contribution did not offset this result.

What has since become apparent is that the redevelopment did not build upon or integrate with the existing social infrastructure, communities and local economy. For example, the jobs created, real and potential, were of little benefit to the local population but were mainly likely to be taken up by people commuting in and out of the area each day.[15] Local unemployment, high due to the collapse of the dock industry and other activities such as manufacturing, which the redevelopment was designed to replace, has remained high. One overall conclusion suggests:

> there can be no presumption that property-led economic regeneration, with minimal regard to the competitiveness of inner city residents in the local labour market, will succeed . . . Policy must recognise that a degree of 'targeting' is necessary and that inner city economic regeneration should play careful regard not only to the business development needs of inner city companies but also to the economic, housing and social needs of inner city residents.
>
> (Moore, 1992:135)

LOCAL AUTHORITIES AND LOCAL ECONOMIES

What might be expected to articulate most closely with the social, political and economic realities of localities are those perspectives which focus on the local authority as a unit of analysis. Both policy-makers, central and especially local, and researchers have adopted this level of analysis for some of their activities. In Pyke's ideal type (1992:19) of the industrial district, the local political order is a key component in sustaining the industrial district. Through a neo-corporatist approach, it promotes the co-ordination of businesses, trade unions, financial sources and public sector institutions such as local educational provision, to produce an integrated local economy. In the UK, there is ample evidence, both from the past and more recently, that local government has been aware of the part it can play in promoting local economic activities and, as noted above, researchers and theorists have had similar views.

In this book the concern is with the small firms and the local economy currently and its future rather than with the past and the long history of 'municipal enterprise' in Britain. In the late 1970s, local authorities all over the UK reacted to economic decline, restructuring and recession by adopting positive economic strategies. They often saw themselves as 'states within a state', able to initiate their own economic policies which not only need not reflect national economic policies but could seek to counter or neutralise them (Cockburn, 1978) Local authorities had resources from central government with local discretion on their use and from local revenue raising such as 'the rates'. They also had the political legitimacy to be able to challenge central government policies, particularly where these affected the local economy and community (Greater London Council, 1985; Pickvance, 1990:8).

The economic strategies of several major urban authorities attracted considerable attention. The Greater London Enterprise Board (GLEB),for example, was set up by the Greater London Council (GLC) in 1983 as a private company to implement the Council's industrial strategy. The latter explicitly aimed at investing in activities which would save or create new long-term jobs in London's economy, particularly in areas and industries and among social groups suffering high unemployment. It encouraged new forms of ownership and control such as producer co-operatives and worker participation generally. Yet it also insisted that these social and community aims should be combined with rigorous investment appraisal. It backed its aims with loans, equity participation and grants plus expert advice. The Board's part-time directors were drawn from both the public and private sectors (GLC, 1983; GLEB, nd:7). The funds available to GLEB were substantial[16] and the approach it adopted was widely regarded as likely to have a significant impact on London's economy (Duncan and Goodwin, 1985; Cochrane, 1987).

As Rainnie (1991) has shown, the GLC was ambivalent in its views on the role of small firms in its economic strategy. In some of its earlier pronouncements, it was far from positive to small firms:

Small firms have contributed a minor share of new gross employment. Their employment impact is confined to a few sectors. Their contribution to the re-investible surplus is less than large firms.

(GLC, 1983:16 quoted in Rainnie, 1991:2)

It went on to argue that small firms often provided poor pay and conditions and trade unions were unable to gain a foothold to defend employees. Central government's promotion of small firms was seen as

a class strategy designed to weaken organised labour in large enterprises and to strengthen a *petit bourgeoisie* which had been in long term decline.

(GLC, 1983:15–16 in Rainnie, 1991:2)

However, in practice, argues Rainnie, GLEB did support small firms. Retrospectively, it is difficult to see how GLEB and the GLC could have avoided promoting small businesses. As other research has shown (Daly, 1990 and 1991) the net increase in small firms and self-employment was high in the South East and, to a lesser extent, Greater London. Small firms were represented strongly in the growth sectors of the economy, business and personal services, which were also growth sectors in London's economy in the period. For the UK as a whole for much of the 1980s, small firms were also net creators of jobs while larger firms were losing jobs (Daly et al., 1991). It is unlikely that the picture was any different in London.

The size distribution of businesses in the UK shows that over 96% of all businesses employed less than 20 people in 1991 (McCann, 1993). Between them, this 96% of businesses was responsible for over a third of employment outside central and local government. True, small firms were responsible for a much less important proportion of total turnover but, even so, it was just under 20% according to the slightly earlier estimate of Daly and McCann (1992). Given these data, it is difficult to see how *any* economic strategy, national or local, could ignore the small business. In other words, the GLC's initiatives could not afford to ignore small firms in practical terms.

Sheffield, one of the localities from which empirical data was collected for the analysis and main arguments presented later in the book, offers another well documented example of local economic intervention strategies. The recent economic history of Sheffield has been well documented, particularly the decline in steel manufacturing and associated products (DEED, 1989a and 1989b). By the mid-1980s, it was by most measures a depressed local economy.[17] The council, Labour controlled, as were most of the local authorities in Britain which adopted highly proactive local economic policies in the 1980s, responded by setting up an Employment Department, which, like the GLC's initiative, sought to combine political and economic objectives in promoting local economic activities (Blunkett and Jackson, 1987; Dabinett and Ramsden, 1993).

Many of the activities of the department were defensive rather than the positive promotion of a new local economy, that is, they were heavily preoccupied with rescuing firms about to fail in order to preserve jobs. This made aligning any aims of investing on sound market principles with political objectives difficult, especially as the latter was much concerned with preserving declining traditional industries such as steel (Goodwin, 1989:166–167). A good deal of these efforts were directed towards large firms where failure would result in the loss of large numbers of jobs. Small firms, therefore, and their promotion, was not especially stressed. Again, however, Sheffield's efforts were regarded as serious and significant by those with a strong theoretical concern for the functioning of local economies in Britain.[18]

Just how efforts such as those of the Greater London and Sheffield City Councils promoted the idea of a local economy can be debated at length.[19] First of all, the declaration of a 'local' economic strategy confined to some geographical area demarcated by local government boundaries does not automatically demonstrate anything very much about the existence of a local economy in any substantive sense. They may, for example, simply enhance, or seek to enhance, levels of economic activity through supporting particular firms or by attempting to induce a general multiplier effect on economic processes in a particular area. In short, a local authority economic strategy does not require or generate a local economy: even if it were to be successful at, for example, saving or generating jobs within its administrative boundaries, this demonstrates little or nothing about the character or cohesiveness of economic activities within the designated area.

Second, beyond the analytical distinctions made above, theoretical and empirical assessments of the effectiveness of local authority economic strategies in the 1980s are also mixed. For instance, a number of theoretical objections have been mounted on the obvious premise that 'no local economy is an island unto itself'. The notion that a local authority can achieve sufficient control and influence over economic activities in its area to significantly alter the direction and performance of these activities is argued to be implausible. This is particularly stressed in relation to Britain since it is argued that Britain's national economy is highly centralised and has been for most of this century. More concentrated than, for example, the economies of many other industrial societies (Eurostat, 1992:8–9; Storey, 1994).

Of course, there are clearly spatial variations in the UK's economic mix and performance, some of which have been persistent and pronounced as earlier sections noted, but these now increasingly arise from the operation and character of the economy at the *national* level rather than as a result of failures or otherwise of local economy management by local governments:

> local authorities possess only a very limited economic power and can only exercise what powers they have in very small geographical areas. They cannot significantly alter labour or commodity markets at a scale relevant to a national, let alone an international, production system.
>
> (Goodwin, 1989:161)

To put the above further in perspective, doubts are increasingly also expressed about the ability of *national* government to control and direct the UK's national economy. Deregulation, the decline in the insulation of the UK economy from the world economy as a result of European Community membership and economic globalisation tendencies have, it is widely argued, enfeebled the control UK governments have over the national economy (Coakley and Harris, 1992; Coutes and Godley, 1992). If this is the case, can local authorities' efforts be much more than 'trying to drain an ocean with a teaspoon' to adopt Cochrane's (1983) phrase?

At the level of the empirical assessment of local authority economic policies in the 1980s, the results appear to be equally pessimistic. GLEB and the GLC have probably received the most detailed attention at this level. The failure appears to have been both economic and political. As noted earlier, Rainnie (1991) has assembled much of the detailed evidence and argues that the economic reconstruction and revitalisation that the council aimed for simply did not occur. In part, this was due to the sheer size of the task the council had taken on: London's economy is large, larger than that of many national economies, even if the City of London is excluded. In part, it was also due to attempts to work against the market and central government policies by, for example, directing much of its support to improving pay, working conditions, strengthening trade unionism and community particip-ation (Nolan and O'Donnell, 1990). In a situation of a declining national economy, these objectives added to the difficulties of an already very diffi-cult situation for council and the GLEB.[20]

The above is not to say that the efforts of local authorities in the 1980s to revitalise their local economies had no impact at all. They did promote new industry and new jobs but only on a limited scale. For instance, Mawson and Miller (1986:170) estimated that between 1981 and 1984, the five main en-terprise boards created by local authorities (including GLEB) created or saved around 8,000 jobs. Moreover this was at a lower cost than other regional policies but, as Mawson and Miller point out, the number of jobs was low relative to the needs of the areas concerned. Moreover, such esti-mates are prone to error and overstatement since it is always difficult to know whether all the jobs created were additional. Some were undoubtedly jobs displaced from elsewhere, either in or outside the local authority's area, or would have been created anyway by firms who preferred to use the cheaper funds available from an authority rather than their own.

Whatever the assessment of local authority attempts to generate an integ-rated local economy in the early 1980s, the late 1980s and early 1990s show the arguments losing force rapidly. A major reason for this was the policies and actions of central government. The most spectacular of the policies was the decision to abolish the GLC and the Metropolitan counties in 1985.[21] Some (eg, Dickens, 1988:178) suspected their abolition was, in part, due to the attempts of these bodies to adopt economic strategies contrary to central government policy and ideology, which emphasised the overwhelming im-portance of market freedom to produce an efficient, restructured economy. Central government was strongly against any notion of economic strategies containing explicit social aims which would deflect or constrain market forces. Moreover, it was also against public provision by local authorities of services which could be provided, more efficiently in the view of central government, by private sector sources. The shift towards privatising local authority services is likely to have the effect of reducing local authorities' ability to impact on local economic activities still further (Abbott, 1993).

Government also reduced local authority control over revenues, reducing opportunities for funding economic activities. The replacement of domestic rates by a 'Community Charge' or 'poll tax' combined with increasingly strict controls ('ringfencing') on local authority budgets and expenditure were clear examples of this firm assertion of central government control (Pickvance, 1990:13). The Community Charge has now been replaced by the Council Tax where, again, the amounts levied are rigidly controlled by central government to remove local authority discretion.

At the same time, local authorities have also lost the ability to levy property taxes on business premises, another source of income over which they had discretion. This has been replaced by a Unified Business Rate whose level is dictated by central government (Cochrane, 1989:129). Other central government funding has also been 'ringfenced' to lower or remove local authority discretion on how the funding is spent. Overall, there have also been reductions in real levels of authority budgets to promote greater efficiency (Cochrane, 1989:128–129).

As might be expected, despite abolition, local authorities, particularly some of those in the areas covered by the former GLC and Metropolitan County Councils, have attempted to retain some influence over local economic activities and some observers continued to believe that they could remain significant forces (see, for example, Marshall, 1987; Dickens, 1988:Ch. 6; Cooke, 1989a). However, the trend since the late 1980s has strongly favoured central government policies seeking to reduce local authority autonomy across the board. The return of a Conservative government in April 1992 sealed the previous policies: local authorities no longer have the autonomy or resources to mount a local economic strategy of any significance and this has reduced whatever integrating force they contributed to anything that might be seen as a coherent 'local economy'.

CENTRAL GOVERNMENT REPLACES LOCAL GOVERNMENT

It might be argued that the above is over-pessimistic. In a wide variety of ways, central government has itself greatly increased its intervention in local economic activities bypassing local authorities. London again provides clear examples of these central government initiatives, which often claim to be rejuvenating particular localities. Mainly they share a common pattern of being run by non-elected bodies set up for the purpose, whose members are appointed by central government with many coming from industry (Lloyd and Newlands, 1988; Cochrane, 1989:122).

The best known instance in London is the London Docklands Development Corporation set up in 1981 to oversee the redevelopment of the huge riverside area which had become derelict with the closure of the docks (Brownill, 1993; Deakin and Edwards, 1993:Ch. 6). This was one of a series of urban development corporations in cities across the UK including Sheffield, Merseyside, Manchester, Tyne and Wear and the Black Country. In 1987–1988 they had budgets of £126 million (Cooke, 1989b:303). Their main thrust was property development, encouraging the private sector to build offices, leisure facilities, shops and accommodation mainly for sale or lease. They operated to ensure that development was coherent in market terms, encouraging government support for infrastructural provision and were intended to neutralise any local authority opposition.[22]

To the above can be added a mix of other central government initiatives including: enterprise zones, free ports, City Action Teams, Training and Enterprise Councils (TECs) plus other initiatives which have received central government subsidies or other support such as Business in the Community and enterprise agencies which have also had support from the private sector.

There are few indications to date that TECs are having a dramatic impact on the economies of the localities in which they are situated (Emmerich and Peck, 1992). Most of the other initiatives mentioned above, however, have been around much longer. For instance, enterprise zones whose planned 10-year lives have now nearly all come to an end do not appear to have had any great success (Balchin, 1990, 89–90; Hall, 1992:153–4; Deakin and Edwards, 1993:123–4). Overall, as one observer has summed up the impact on one geographical area:

> in Merseyside, for instance, which has had every new scheme, economic decline has not even been halted, let alone reversed. In general, these initiatives seem to have shifted jobs around rather than created new ones as some firms have relocated to take advantage of the subsidies.
>
> (Goodwin, 1989:163)[23]

Another assessment puts broadly the same criticisms in more trenchant terms in relation to one of the main initiatives:

> UDCs (Urban Development Corporations) . . . represent a totally centralist solution to urban problems and one, moreover, which under a right wing government rests on transforming deprived working class neighbourhoods into middle class playgrounds composed of yachting marinas, expensive shopping plazas and elite culture facilities.
>
> (Cooke, 1989b:302)

The above indirectly reintroduces the theme of 'embeddedness' discussed earlier. It was argued that, as well as economic activities and transactions, the local labour market and local consumption (the 'local economy') non-economic relations need to be considered. These, it was noted, are often summed up in rather ill-defined notions such as 'community' taken to refer to settled populations with a wide variety of kinship, social and political links plus a cultural awareness or identification with the local geographical area corresponding to that designated as the local economy.

'Local economy' and 'community' in the above senses interpenetrate, mutually supporting and reinforcing each other especially where they approximate to a notion of an 'industrial district'. Even where the approximation does not exist, the 'local economy' and 'community' will have some, even if only a vestigial, relationship with each other.

Clearly, the critics of central government measures quoted above are arguing that they do not promote a local economic community and even operate to undermine existing economic and non-economic links in the given areas. In other words, the measures have not made much of an impact economically in many cases but have, through their operating practices, neglected the non-economic requirements needed to rebuild a local economic community in a fuller sense.

RESEARCHERS AND LOCAL ECONOMIES

Earlier it was argued that much of the regional and urban policy analyses that have dominated discussion of spatial differences in the UK economy were too dependent on aggregate analysis. This produced highly quantitative overviews of spatial characteristics devoid of much of a sense of people living their lives in the areas concerned or, more generally, of the non-quantitative aspects of economic and non-economic life.

In 1984, however, the Economic and Social Research Council (ESRC) established a large-scale research programme to carry out detailed studies of a variety of localities in the UK. The localities selected were: Swindon, Cheltenham, Lancaster, the Isle of Thanet, Merseyside, Birmingham and Teesside (Cooke, 1989a; Harloe et al., 1990). Each was studied in depth by researchers drawn from research centres and universities throughout the UK.[24]

Each study detailed the history of each locality particularly its economic changes and local politics over the last few decades. There are scattered references to the people living in the areas, often with quotes from the people themselves, but the analysis remains general. Where businesses are referred to, it is almost always the largest firms: rarely is there any reference to small firms or a small firm presence in local economic activities. Much of the analysis is concerned with the ways in which local economic change is related to the economic restructuring and globalisation effects occurring more generally in the UK.

Like so much research on spatial phenomena in Britain carried out in the 1980s (the research in the ESRC programme on the Changing Urban and Regional System was carried out between 1985 and 1987) it has dated, so rapid has the pace of change been as restructuring and severe recession dissembled Britain's economic and social structure.

There are claims made that the studies offer:

> an in-depth analysis of the ways in which localities function internally and how they articulate to the wider national and international processes of change . . . to illustrate the argument that . . . localities [are not] the mere recipients of fortune or fate from above [but] are actively involved in their own transformation . . . they are the sum of social energy and agency resulting from the clustering of diverse individuals, groups and social interest in space.
>
> (Cooke, 1989b:296)

However, they do not deliver this picture. At best the studies are firmly at what might be called the 'macro-local level'. That is, they take geographical areas, 'Swindon', 'South Birmingham' etc and analytically synthesise a local economy and to a much less well defined extent, an associated community in the sense of a set of non-economic relations between those living and/or working in the local economy.

The studies do not really achieve a portrait of an integrated local economic community whose members have a sufficiently well developed sense of self-identification with the area to form the basis of collective action to make their own economic destiny except in a very limited way. For instance, Cheltenham is portrayed as marketing itself in terms of a 'Regency image' based on its history and architecture to attract new businesses and a skilled middle class labour force (Cohen et al., 1989). But the extent to which the local population play any part in this image generation or how it is incorporated in their own awareness of locality is not analysed. Indeed, the authors admit:

> local policies and local features hold diminished importance for the increasingly globalised operations of the multi-national engineering corporations who . . . provide a significant proportion of Cheltenham's employment.
>
> (Cohen et al., 1989:125)

In terms of the opportunities offered by the ESRC initiative, it has to be said that the researchers missed an opportunity to explore in depth the ways and extent to which economic activities are local and integrated with people's lives in the same locality. Of course, it may be unfair to offer such a criticism if the researchers' aims were to investigate other matters, such as national economic restructuring and the effects of globalisation, for example, but the use of terms such as 'locality' and the promise of a detailed characterisation of a place ('Swindon' etc) demand more than hints and allusions to the non-economic lives of ordinary people.[25]

Sociologists have long been interested closely in localities in a mainly non-economic sense, though often with frequent links made with the economic, through their theorising and research on 'urbanism' (Saunders, 1979; Lee and Newby, 1983; Crompton, 1993:42) and rural life (Newby, 1977; 1979; 1988; Cohen, 1983). More recently, however, detailed attention in the form of empirical studies of particular localities has been less common with more attention being given to theoretical issues (Savage, 1989; Crompton, 1993). This theoretical discussion has interesting implications for some of the main concerns of this book – the extent to which we can still usefully talk about local economies embedded in local communities as defined earlier, that is, as a set of social and cultural relations between people aware of, and identifying with, a particular geographical area.

One result of the above, more theoretical, approach to sociological aspects of 'locality', is to demonstrate just how problematic these issues are. For instance, one theoretical elaboration that has been argued is that local cultures are better conceptualised as symbolic rather than embodied in actions and behaviour. Thus, people in a local area may believe they possess qualities and attributes which distinguish them from people living in other localities or parts of Britain and this is an important element in any identification with place they hold. People in Yorkshire, for example, may have a cultural identity linked to the notion of 'Yorkshire' centred on symbols such as bluffness of speech, physical stamina or toughness, strength of character, warmth and directness in personal relations. To heighten this awareness, these attributes may be set against the deviousness, physical softness, lack of directness and coldness of personal relations among people who live elsewhere in Britain and especially in the South.

Cohen (1983) distinguishes the cultural level expressed in the above way from the 'practical community', that is, the actions and behaviour of people in their relations with each other. To put this another way, the imagined community in people's minds may differ greatly from the actual community constituted in everyday living: nor need the two – symbolic culture and day-to-day behaviour – be related to each other in any direct or clear fashion.

Savage (1989:260–67) sums up another long debate in sociology between two views which touches on a further aspect of the discussion of the significance of locality. First, he summarises the view of those who argue for an emerging 'mass society', that is, a growing uniformity in ways of living and thinking deriving from several influences. The latter include mass media and especially television's effects, privatised ways of living centred on the home, the increasing importance of a world economy in employment and consumption terms and a national educational system. All these are said to have led to a decline in the significance of locality for people, the 'loss of community' much discussed not only among social scientists but also in popular discourse and the media.

The alternative view suggests that the mass society thesis is too simple and/or overstates. For instance, the mass media may heighten a sense of locality because it may accentuate awareness of differences between places and people. This can occur, for example, where it emphasises stereotypes of such differences as it often does in comedy, drama and news programmes.[26] Nor do people simply receive the media passively: they interpret what they receive in terms of their own direct experiences and the framework of meanings and values which form part of their interactions with immediate others. More directly, some media output such as local newspapers and local radio, seek to reinforce awareness of place.

Which of the above two views is most persuasive is a matter of debate and continued empirical questioning – a questioning which has largely not occurred in exploring spatial economic concerns. There *is* evidence (Social Trends, 1993) of increasing uniformity of leisure habits, the decline of locally based leisure activities such as those based on the pub or local associations such as drama societies or local political parties.[27] Young people especially (the adults of tomorrow) are linked increasingly closely to influences emanating from outside the immediate locality such as computer games, music and 'youth' as portrayed by television and the media as well as nationally prescribed education. But even if such extra-local influences and uniformities of thinking and behaviour are increasing, it could still go with *some* awareness of locality and spatial differences. The question is then the extent to which awareness of locality impinges on everyday thinking and behaviour and whether it is stronger or weaker in relation to the economic as compared to the non-economic.

In this book the initial concern with economic relations and their links with the non-economic is a context for analysing the small enterprise and its spatial relations with other firms, large and small. It might be, for instance, that the economic is undermining the non-economic. We know, for example, that local shops, especially small specialist shops, are giving way steadily to national chain stores with their uniformity of shop style, selling patterns and stock (Howe, 1991). This has a strong spatial dimension especially with the proliferation of out-of-town supermarkets and shopping developments. Businesses may be less connected to local economies and offer fewer opportunities to develop non-economic relations. What is especially interesting is whether and to what extent small businesses are upholding or are a part of any diminution of place in both economic and non-economic relations.

CONCLUSIONS

This chapter has been concerned mainly with examining recent thinking on local economies and localities and the role of the small firm. The aim is to provide a detailed background for the following presentation of results from research on a range of contrasting localities focusing on the integration of the small firm into the wider economic environment and the extent of its relations with large firms. Despite the enormous range of literature drawn from several specialisms touching on these issues, the overall conclusion which might be drawn from the examination in this chapter is that the literature largely fails to come to grips with the substantive level of economic relations and the latter's links with non-economic relations.

Conceptually, notions such as 'local markets', 'local economy', 'community' and their variants, for example, 'local economic community' or 'local labour markets', have been shown to be poorly defined and or very difficult to pin down in any agreed fashion. But the main criticism which might be levelled against this thinking is that those involved did not try very hard. The abstractions employed are thrown into the analysis with little attention to rigorous conceptualisation with the inevitable result that fuzzy conceptualisation produces fuzzy analyses.

Real people running and working in real enterprises, especially small enterprises, do not receive much attention. If the units of analysis are vague, it is not only due to the lack of conceptual clarity but the general avoidance of the substantive level. Top-down aggregate analyses based on synthetic constructs such as 'region' or 'travel-to-work area' are unlikely to reach very far down to ground level realities beyond the thin hints offered in quantitative contrasts.

The major exception to the above is the now voluminous discussion of the industrial district thesis. Whatever the utility of the thesis in discussing areas in Italy or elsewhere outside the UK, the examination in this chapter of the thesis' applicability to contemporary Britain showed that it was hopelessly overstretched to the point of distortion. While a case could be made for the thesis as an economic history tool, neither the economic nor non-economic conditions postulated from any reasonable ideal typical formulation seem likely to be satisfied in late 20th century Britain. One suggested example, the high tech small business concentration around Cambridge, was examined to demonstrate this point. Others could have been selected with the same results. In later chapters other elements of the critique of the thesis will be developed in relation to the behaviour of small business owners and large firms in the localities studied.

The weakness of the industrial district thesis' applicability to Britain was further illustrated in the examination of the impact of central government policies and especially local authority policies for economic intervention at the local level. The impact of central government policies with their over-emphasis on the economic, and especially property development, at the expense of the non-economic, has clearly been limited. It is doubtful whether any of the policies have succeeded to any marked extent in pulling together economic relations and communities in any of the localities, labelled 'inner cities', 'enterprise zones' or 'docklands redevelopment areas', upon which they have been focused.

Local authority policies and experiments such as the GLC's economic strategy of the early 1980s were more interesting, in that they were closer to the ground or substantive level relations. Brave though these interventionist approaches were, they foundered in the face of the size of the areas covered and the severity of the problems they were trying to counter. These were then compounded by the attempts to swim against a powerful ideological tide of free market, non-interventionism emanating from a determined central government with a large majority and, finally, the dissolution and emasculation of local authorities by the same government.

Small firms were often mentioned in central and local government local economic policies, usually in positive terms. For Conservative governments in the 1980s, small-scale enterprise embodied the main values of a market economy (Goss, 1991:8–11). In many of the policies implemented such as those aimed at rejuvenating inner cities or the more recent TECs, small firms are prime objects of support and encouragement (Deakin and Edwards, 1993). Again, however, considerable doubts have been expressed about the extent to which small firms have been helped or promoted (Bannock and Albach, 1992; Emmerich and Peck, 1992).

The promotion of small firms was supposed to have a positive impact on localities and local economies. Just as a revival of the small firm sector could lead the national economy to recovery, so it could local economies, though just how this would happen was not always very clearly spelled out. There was a chain of assumptions surrounding such policies. More small firms meant higher levels of economic activity and more jobs and since small firms were also assumed to be integrated into the local economy around them, the locality must benefit.

This last argument brings the analysis to the crux of this book, the examination of the functioning of economic activities in localities and the role small firms play both in relation to localities and to other firms, small and large, in them. The approach is very different from the bulk of approaches discussed above since it very explicitly adopts the substantive level as its starting point, the level that has been missing from the debates to date.

Notes

1. This should be regarded merely as a sensitising definition. We are aware that the notion of 'community' continues to prove conceptually elusive to the extent that some writers – particularly sociologists who have had a long and close interest in the concept as key to their discipline – suggest it is of no utility. Stacey, for example, who carried out two classic studies of Banbury in Oxfordshire (Stacey, 1960 and Stacey et al., 1975), nevertheless felt able to argue 'It is doubtful whether the concept 'community' refers to a useful abstraction' (1969:134). See also the somewhat convoluted struggle to retain the notion in Lee and Newby (1983:65–66). The latter author is also known for a classic study of a locality (Newby et al., 1978). For a more recent discussion in relation to administrative areas, see Coombes et al., (1993).

2. The debate on the processes behind the changing industrial structure is widespread throughout the social sciences and is of varying complexity. Competing schools of thought (regulationists and institutionalists) provide sharply contrasting explanations for the restructuring process (see Allen and Massey, 1988 for an overview). However, it is the industrial district thesis which gives smaller businesses a central role in the economy within a spatial context.

3. The literature on this thesis and its variants is voluminous. What follows is an interpretation focusing on the role of the small business.

4. It is well established in the literature that small firms provide less formal qualification-based training primarily because of expense, opportunity cost and inadequate appropriateness of the training on offer (Blackburn, 1990; Curran et al. 1993a; Skills and Enterprise Network, 1993).

5. Much of the recent writing on 'industrial districts' has been influenced by the economist Alfred Marshall whose most influential works on this topic were published in the 1920s. (See for discussions, Ballandi, 1989; Amin and Robins, 1990; Harrison, 1992). Marshall's writing was based on his observations in several countries. In England he cited, among others, the Lancashire textile industry around Rochdale as well as the Sheffield cutlery industry as examples of 'industrial districts'.

6. Interestingly, Massey et al. contrast Cambridge with the West Midlands where they argue that high tech firms, particularly those associated with the Aston Science Park, have a higher level of linkages with the local economy. However, they stress that the level and character of such linkages should not be overstated (Massey et al., 1992:185).

7. The discussion here is of the so-called 'Cambridge Phenomenon' but concentrations of high tech small firms exist elsewhere in the UK although claims that they constitute putative industrial districts are made less frequently. See for an analysis of another concentration, the discussion of Scotland's 'Silicon Glen' by Oakey and Rothwell (1986) and Turok (1993).

8. This point is illustrated by findings offered elsewhere that the absence of a sufficient support infrastructure has left many science parks 'to become no more than managed workspaces' (Bennett and McCoshan, 1993:104).

9. Even those who have been highly critical of the role and performance of high tech small firms and high tech economic concentrations have neglected these issues. (See eg Oakey (1991) and the more recent critical study of science parks by Massey et al. (1992). The latter are more aware of these issues but restrict themselves to a rather old-fashioned discussion of the class situations of those working in high tech firms (1992:Ch 5) and an examination of central government policies on new technology and its support.

10. The discussion above was confined to the Cambridge area and there may be other candidates in other areas of high tech small firm concentration but there seems little likelihood of them being industrial districts in Pyke's sense. Another study of linkages between academic institutions and industry in the South West of England shows a dramatic fall-off in links as size of firm reduces – results that are far removed from any notion of an industrial district (eg Bishop, 1988).

11. It is also worth stressing how the South East also illustrates the way in which services activities can be spatially mobile. For instance, in several kinds of activities, notably financial and insurance services, from the 1960s onwards there were large decentralisations of clerical and administrative functions away from London (the City in particular) to suburban and provincial locations within, but often well outside the South East (Allen, 1988). Government itself adopted a similar decentralisation strategy in the 1960s and 1970s, (see Hardman, 1973) moving the bulk of those working in some of the major departments such as employment and social security outside London and the South East, a policy which continued in the 1980s.

12. Hall (1992:112–113) labels this as a period of great policy reversal, in which one of main 'sticks' of regional policy, industrial development certificates, was dropped and the boundaries of assisted areas were cut back from covering 43% of the UK to 25%.

13. Moore (1992:123–124 and 126) lists 30 inner city schemes and initiatives run by 6 government departments ranging from City Action Teams to garden festivals. They represent a remarkable set of interventionist strategies from the series of post-1979 governments dedicated to allowing market forces to operate as effectively as possible. Several other initiatives, though not directed specifically at inner cities, added to the above in offering aid to inner cities.

14. These totals still underestimate since not all schemes which have an impact are included. (There have been so many with frequent changes that it is very difficult to be precise). They also exclude local authority inner city regeneration strategies – discussed below.

15. The failure of Canary Wharf and similar dockland commercial development to successfully attract business and jobs (to the extent of virtually ruining the Canary Wharf developer, Olympia and York) was in part due to the failure to provide adequate public transport to allow commuters to more easily enter and leave the area. Had the transport been built, the effect of creating jobs for those outside the locality would have been accentuated. (This may still occur if and when the public transport infrastructure is built.)

16. For example, under the Local Government Act of 1972, the GLC was able to raise a two pence rate to provide funds for its economic policies. In 1983–1984

this provided about £30 million according to Dickens (1988:199). The council was also able to use other funds and its expenditure on goods and services to support its economic strategies, for example, through its contract compliance policies.

17. For instance, on the index of local prosperity constructed by Champion and Green (1988), which divides Britain into 280 Local Labour Market Areas and ranks them from the most prosperous (1) to the least prosperous (280), Sheffield ranked 262. See also DEED (1989a) and Sheffield Economic Bulletin (1990).

18. On this besides Duncan and Goodwin (1985) and Cochrane (1987) cited above, see also Boddy and Fudge (1984) and Pickvance (1990).

19. The Greater London Council and Sheffield City's efforts were not by any means the only examples of attempts at local economic strategies. Others often discussed alongside the above include the West Midlands County Council and Enterprise Board (West Midlands County Council Economic Development Committee, 1984) and the Newcastle area (Rogers and Smith, 1977; Shaw, 1993) plus a whole raft of similar kinds of schemes (Hausner, 1986; Imrie and Thomas, 1993).

20. The above could be extended by detailed considerations of Sheffield and other major local authority attempts at interventionist local economic policies such as those in the West Midlands. However, the assessments would be very similar (Goodwin, 1989:162–168).

21. This included the West Midlands Metropolitan County, seen above as another major instigator of a local economic strategy, as well as those of Greater Manchester, Merseyside and Tyne and Wear, all to a lesser or greater extent in favour of local economic intervention. Sheffield City Council remained in place though, as described below, central government much reduced its power to intervene economically.

22. Not all local authorities opposed urban development corporations and some have had mixed attitudes. For instance, some authorities have objected to an over-emphasis on commercial and industrial interests which they argued neglected social concerns and the needs of local populations in the areas. Others have welcomed the corporations for the economic boost and positive image they provide not only for the area covered by the development corporation but more generally. For their part, the corporations have also sometimes worked closely with local authorities in practice rather than ignored them or seen them as 'the enemy' (Cochrane, 1989:156–157).

23. The same author offers an equally thumbs down view of the Docklands Development Corporation:

> although London's Docklands has seen a major development, questions are being asked about its nature. It seems that existing residents have hardly benefitted at all, as most jobs created have gone to those living outside the area and most economic gains to international finance companies, property developers and construction companies.
>
> (Goodwin, 1989:163)

Since the above was written, of course, there are doubts whether the last three mentioned above have been beneficiaries at all since several of the companies involved have suffered huge losses or even failure.

24. These were not, of course, the first detailed studies of localities in Britain. There has been a strong tradition of such studies which produced some outstanding work (see, eg Mogey, 1956; Dennis et al., 1956; Frankenberg, 1957; Stacey, 1960; Stacey et al., 1975). However, the kinds of localities studied in this earlier work have now mostly disappeared or undergone such fundamental change as to make the studies poor indicators of social and economic life in contemporary Britain.

25. As remarked above, even the characterisation of economic relations by the researchers was inadequate since so little attention was given to the large number of small enterprises which exist in the areas covered. These provide substantial proportions of jobs and output in the localities selected for study.

26. Savage (1989:266) offers television programmes such as *Boys From the Blackstuff*, *Minder* and *Only Fools and Horses* as examples of television output which provides 'an imagery of place' but this raises the question of whether the imagery might be perceived by much of the audience as imaginary and, hence, less effective in reinforcing a sense of place or of portraying real people. Conceivably, it can be both: people may be aware of a stereotype qua stereotype yet still believe it contains essential truths.

27. Although the decline in political party membership in the UK is widely accepted, exact data is not easy to come by. However, the *Guardian* (5.10.93) reported that a member of the Conservative Party's national union executive had revealed that party membership had fallen from 1.5 million in the mid-1970s to 500,000 currently.

2

INTER-FIRM LINKAGES AND LOCAL ECONOMIES

INTRODUCTION

In the previous chapter a number of macro views of the role small firms play in economic activities were examined. Particular emphasis was given to some of the currently fashionable theses such as 'industrial districts' and the high technology small firm's contribution to local and national economic activities. Some of the principal conceptual tools of macro analysis were also discussed critically such as 'region' and 'regional analysis'. However, these by no means exhaust the examination of relations between small firms and the wider economy and community. In this chapter the focus is on lower levels of generality and especially on theories and research concerned with *specific* relations between firms and between firms and localities.

Inevitably, there are connections between this and the previous chapter. Much of the global theorising of the industrial districts thesis or Post-Fordist theory, for example, contains assertions about specific firms and their inter-relations within particular localities. A good deal of this discussion is best described as argument by illustration: the selective use of often superficial descriptions of alleged relations to bolster a more general argument. In this chapter the examination of inter-firm relations, especially small firm–large firm relations, is much more focused and tougher criteria of assessment are applied than by many of those theorising about 'the second industrial divide' or the like.

Similarly, it seems that theorists and researchers find it increasingly difficult to discuss inter-firm relations such as forms of subcontracting without bringing in references to Post-Fordism, 'flexible specialisation', 'the crisis of mass production' etc and suggesting what their thinking and findings contribute to the higher level debates.[1] Where these issues arise in examining inter-firm economic relations it is difficult to avoid such references but this chapter's discussion is firmly at the lower level of generality.

SUBCONTRACTING RELATIONS

Without doubt the most commonly used notion in analysing relations between small and large firms is 'subcontracting'. So commonly is it used, that
many might believe that this is the *only* relation between small firms and the
wider environment, that is, that small firms exist solely to serve the needs of
other, usually larger firms. Often this is also linked to notions of locality
since small firms' larger customers are often assumed to be within a short
distance perhaps for historical reasons or to ensure rapid response by the
small firm to the large firm's needs. Moreover, a good deal of recent writing
has argued that subcontracting is on the increase due to larger firms prefer-
ring to outsource more than in the past, especially in certain industries (See
eg Atkinson and Meager, 1986; Thorburn and Takashima, 1992).[2]

It is not always clear what is meant by 'subcontracting' since it is often
used very loosely or data are offered to show the level of, or changes in,
subcontracting relations without specifying what is being measured. Coun-
tering this vagueness, several theorists in the 1980s became concerned about
this lack of clarity and attempted to introduce some precision in discussing
'subcontracting'. These range from somewhat rough and ready attempts to
distinguish subcontracting from other forms of inter-firm relations to much
more refined views offering typologies of sub-contracting relations. Some
are supported by sophisticated theoretical arguments, sometimes with empirical support, for the predominance of one or other type or even the
absence of sub-contracting relations in some areas of the economy.

One common approach to situating sub-contracting among inter-firm relations generally is to see it as some kind of 'intermediate' relationship. An
early, widely cited view sees subcontracting as:

> Occupying a middle ground between arm's length market transactions
> between firms (regulated by the price system) and the direction of
> activities within firms (regulated by a fair measure of conscious plan-
> ning), [there are] a wide range of relations based on co-operation or
> affiliation . . . [linking] firms with one another.
>
> (Friedman, 1977:118)

Friedman points out that the diversity of relations which might be labelled
'subcontracting' makes estimates of their importance difficult. He also tries
to pin down the term further:

> I shall use the term loosely to refer to situations when suppliers produce
> parts and components to specifications set out in advance by the large
> manufacturers, whether materials are issued or not, and whether the
> contract is directly with the large manufacturer or through some inter-
> mediary contract with another supplier.
>
> (Friedman, 1977:119)

Friedman's approach is interesting because he was discussing the UK
motor industry, an industry often used to illustrate discussions of

subcontracting relations and one which, as will be demonstrated below, is particularly favourable to arguments stressing the importance and extent of such relations in the UK economy.

To show the persistence of definitions of the above kind, albeit with further refinement, we can cite Thorburn and Takashima (1992:1):

> Industrial subcontracting is the provision, by one firm to another, of relatively specialized inputs, which are then incorporated into the final product of the buying firm. These inputs are distinguished from inputs of a standard kind such as raw materials or electric power, which can be purchased on the open market . . . It has the implication of a continuing (though not necessarily continuous) relation between the buying firm . . . and the subcontractor which may be backed by legal contract, or trust, or both. Often, though not always, the supplying firm may be small in relation to the principal.[3]

The differences between Friedman and Thorburn and Takashima are minor though three might be highlighted. First, the more recent definition drops the reference to the 'principal' (or buying firm) specifying the parts or components. This very sensibly allows for cases where the subcontractor originates the design and development of products or services sold and the purchasing firm is merely a consumer, even if a sophisticated one. Second, and much more important for the interests of this book, Thorburn and Takashima explicitly refer to size of firm, noting that subcontractors need not be small in relation to the purchasing firm.

Third, Thorburn and Takashima include a time dimension by asserting that a subcontracting relationship is a continuing relationship and, rather less directly, refer to the closeness of the relationship. They appear to suggest that the relationship between the firms may be intermittent. This implies that firms need not have much more than a market relation which is revived from time to time. This, in part, goes against any notion that subcontracting relations necessarily involve close relations between the firms or that the subcontracting firm is always dependent upon the purchasing firm.

It should be noted that the above definitions are examples from a very extensive literature on conceptualising subcontracting (see, for instance, Taylor and Thrift, 1982; Holmes, 1986; Imrie, 1986; Blackburn, 1992; Rainnie, 1992) but are broadly representative of the most widely accepted approaches. However, definitions of this kind need a theoretical context, the why and how of this kind of inter-firm relation and its links with other aspects such as locality and size of firm. Fortunately, economic geographers have focused on this set of issues and have provided a starting point for the development of a theoretical context. In addition, economists and economic sociologists have been attracted by the issues raised. The result is a theoretically complex set of interpretations which, in our view, over-states the importance of subcontracting and its importance in economic activities within geographically delineated areas.

THEORIES OF SUBCONTRACTING

In the stereotypical subcontracting relationship, that is, large firms using small firms to provide and supply goods or services, the theoretical emphasis is on flexibility and cost reduction advantages accruing to the larger (purchasing) firm. For the small (supplier) firm, the reward is having a secure customer for its output but it is usually readily admitted that the bargain is unequal with the larger firm receiving most of the benefits. 'Flexibility' here is a complex notion. It may, for instance, refer to what Holmes (1986:89) calls 'production smoothing' by the large firm where it faces cyclical or fluctuating demand for its products. The firm, in other words, maintains a level of productive capacity for which experience indicates there is a permanent level of demand. When demand raises above this level additional capacity is purchased from other, usually small, firms.[4] The car industry is often offered as a prime example of this situation (Friedman, 1977).

A rather more complex set of theoretical ideas, not mutually exclusive with the above, concerns the different technical and production characteristics of the separate stages of producing a good or service. To take an obvious example, few mass production manufacturers make their own steel because the economies of scale involved mean very high levels of investment and they would produce much more than they could ever use. They *could* supply other users but this would make them steel makers rather than just producers of whatever manufactured good they are in business to produce, a complication which would make for considerable managerial diseconomies of scale. This example reinforces the point that the subcontractor need not be small or smaller than the purchasing firm.

Another common example is an occurrence further down the production chain where specialist services or products are required. In the electronics industry, for instance, the large number of tasks and stages required to produce a complex end product such as a personal computer includes several where the minimum efficient scale of production is much higher than the needs of the individual assembler and marketer. Some of these tasks/stages are also technically sophisticated, need constant R & D support and require considerable investment. Not surprisingly, specialist producers exist who undertake many of these tasks from manufacturing disc drives and microchips to writing software. Again, it is worth underlining the point that specialist producers of these types need not be subcontractors or smaller than the firms which buy their output as the computing and electronics industry illustrates clearly. For example, Intel has a turnover and assets which dwarf most of the purchasers of its microchips (Times 1000, 1992). Nor, as this industry also shows, need they be geographically proximate (Henderson, 1991).

One of the more sophisticated attempts to integrate subcontracting into a comprehensive economic theory of the firm and its relation with the economy is transaction cost theory most closely linked to Williamson (1975; 1979). Again subcontracting is made intermediate between simple, discrete market transactions and vertically integrated production within the enterprise. Put simply, the principle involved is the minimisation of production costs by making choices between internal production and subcontracting but with consideration of other factors such as limited knowledge, rationality, trust and opportunism on the part of those involved. For instance, Williamson (1979) assumes that economic actors will be opportunistic, that is, seek advantage over others by deliberately breaking contracts or exploiting information if they believe they can do this without penalty. A broken contract may not result in the injured party resorting to the courts, for example, because of the time and expense involved. Trust, on the other hand, may be needed for long-term relations, reducing opportunism, or there may be sanctions applied by third parties such as other firms who feel they might become victims of such opportunism. These considerations add a welcome non-economic input to the discussion of subcontracting.[5]

A very fashionable area of subcontracting theory stresses the labour aspect of subcontracting. This is by no means new: every school economic history text is full of examples of using cheap, external sources of labour, that is, labour obtainable on a lower cost than employing it directly, but in the 1980s this was elevated almost into a new theory of the economy.[6] The principle of reward and labour cost differences between directly employed labour and labour power supplied by other, usually small, firms or homeworkers or other kinds of self-employed persons underlay the much discussed 'flexible firm' model of Atkinson and Meager (1986). In the ideal type, the 'flexible firm', (usually large) seeks three kinds of analytically distinct but closely related labour use advantage from subcontracting:

i)   *Numerical Flexibility.* This refers to being able to increase or decrease the effective size of its labour force quickly with few bureaucratic or cost disadvantages.

ii) *Functional Flexibility.* The ability of the firm to increase or decrease the numbers of workers performing particular kinds of tasks. This might be achieved, for instance, by switching directly employed labour between tasks or through subcontracting arrangements.

iii) *Rewards Flexibility.* The move toward individualised labour contracts reflecting employers' assessments of the value and performance of individual employees. Again this may be internal to the firm but may also exploit the lower levels of rewards (wages and salaries and other benefits such as paid holidays, sick pay and pension levels) thought to be found most often in small firms.

One reason why this kind of subcontracting received so much attention in the 1980s and continues to do so in the 1990s is that it became prominent in the public sector. The privatisation of public services provided by central and local government has been carried out for a number of reasons but a major one has been labour flexibility (Marsh, 1992:Ch. 7 and Ch. 9).[7]

In the private sector (again supported strongly by government through changes in employment and trade union legislation) it has been extended, most recently, in retailing where several high street retailers such as the Burton Group, decided in the early 1990s to convert their full-time labour force into part-timers, on call for any number of hours from zero to full time in any particular week.

Clothing manufacture, which is very commonly cited in discussions of subcontracting, has several of the characteristics argued to promote such relations: very unstable, unpredictable markets, large differences in economies of scale at different stages of production, large differences in capital investment and labour costs between firms in the production chain, and very large and very small firms (Rainnie, 1989; Winterton and Winterton, 1990; GLC, 1985:Ch. 4). At one end of the production chain are very small producers – for example, homeworkers operating efficiently with a single sewing machine. Their output and that of an array of other small, end-of-the production-chain producers, goes most commonly to other small firms who wholesale finished garments to retailers. The latter are often very large enterprises, the high street retailers whose names are familiar to every consumer, with Marks and Spencer, said by Rainnie (1989:96) to have over 600 suppliers and to take 20% of the British clothing industry's output, probably the best-known example.

THE NEGLECT OF LOCALITY IN SUBCONTRACTING STUDIES

What is noticeably absent from attempts to develop a theoretical context for subcontracting relations is much of a systematic emphasis on locality:

> on the basis of my initial research . . . very few, if any, non-trivial *general* theoretical tendencies concerning the spatial configuration of sub-contracting relationships can be identified.
>
> (Holmes, 1986:98 emphasis in the original)

One reason, it might be suggested, is that the locational aspect of subcontracting in economic terms is so obvious as to need little theorising: subcontractors and principals are likely to be geographically near each other since this minimises costs. But on closer examination this appears not to be entirely the case (see for example, Mair, 1993).

As the last chapter showed, traditional 'industrial districts' in the UK were made up of clusters of firms undertaking similar and different stages of production. But in this century it has become much more common for subcontractors and purchasers to be geographically distant. For example, in electronics and clothing manufacture, two industries with very extensive inter-firm linkages, cross-national subcontracting is now often found.

On the other hand, one fashionable form of subcontracting, discussed in more detail below, the so-called 'just-in-time' linkage pioneered by Toyota in Japan, has a strong locational/spatial element. Here the subcontractor has to produce constantly varying numbers of components to be delivered at very short notice to the purchasing firm. This allows the latter to maintain very low stock levels (with substantial cost benefits) but requires very quick and sensitive responses from the supplier. A corollary of this relationship, if it is to be effective, is that the supplier and customer must be spatially close.[8] There is evidence, however, that this is very much a 'Japan' phenomenon and transplants to North America (Mair et al., 1988) and the UK have not led to the development of a local cluster of suppliers.[9] In short, in theorising about subcontracting relations between firms, it is unclear what the local economy component of this kind of inter-firm linkage might be. Recent research appears to show both a decline in the importance of local economies in inter-firm relations *and* its possible increase in some kinds of links.

A CRITIQUE AND SOME FURTHER THEORISING

At the beginning of the above section, it was argued that the importance of subcontracting as a form of inter-firm linkage was exaggerated. There are several reasons which might be responsible for this. For instance, it might be the result of a reaction against the unsatisfactory and over-simple, atomistic models of inter-firm relations in classical economic theory. Or perhaps it reflects assumptions about the essentially subservient role of small firms in a modern advanced economy. (The term '*sub*contracting' itself has an implicit notion of the supplying firm – usually assumed to be a small firm – being subservient to the purchasing firm.) Or, alternatively, it might reflect the increased attention given to Japan as a model of economic success in recent years since subcontracting is widely seen as a core component of the Japanese economy (Mitsui, 1992; Thorburn and Takashima, 1992). Or, finally, it may be a by-product of the kinds of theories, especially those linked to Post-Fordism, discussed in Chapter 1.

Whatever the reason or combination of reasons producing the concentration on subcontracting and especially its link with small firms, the picture needs redrawing. First, much of the theorising and even more of the research deployed in its support, is linked to the manufacturing sector. Within the manufacturing sector, there is often a selective emphasis on a few industries, especially car-making (eg Friedman, 1977; Thorburn and Takashima, 1992) and clothing manufacture (eg Rainnie, 1989). Yet manufacturing is now only a small part of the UK economy. By the mid-1980s, indeed, its contribution to National Income had fallen to around a quarter (Ball et al., 1989:86) and has fallen further since. The car industry contributes relatively little to National Income compared with its heyday in the 1960s, despite the recent small resurgence produced by Japanese manufacturers Nissan, Toyota and Honda establishing UK plants.[10] In short, neither manufacturing nor motor car making can be taken as typical of the UK economy. Similarly, neither can the other commonly cited industries used to illustrate subcontracting theory, such as clothing manufacture or electronics.

Second, and even more relevant, the vast majority of small firms are not in the manufacturing sector. For instance, taking firms employing under 25 people as 'small', Curran and Burrows (1988:55) calculated that almost 90% of *all* small businesses were in services or construction. This suggests that whatever links small businesses have with the wider economy, they are certainly not over-represented in manufacturing. The proportion in construction, around one in four according to Curran and Burrows, are, however, likely to be involved heavily in inter-firm relations of the subcontracting variety not only as suppliers but also as principals since many construction firms in the private dwelling building and repairs sector are also small (Norris, 1984). But the remainder, the great majority of small firms, are in services.

Subcontracting relations in the services sector have not been neglected entirely though they have received considerably less attention than those in manufacturing. O'Reilly (1992) provides a study of subcontracting in the financial services sector (banking) in Britain and France showing that this has broadly followed the patterns discussed earlier in relation to manufacturing. In both countries banks have subcontracted non-core activities (catering, security, courier and messenger services), turned more to 'production smoothing' subcontracting to iron out fluctuations in work flow, and bought in expertise in the use and application of IT. The overall tendency was for these shifts to be more evident in France than Britain. What is not clear is how much of this external sourcing has gone to small firms. In the UK it is unlikely that small firms have captured many of the new opportunities. For example, contracts for staff catering in larger centralised enterprises such as UK banks as well as the supply and maintenance of IT equipment, are likely to be negotiated at regional or national level, greatly reducing the chances of small businesses winning such contracts.

One other selected inter-firm relationship, which some would see as subcontracting in services, is franchising, which has shown substantial expansion in the UK since the 1960s (Felstead, 1991:69). While a precise definition is hard to come by, one view might be that it consists of: one business (the franchisor) entering into contractual relationships with franchisees (typically self-financed, small independent owner-managers or sometimes other large organisations) who operate under the franchiser's trade name to produce and/or market goods or services according to a format specified by the franchiser. The franchiser may be a small or large firm.[11]

It has been suggested that this 'contracting forward', that is, transferring the final stages of production and distribution to other firms may occur for a variety of reasons. One set of reasons parallels those often cited in the theoretical analysis of subcontracting in manufacturing, the importance of divergent economies of scale. In this instance, relatively stronger economies of scale accrue to earlier stages of production of the good or service but there are few economies or even considerable *dis*economies of scale at the final stage of distribution. One clear example is where the final stage contains a strong personal service element as, for example, in catering. Large organisations often find it difficult to ensure a high quality, committed customer service in many areas of services and a solution is to share the returns with another, often a small firm owner-manager who operates the outlet on personalised management basis.[12]

Interestingly, one other long-standing example frequently discussed is car sales. Typically car manufacturers rarely sell their products directly to the consumer but operate through tied or franchised outlets. The reasons for this have been argued to be linked to the complexity and emotionally charged content of the transaction (Marx, 1980), for example, part-exchanges and the effects of local market forces. Manufacturers, it is argued, cannot manage the sales and support processes involved in selling cars from a distance and have preferred to externalise this final link in the producer to consumer chain.

Even taking into account inter-firm relations such as franchising as examples of subcontracting, it is difficult to see how most small services firms could be defined as 'subcontractors'. The great bulk are in catering, retailing and repairs (Curran and Burrows, 1988) where although subcontracting exists, it hardly dominates. For very large numbers of these businesses, private consumers are their sole market or they have a mix of business and private customers where business-to-business relations are only part, perhaps only a minor part, of their markets. Even those small firms who have other businesses as customers are not necessarily subcontractors even within the wide definitions discussed earlier, Most theorists (as Williamson's transaction approach illustrates for example) allow for a category of discrete market transactions between firms which entail no close or prolonged association between the parties.

The point that not all businesses-to-business, still less all small business-to-large business relations, fit the subcontract paradigm has been recognised more formally in attempts to construct typologies of small business–large business relations. One of the best-known attempts has been offered by Shutt and Whittington (1984), which has been subject to further refinement by subsequent theorists and researchers, notably Rainnie (1989:85). In the Rainnie version, the typology of small firm–large firm relations has four categories:

i)   *Dependent.* Small firms which largely serve the interests of large firms – subcontractors whose viability depends wholly on the purchasing decisions of the large firms. The Marks and Spencer supplier exemplifies this category for Rainnie.

ii) *Competitive Dependent.* Small firms in manufacturing and services who compete with large firms by intense exploitation of their equipment and especially their labour by 'sweating' practices. Despite a degree of independence their strategies and survival are influenced heavily by their larger competitors.

iii) *Old Independent*. Small firms operating in niches of demand unlikely
      to be invaded by large firms, for example, because potential profits
      are too low to be worth the bother of entering the market. An ex-
      ample offered by Rainnie is the small jobbing printer.

iv)   *New Independent*. Small firms operating in new and developing mar-
      kets which have not attracted large firms though they may well
      suffer the attention of the latter if the market expands further. Ex-
      amples of these processes are common in the history of the elec-
      tronics industry where a cycle of small firm market innovation
      followed by large firm entry and domination has been common. (see
      e.g. Rothwell, 1986)

This is a very helpful systematising of the range of possible relations
between small firms and the market. However, it has limitations. For instance, Rainnie was unable to offer indications of the distribution of small
firms between the categories or of the historical trends which may have
occurred or the likely future trends. The emphasis on the subcontracting role
of small firms in much of the literature, for example, would place a high
proportion, or even a majority, in the dependent category. This, we believe,
is not the case: it is much more likely that the majority are in one or other of
the next three categories, as the evidence in later chapters makes clear.
Rainnie's theoretical perspective is neo-Marxist, which assumes that a normal characteristic of the operation of capitalist market economies is that
larger enterprises dominate and exploit smaller enterprises. Small firms that
show apparent independence are either at the margins of the economy or
can be picked off by larger firms when the latter choose to do so.

Our contention is that the level of economic integration and the ability of
larger enterprises to dominate smaller firms in the above way is over-stated.
The historical trend, certainly over the last decade and a half, has been to
demonstrate the relative strength of small firms and the relative weakness of
large firms in terms of neo-Marxist assumptions concerning the operation of
capitalist market economies (Curran, 1990).

A more recent but less satisfactory attempt at a small firm–large firm
relations typology, is summarised by Penn (1992:211–212). Here the underlying assumption is that co-operation rather than exploitation, is the major
feature of normal relations between small and large firms. The typology
suggests four main forms of relationship:

i)   *Satellite*. Here small firms provide a series of functions for large firms
      such as supplying components or doing other work on behalf of the
      large firm with the relations co-ordinated through the market.

ii)   *Active Engagement*. Seen as a new form of small firm–large firm rela-
      tionship of increasing importance. Here the relationship is close with
      the large firm closely monitoring the small firm to ensure quality and
      technological innovation. The small firm functions to supply the
      large firm with components and services. Examples cited from the

literature are small firms which exist to serve the needs of Nissan and Komatsu in the North East.

iii) *Subordinate Co-operation*. This is also described as a 'new form of relationship' (1992:211) and a key example is seen as small firm–large firm relations in the clothing industry where firms such as Marks and Spencer are dominant customers of a host of small firms. This has led, it is alleged in the literature, to increased co-operation *between* small firms to improve their capacity to respond to large retailers.

iv) *Independent Co-operation*. Here small firms act in concert to create an alternative to the classic satellite dependent relationship and thus increase their independence in relation to large firms. The examples offered are drawn from the literature on Post-Fordism and the 'Third Italy' discussed in detail in the last chapter.

To be fair, Penn's typology was generated from recent international literature on small firm–large firm relations as a test bed for examining contemporary inter-firm relations in Rochdale, a 19th century industrial district based on textiles and textile machinery manufacture.[13] He concludes, in effect, that the typology has little relevance to Rochdale's inter-firm relations:

we did not find much evidence of the . . . much vaunted new forms of inter-firm relations . . . *active engagement* or *subordinate co-operation*.

(1992:224 emphases added)

Nor did he find evidence of *active management* relations. Instead, the commonest relationship by far was the classic satellite relationship but even this was showing clear signs of decline in the Rochdale local economy:

the historic residue of inter-industry linkages remained a significant feature . . . [but] there has been a progressive uncoupling of the constituent parts.

(1992:225)

Penn's typology reproduces several contemporary fashionable emphases, but it also remains firmly in the tradition of much of the subcontracting literature discussed earlier in the chapter with its almost exclusive concern with inter-firm relations within the manufacturing sector. The weakness of this emphasis, given the importance of the services sector in the UK economy and the high proportion of small firms not in manufacturing, was also demonstrated earlier.

Inter-firm relations, particularly those between small and large firms, therefore remain poorly theorised despite attempts to classify them more systematically, as for instance Rainnie's, and to move away from the distorting effects of the over-concentration on the subcontracting form of such relations. The number of smaller businesses has increased very sharply since the mid-1970s and, other things being equal, it might be argued that this trend suggests the small enterprise sector is growing more independent, more central to the economy and more likely to display a widely varying set of relations with other actors in the economy, including large firms. But, equally, it might be argued that while such an increase in small firm numbers has occurred, this is also reflected in increases in the proportion of small firms involved in subcontracting or other forms of dependence on large firms.

TRENDS IN SUBCONTRACTING AND SMALL FIRM DEPENDENCE

The debate on whether subcontracting relations are on the increase and especially if small firm–large firm subcontracting is becoming more or less common, has been fierce over the last 15 years. It has been linked closely with the so-called 'flexibility debate' (Pollert, 1988a and b; Rainnie, 1989 and 1992). Proponents of the flexibility thesis argue that the 1980s witnessed a massive increase in co-operation between firms, including small firms and large firms, due to a fundamental reordering of relations between firms in capitalist market economies. As Rainnie puts it:

> Subcontracting in this model changes from a win:lose situation with the large firm dominant, to a more long-term, inter-dependent, high-tech relationship, supposedly a win:win situation.
>
> (Rainnie, 1992:223)

In other words, subcontracting as a mode of articulation linking the small firm to the wider economy remains at least as important as it always has been.

We have noted already that there are considerable difficulties in estimating the importance and extent of subcontracting for small firms but the question of whether it has been on the increase or decrease might be considered separately. In short, we may not know the base from which the trend starts but may be able to estimate whether the trend is up or down. There are no reliable aggregate statistics on the amount of subcontracting and any estimate would be problematic because of the difficulty over definition.[14] Moreover, due to the interest generated by the flexibility debate, a considerable amount of research has been undertaken which offers information on subcontracting levels.

Most of the research, predictably, concentrates on manufacturing. What is particularly interesting, however, about the findings is their lack of consistent support for any clear answer to the question posed in the above paragraph. One of the clearest assertions of an increase in subcontracting in the UK over recent years comes from Thorburn and Takashima (1992) who examined three sectors, engineering with special reference to machine tools, the motor industry with special reference to passenger cars, and electronics with special reference to computers.[15]

Their findings indicate that in the engineering sector, the claimed increase in subcontracting by principals was clear cut and recent. It arose, they argue, from a radical thinking by firms of their strategies in the face of increased competition from abroad and recession. The subcontractors, on the other hand, showed various forms of relations with purchasing firms. One-off orders were very common and the longest formal contract found was 1 year: 'orders of one or two months perhaps with projections for a similar period in the future were the most common arrangements after one-offs' (Thorburn and Takashima, 1992:68). In other words, close relations of the kind often attributed to inter-firm relations in Japan were not found. All the sub-contractors tried to avoid over-dependence on any particular individual customer and to maintain 'distance' between themselves and purchasing firms.

The motoring industry has a history of extensive outsourcing going back to its earliest beginnings with levels of subcontracting rising and falling over the years (Turner, 1964). Thorburn and Takashima (1992:74) interviewed two UK principals only, and found some increased subcontracting in the late 1980s but this started from a high base. Evidence was found of drastic reductions in the numbers of suppliers and attempts to hold prices down, as part of continuing contract relations though not of the Japanese practice of progressively driving down prices in return for long-term agreements. The subcontractors themselves who were interviewed on their motor industry work received mainly one-off or short-term contracts and were somewhat sceptical about the long term given the instabilities resulting from recession. Little evidence of close relations was found though the purchasing companies claimed close relations with some of their suppliers.

Like the motor industry, the electronics industry has a tradition of inter-firm contracting (Scott, 1983; Scott and Storper, 1986; Scott and Kwok, 1989). In computing manufacturing it is also common, and one of the principals in the Thorburn and Takashima study, IBM UK, is still the key manufacturer in the industry. The researchers report a sharp increase in outsourcing by IBM since 1980 but the four other principals involved showed little overall change in the last decade. IBM's relations with suppliers are relatively close with a good deal of monitoring of supplier performance and normally long-term orders. However, the company emphasised that relations were on a commercial basis, that is, the length of time a relationship had existed was always subordinate to market considerations. The other principals gave mainly only one-off orders and did not wish for close relations with suppliers.

The electronic subcontractors supplying printed circuit boards but also some specialised products were very aware they were in a highly competitive situation with customers willing to switch suppliers. They were also aware that increasingly the latter were coming from outside the UK, especially the Far East, allowing customers to be ruthless in driving bargains. Orders were commonly one-offs though with some longer term contracts up to 18 months. They stressed their independence from customers in terms of the technological superiority of much of their work. They also sought final consumers for some of their products to widen their market and escape from the dependence associated with subcontracting. In short, there may have been an increase in subcontracting as a sourcing strategy but other influences such as recession and increasing competition kept relations clearly very market-based.

Thus, despite the authors' clear belief that there has been an increase in subcontracting, closer analysis shows that the picture revealed by their findings is rather less clear. Assertions of switching to more outsourcing by principals is contrasted with less confidence among subcontractors of such major changes. Subcontractors stress continuity with the past or even a worsening situation due to recession and foreign competition. Similarly, there is little evidence of closer relations between purchasing firms and subcontractors: *some* principals do have close relations with their suppliers but whether this represents a sea change or simply the management strategies of particular firms is not easy to say.

Equally clear is the lack of enthusiasm on the part of subcontractors for such relations: maintaining their distance, seeking alternative markets and customers to avoid over-independence and an awareness of the implicit opportunism and instability inherent in purchaser–supplier relations in their industries, were very pronounced. Nor was locality mentioned much by their respondents. Indeed, references to the globalisation of manufacturing and supplying relations were much more typical.

Thorburn and Takashima (1992:12–13) note other research carried out on subcontracting and small businesses in engineering which reported an increase in subcontracting by half the principals surveyed over the previous 5 years (Lyons, 1991a and b; Lyons and Bailey, 1991). On average, the increase among these 50% was 47%. The other 50% of principals had either maintained or reduced their levels of subcontracting. Unfortunately, this was mainly a mail survey. Mail surveys of small firms are notoriously difficult to conduct successfully and are far from ideal when investigating subjects as complex as inter-firm relations. Nevertheless, even at face value, the findings only offer limited support for the notion that there has been an increase in subcontracting and the study draws on only a very limited number of other studies to support this finding. Again we should note the emphasis on manufacturing, a sector in which only a small proportion of small firms are located.

Even if it is accepted that outsourcing has become a much more conscious and systematic process on the part of purchasing firms, for example, through the advent of new approaches such as 'preferred supplier' lists and insistence on BS 5750 accreditation of suppliers, this does not necessarily mean a major increase has occurred. Preferred supplier strategies usually mean a drastic reduction in the number of subcontractors used by the purchasing firm. Being a 'preferred supplier' does not logically entail any increase in the closeness of relations between the firms or any reduction on the part of suppliers of a strong commitment to independence. BS 5750 approval similarly does not necessarily tie firms any closer to each other. Indeed, there is limited evidence that some small firms seek BS 5750 approval primarily as a marketing device to increase their independence and widen their customer base (Holliday, 1993).

Recession and market instability, both severe for much of the last 15 years, are not ideal conditions for the promotion of close, long-term, ordered relations between suppliers and purchasers. Both produce insecurity and opportunism in market relations. Both are likely to lead to more 'one-off' relations, closer to the simple market transaction end of the continuum than the total incorporation and integration end of the continuum of inter-firm relations. Inter-firm relations can become disorganised and less stable even if the absolute number of such transactions is on the increase. Equally, whether such phenomena can be subsumed under a persuasive conceptualisation of 'subcontracting' might be regarded as debatable.

Of course, Thorburn and Takashima are not the only researchers to have tackled the issue of whether subcontracting is on the increase in the UK economy. Milne (1991), in a study of the UK 'whiteware' industry,[16] which still has a substantial market in the UK though foreign competitors have made serious inroads, focused on the question of whether UK firms have adopted different manufacturing techniques and especially flexible and vertically disintegrated strategies to cope with increased competition (Milne, 1991:242). He concluded that while firms had introduced major changes in R & D, marketing and distribution in order to achieve product development, higher quality and better work flow:

> Levels of subcontracting within the sector have, in general, not shown any tendency to grow and have, in the case of many of the more innovative manufacturers, declined as certain core activities are brought back in-house or on-site. The development of JIT [just-in-time] based supplier relations has spread . . . but has yet to reach any level of real success as most of the companies are unable to exert the necessary types of control over their suppliers.
>
> (Milne, 1991:248)

He notes that, traditionally, the UK whiteware industry was heavily located in the London and West Midlands areas. This has declined only slightly in recent decades but incoming far eastern manufacturers are establishing new factories in other regions, particularly to manufacture microwave ovens. In other words, there is drift towards less spatial concentration, subcontracting patterns show no evidence of becoming more localised around purchasing firms and subcontracting itself is not on the increase. Thus, contrary to Thorburn and Takashima's findings, the evidence offered by Milne suggests doubts about assertions of major growth in subcontractor–supplier complexes and the further arguments concerning closeness of supplier–principal relations.

Elsewhere, Penn and Francis (1992) also examine the issue of whether there has been an increase in subcontracting in the UK in the 1980s and

again are sceptical on the basis of research in which they have been involved. For instance, a comparative study of paper mills in the UK and
Finland (Penn, Scattergood and Lilja, 1992) showed that, while there had
been experiments in outsourcing, particularly of support services, the most
recent trend was to take these activities back in-house. This was found
necessary mainly to establish control over the quality and delivery of the
these services

In a further survey of 180 firms in 6 localities in 1988–1989, 30 establishments were investigated in terms of their use of subcontractors. The economic sectors covered both manufacturing and, unusually in research on this
topic, services. Levels of subcontractor use varied considerably though there
was no obvious sectoral bias or size effect (Penn and Francis, 1992:6). Differences within sector, conversely, were very marked with metal working
establishments recording the highest levels. There was, however, a locality
effect. In Coventry, for example, 2 out of 3 (66.7%) establishments surveyed
used subcontractors but in Swindon the equivalent proportion was 20.8%
(Penn and Francis, 1992:7). They argue that such locality differences were
the results of local labour market differences rather than the impact of competitive forces. Overall, most establishments in the survey neither used subcontractors nor acted as subcontractors themselves.

The concentration of subcontracting among metal working establishments
is noteworthy. Research reporting an upsurge in subcontracting and inter-
firm relations such as that of Thorburn and Takashima, has often been
highly reliant on data drawn from samples where metal working or metal-
working-related firms, were strongly represented. Again, broadly in line
with Thorburn and Takashima's findings, rather more than half of the
establishments had increased their outsourcing during the previous 5 years.
Yet this also included public sector organisations where some of the increase
may have resulted from political fiat rather than economic influences. Penn
and Francis also warn strongly against accepting simple counts of the proportions of firms involved in subcontracting activities. In most of the instances where subcontracting was recorded it represented less than 5% of
total activities of the establishment:

> our results suggest that subcontracting remains a relatively insignificant
> part of most of the British economy with the exceptions of metal work-
> ing and energy establishments.
>
>   (Penn and Francis, 1992:15–16)[17]

One final example illustrating the ambiguities of the findings attempting
to assess the extent to which subcontracting and/or closer inter-firm relations have developed in the UK over recent years is provided by Marshall
(1989) in a paper which very interestingly combines the motor vehicle industry, the subject of several of the previous studies discussed, and services.

Increasingly, manufacturing industry has developed more sophisticated
white collar functions – design, marketing, distribution and customer

support – but equally increasingly, in-house services and outsourcing have become spatially related to the manufacturing function in new ways. Traditionally, the accepted view was that head offices of large firms were located close to London (or, less frequently, major regional centres) while manufacturing was located elsewhere in branch plants in peripheral locations (eg Massey, 1984; Goddard and Coombes, 1987). This sometimes generates two supply chains each spatially related to the separate sets of functions: managerial and control functions stimulated the development of local specialist services ranging from catering to international airports while production units in different locations spawned subcontractors to serve their needs. Marshall argues that these models are now widely accepted as increasingly outdated.

Recently another view has emerged stressing important departures from the above model. One important way in which change has occurred, it has been argued, is that, internally, management structures, aided by IT, have been simplified to cope with recession. At the same time the contracting out of services linked to white collar functions has increased. However, for Marshall this model is also too simple and he uses a study of the motor vehicle 'aftermarket', that is the market for replacement parts, equipment and accessories, to illustrate his thesis. The main concentration of supply activities feeding this market is in the West Midlands, home of so much of the former UK vehicle making industry. At the other end of the chain are the retail outlets (eg Halfords) and service outlets (chains such as Kwik-Fit to the backstreet one-man repairer). In between are the wholesalers and factors, national and local. Marshall (1989:144) argues that there has been a trend towards emphasising the service end of the chain and making the production and distribution of components more responsive to the needs of the service outlets and final consumer.

Recession has had a similar impact on manufacturers in this sector as elsewhere. Management structures have been de-layered, managers made more accountable, non-production workers reduced in number with more contracting out of production and support services. Firms have also scrutinised closely their distribution functions with some withdrawing completely, or in part, to create opportunities for specialist distributors. But this has not meant any overall fragmentation of functions. For instance, at the service/retailing end of the chain, several major distributors have brought in-house some service activities. Thus Marshall cites examples of training, packaging and consultancy services to businesses further down the chain. Market research and computing are either internalised or created as new activities by distributors. This increases their sensitivity and effectiveness in relation to consumers (private and business consumers such as small repairers).

Among retailers such as Halfords, internalisation *and* contracting out has been common (Marshall, 1989). For instance, several have expanded back into distribution to increase efficiency and the control of stock supplies while, alternatively, some suppliers have been made responsible for delivery direct to outlets and other activities such as payroll have been contracted out. Earlier Marshall mentions the strong tendency for end of chain businesses to integrate further consumer services into their operations. Halfords, for example, now has a chain of servicing centres in addition to its traditional outlets selling parts and materials to the DIY market. Specialist exhaust and tyre replacement outlets such as Superfit have also expanded into providing full servicing.

Spatially, many of the changes at the manufacturing and distribution stages have meant relocation and a separating of functions geographically. Jobs were lost in one area but sometimes gained in others as, for example, when transport operations were contracted out to national transport distributors located elsewhere. 'Locality' in the conventional sense of local economies defined by local authority or travel-to-work areas, would be irrelevant to moves of these kinds.

Marshall demonstrates, therefore, that subcontracting and inter-firm relations need to incorporate services activities as well as manufacturing to provide a more adequate analysis. He also demonstrates that there is no overall simple trend towards contracting out and that one reason for the over-simplification of much of the literature dating from the mid-1980s is its over-concentration on manufacturing activities. There are, he argues, clear discernible influences on decisions to outsource or internalise services activities. For example, where the service is deemed highly significant to the business or the need unpredictable but important, internalisation is likely.

Examples of studies such as the above show that inter-firm relations are unlikely to be explained simply in terms of some variety or other of flexibility theses. The bringing in of services to the analysis – both services in the manufacturing firm and services as the prime economic activity of the enterprise – adds richness but also destroys simple interpretations. It also shows again how irrelevant conventional notions of 'the local economy' are when examining inter-firm relations at this, real life level compared with the generalised level of the 'industrial district' analysed in the last chapter. One other weakness here, of course, is that size of enterprise has also been largely neglected.

CONCLUSIONS

In this chapter the concern has been with relations between firms, the reality of business links between firms as opposed to the macro-level, economy-as-a-whole perspective of the opening chapter. The major theoretical emphasis, subcontracting relations, has been examined alongside recent attempts to decide whether inter-firm relations are becoming closer and more common. The analysis has also touched on several other issues relevant to the contemporary discussion of inter-firm relations such as the flexible firm thesis and just-in-time links, both employed as ways of conceptualising trends in relations between firms.

How the main concerns of this book, the small firm and locality, can be integrated into these discussions is also a central issue. The results are inconclusive with the theoretical level failing to be sufficiently encompassing, the empirical studies apparently supporting several views, and an almost virtual absence of consideration of the dimension of locality. Small firms *are* mentioned but their presence is often implicit rather than systematically accounted for.

Although 'subcontracting' is much the most used term in discussing relations between firms, it is often over-general. In some definitions, for example, the difference between a one-off market transaction and 'subcontracting' appears to be very thin. For instance, the Thorburn-Takashima definition quoted at the beginning of the chapter allows transactions to be intermittent and based on no written contract. Some might see this as stretching the notion of 'subcontracting' to an unacceptable degree.

In our view the phrase 'subcontracting' is best taken to mean the supply of items and/or services on the basis of written agreements which specify the type and delivery of the items and/or services over some period of time but exclude one-off orders. Where orders are repeated, that is, a similar order is placed at some later time but there is no commitment, whether verbally or in writing, that a repeat order will be made, then the relationship is treated as a 'one-off'. Even if there are informal expectations that repeat orders might be made, it is argued that this should not be treated as 'contracting' in the above sense because the supplier cannot be confident enough to plan ahead organisationally, for example, to stockpile resources and labour) to prepare for further orders.

Most conceptualisations of subcontracting do not take into account the potentially differing understandings and expectations of the parties (firms) involved. While the principal (purchasing firm) may have in mind a continuing relationship based on placing orders as and when requested with perhaps substantial gaps between orders (several months or more than a year, for example) does the supplying firm share this view? It is noticeable that in the studies of subcontracting discussed so far, while the purchasing firms frequently saw relations with supplying firms as ordered, close and long term, supplier firms often saw these relations as more distant, less ordered and had less confidence in their continuation particularly under conditions of recession and increasing competition from imports. Suppliers were frequently reluctant to develop relations of dependence with purchasing firms and some adopted strategies seeking other customers and markets to offset any reliance on purchasing firms.[18]

Even where subcontracting links are found, the extent and length of such relations appeared to be much less than would be warranted by the very frequent use of 'subcontracting' to describe the major way firms are linked to each other. This seemed to hold even for manufacturing given by far the most attention in both theoretical discussions and empirical studies. While some writers emphasise 'flexibility' and 'just-in-time' relations as demonstrating increases in subcontracting and the closeness of inter-firm relations, the evidence for this is only limited. On balance, the flexible firm thesis suggesting an increase in outsourcing of services and to a lesser extent, productive capacity, does appear to have some support. Of course, it does not follow that this increased outsourcing has gone to small firms or to local firms. Just-in-time arrangements as a new and important mode of inter-firm articulations in the UK seem to receive little empirical support from the studies cited.

The major weakness of much of the subcontracting literature is its over-concentration on manufacturing. This not only neglects the decline in importance of manufacturing in the UK economy but where the concern is with small firms, it neglects the key point that the great majority of small firms are not in manufacturing. Moreover, the indications are that subcontracting is less important as a mode of inter-firm linkages in services. One obvious reason for this is that many enterprises in services integrate into the market through links with private consumers rather than business customers.

More generally, an artificial dualism introduced by the over-concentration on manufacturing implies manufacturing firms are not closely integrated with services or that their services aspects are secondary. Indeed, they are often called 'peripheral' activities in the flexible firm thesis for instance. Yet, as some of the most recent research (Marshall, 1989, for example) shows, in an economy where services have become so important, it is necessary to see how manufacturing serves services, that is, to trace inter-firm relations *across* the boundaries between sectors without assuming one sector (manufacturing) is more 'real' than the other. When this is done simple notions of a straightforward trend towards more subcontracting become even more doubtful as Marshall demonstrated.[19]

Two other weaknesses also stand out in theorising and research on inter-firm linkages. First, the assumption that small firms exist by and large to serve the needs of larger firms is rarely tested rigorously. Often particular industries are cited as supporting this 'obvious' assumption, construction and clothes manufacture most commonly, but whether this holds more generally is unclear. Much of the literature on inter-firm linkages is not concerned very greatly with size of firm or size of firm is not incorporated systematically. For instance, what are the size distributions typical of inter-firm relations in particular sectors of the economy? Do they vary from sector to sector and to what extent are horizontal linkages (that is, linkages between firms of similar size) more important than the much more emphasised vertical linkages?

Locality is, if anything, even more neglected than size of firm in the literature on inter-firm relations. For instance, very few of Thorburn and Takashima's respondents mention locality as important in relations with other firms. Nevertheless, locality is mentioned indirectly more frequently and in interesting ways. For instance, the fashionable concern in management literature with just-in-time relations between suppliers and principal firms is often linked with an emphasis on spatial proximity: supplier firms need to be close to the purchasing firm to ensure rapid and accurate responses. But research on subcontracting indicates that just-in-time relations are difficult to set up in practice in the UK so this locational aspect does not appear to be critically important.

Other indirect references to locality may be gathered from the frequent mention of the growing importance of foreign suppliers of components and services. This means that 'locality' in the conventional sense, that is, some geographically demarcated area within the UK, such as a region or smaller area, may well be becoming less important. Put another way, these references provide support for the globalisation thesis. However, gauging the exact significance of these changes is difficult since virtually all the mentions refer to the manufacturing sector rather than services where globalisation is likely to be very much less marked, though competition from less developed countries in areas such as data entry and software is increasing (Wagstyl, 1993).

As Marshall (1989) shows, spatial shifts in inter-firm linkages may well be complex involving increases *and* decreases in spatial proximity. Keeble et al. (1991) and Bryson et al. (1993) in their study of small business services firms indicate that while such firms increased in numbers substantially in the 1980s, they also show less close links to locality, defined in the conventional 'local economy' sense, than other kinds of small firms. Even this is not the end of the story, however, since attention has to be given to what kind of locality is being considered. For instance, O'Farrell and Hitchens (1990) point out there is considerable variation in the market for business services between regions and, we may infer, this also holds within regions.

Finally, the relations between inter-firm linkages in the economic sphere and other kinds of linkages are not explored in most of the theorising and literature. Inter-firm relations are embedded in non-economic relations and the latter may be critical to how inter-firm relations function. To be fair, there is indirect recognition of this point. For instance, the notions of 'trust' and 'opportunism' are brought into the analysis from time to time. Trust in on-going relationships and the extent of opportunism, that is, the tendency for firms to unilaterally engage in behaviour based on simple economic advantage regardless of whether this goes against implied or even formal contractual agreements with other firms, will both be affected by how deeply economic relations are embedded in non-economic relations (Pyke, 1992). It is possible that this neglect in the literature is a tacit recognition of the way in which the economic has become detached from the non-economic but a more explicit confirmation would be preferred. Similarly, there is little or no recognition of the roles the state and political system play in influencing inter-firm relations.[20]

In this and the last chapter, we have analysed a considerable range of theory and research with implications for theorising and empirical study of localities, small firms, the relations between small and large firms, and levels of economic integration. The findings from the study to be presented in the remainder of the book enable us to contribute to this theoretical and empirical debate.

Notes

1. A typical example of this tendency is Thorburn and Takashima (1992) whose work is discussed at length later in this chapter. See also Penn (1992) and O'Reilly (1992) for other examples covering the span of inter-firm relations across manufacturing and services.

2. This alleged tendency is, in turn, linked with a variety of other phenomena (also often seen as recent developments) such as 'just-in-time' supply systems and 'flexible production' and, on a more theoretical level, 'regimes of flexible accumulation'. Reference to these phenomena will be made later in the chapter when research on the extent and involvement of small firms in these activities is examined.

3. This definition understates the continuity and similarity of the views between Friedman and Thorburn and Takashima. In a more recent article, the latter authors offer an almost identical definition to that of Friedman:

   > Subcontracting is an intermediate arrangement which lies between the use of free market transactions for standard commodity inputs and vertical integration, where a firm decides that an input . . . is so specific to its needs that it would not expect an outside supplier to be willing to make it or would not trust it to do so.

   (Thorburn and Takashima, 1993:3)

   The differences between the 1992 and 1993 definitions may be attributed to the different audiences for which each was intended: the above is from an article in the *National Westminster Bank Quarterly Review*, intended for a more general readership.

4. This oversimplifies the situation considerably of course. For instance, in order to ensure that extra capacity will be forthcoming from sufficient suppliers, the latter must be assured that the market has a future. The large firm, therefore, will often need to ensure that some demand exists even in periods of low activity otherwise suppliers have little incentive to invest in, or develop, their capacity to keep up with new technology. Suppliers, however, may also be engaged in other kinds of production free from dependence on large firms or may operate in unrelated markets.

5. A clear example of the approach of transaction cost analysis is provided by Eccles (1981) in an analysis of the building industry, another industry with very widespread subcontracting especially involving small firms and the self-employed labour-only contractor (Scase and Goffee, 1982; Norris, 1984). Eccles introduces the notion of the 'quasifirm' in the building industry, seen as a complex of firms and units of production under the leadership of a general contractor or building developer involved in a project or series of projects.

6. Take, for example, the use of sub-contract labour in the railway industry in the last century (Coleman, 1965).

7. At the time of writing, the privatisation process in the public sector has been brought almost to a halt by a European Community ruling that where employees are transferred from the public sector to private employers as a result of privatisation, their wages and conditions should not be worse (Labour

Research, 1993:23). Both government and firms seeking contracts to provide services have suggested that this makes privatisation much less attractive implying that 'labour flexibility' in the form of lower labour costs, is central to this kind of subcontracting. The authors (with Brian Abbott) are currently undertaking a study of the opportunities provided to small firms by the privatisation of local authority services.

8. The authors have visited Nissan's Sunderland plant where Nissan representatives stated that just-in-time suppliers often have to deliver to the point on the line where the components are used and that a major supplier (of car seats) is located on the same site as the Nissan plant. However, Nissan have not managed to develop the just-in-time system using local firms to anything like the level the company would prefer (Garraghan and Stewart, 1992).

9. Mair, for example, suggests that a 'highly localized spatial concentration in Japan may be uniquely related to that country's poor transportation infrastructures' (Mair, 1993:216).

10. The decline in manufacturing especially engineering and motor car making, with the upturn in the latter resulting from Japanese inward investment, is well documented by Thorburn and Takashima (1992:34–45) as an introduction to their choice of sectors for the study of subcontracting in the UK and Japan.

11. This conceptualisation follows closely that of Curran and Stanworth (1983:11).

12. This is one approach to theorising franchising. Others see it as merely a form of marketing distribution, that is, that the franchisee-operated outlets are simply agents of the franchisor. For a fuller discussion of both conceptual alternatives and theories of franchising, see Curran and Stanworth (1983) and Felstead (1991).

13. Penn's typology might more properly be termed a 'hypothetical typology' that is, a set of linked categorisations based on an overall set of reasoned assumptions derived from previous thinking and research. Such an analytical construct does not imply that the person generating the typology has any commitment to it other than as a basis for testing observations made to assess its utility. In this sense, critical points made against the typology are not criticisms of the originator unless they take the form of arguing that the typology does not reflect accurately previous thinking and research.

14. For example, Thorburn and Takashima (1992:21–22) cite Census of Production data on 'materials purchases' as a surrogate for subcontract purchases but it is the authors' view that this is misleading since it cannot account for the way in which the materials are purchased (they may be off-the-shelf purchases) or the nature of relations between buyer and supplier.

15. Thorburn and Takashima's research was comparative, comparing UK and Japanese subcontracting relations and is particularly valuable for its contribution to the literature on such relations. However, here only the findings on the UK are discussed since this book is about inter-firm relations and local economies in the UK. It should also be noted that Thorburn and Takashima's samples are small, usually less than half a dozen principals or subcontractors for each of the industries covered but their analysis is convincing and very well contextualised in an overview of the relevant industries and their inter-firm relations.

16. 'Whiteware' here refers to the sector of electrical appliance manufacturing making domestic refrigerators, freezers and laundry appliances. The term is derived from the common practice of painting these products white.

17. In this and the previous chapter, we also discussed Penn's detailed study of Rochdale (Penn, 1992) an old industrial district based on textiles where he presented evidence suggesting relations between firms in the locality were becoming less integrated with little evidence of increased subcontracting, indeed, the reverse.

18. In one study of small firms, for instance, just over a quarter of firms interviewed stated that they were reliant on two or three major customers who took over 50% of turnover. Among the services firms in the sample, this proportion was much lower. The authors take this as showing a low level of dependence (Scott et al., 1989:9).

19. For a parallel argument which also takes into account regional factors with some reference to the locational dimension seen in intra-regional spatial terms, see O'Farrell and Hitchens (1990).

20. Again, it is not difficult to make such links. For example, an issue receiving considerable attention currently is payment of debt between firms with representatives of the small firm sector arguing for statutory support for shorter payment periods (see eg the *Guardian*, 7.6.1993). The criticisms made by smaller businesses of slow payment behaviour are often of larger businesses for whom they have carried out work. In Japan, Mitsui (1992:2–3) describes how government developed a large-scale policy initiative backed by substantial resources to strengthen the small business sector from the mid-1960s onwards.

3

A NEW STUDY OF LOCAL ECONOMIES

INTRODUCTION

Investigating small and large firms in specific localities poses a number of formidable methodological problems. Besides the problems discussed in Chapter 1 of what might be taken to constitute a 'locality', there are also problems in saying what are 'small' and 'large' firms and assembling suitably representative samples. Conventional methods have taken a top-down, aggregate data perspective, using VAT registration data, for example. We have already argued that this kind of approach has considerable drawbacks. Aggregate national data sets on economic units are very poor in relation to small firms however the latter are defined. For instance, firms with a turnover of less than £25,400 in 1990 and £35,000 in 1991 (the period in which the data in the present study was collected) did not need to register for VAT. One estimate using NatWest Bank data (Jennings, 1991) suggested that between 40 and 50% were not registered.[1] Other data sets such as the Census of Production do not require the smallest businesses[2] (those employing less than 20) to make a return. However, these businesses constitute over 95% of all businesses in the UK according to McCann (1993:9).

Given the above inadequacies of aggregate data sets, their use to monitor economic activity at the regional level and especially small-scale economic activities, must also be suspect. For instance, VAT registration and de-registration data is often used to analyse economic trends within regions to assess changes in regional industrial mixes (see eg Daly, 1991). But not only does the data exclude large numbers of smaller enterprises in each region, it also fails to allow for differences in the size distributions of businesses within different industries. In manufacturing, for example, businesses tend to be larger, measured by employment or turnover, than in services (Small Business Research Centre, 1992:4). Some regions such as the South East have a higher proportion of economic activities in the services sector than others, for example Yorkshire-Humberside, and these differences increased for much of the 1980s (Daniels, 1988). In other words, top-down analyses of regional differences and trends are likely to become less and less adequate as the focus moves downwards towards smaller local areas. What these considerations suggest is that other approaches are required which focus more directly on small firms and/or specific geographical areas.

THE SMALL ENTERPRISE: CONFUSIONS AND CONCEPTUALISATIONS

Before offering an alternative approach to collecting data to examine inter-firm relations and localities, it is necessary to clear away some of the conceptual confusions which bedevil discussions of the 'small' firm and its role in the economy. There is no official definition of the small business since government departments and legislation employ a wide variety of definitions and researchers have similarly developed a wide variety of definitions depending on the kind of economic activity and issues being studied (Cross, 1983; Curran, 1986; Curran and Stanworth, 1986; Burrows and Curran, 1989).

There are basically two approaches which have been employed in seeking an adequate and persuasive definition of the small business: *qualitative definitions*, which try to capture the meanings and beliefs and behavioural aspects which distinguish a 'small' business from larger enterprises, and *quantitative definitions*, which try to place small firms within boundaries marked out in terms of numbers employed, turnover or some other quantitative measure deemed appropriate. Neither have produced conceptualisations which are entirely acceptable and in practice, the two approaches are often combined within a single definition though there remain plenty of examples of advocates of one or other approach.

An excellent early illustration of the two approaches which remains influential, even if its influence is now declining somewhat, comes from the Bolton Report (1971). This was the last large-scale comprehensive government inquiry on the small firm and its role in the UK economy. The Committee initially adopted a qualitatively based ideal type of the small firm:

> First, in economic terms, a small firm is one that has a relatively small share of its market. Secondly, an essential characteristic of a small firm is that it is managed by its owners or part-owners in a personalised way, and not through the medium of a formalised management structure. Thirdly, it is also independent in the sense that it does not form part of a larger enterprise and that its owner-managers should be free from outside control in taking their principal decisions.
>
> (Bolton Report, 1971:1)

It is easy to quibble with elements of this conceptualisation. For example, leaving aside for the moment what constitutes a 'market', it might be argued nevertheless that some firms which many would regard as 'small' have a relatively large share of their market. However, most people would probably agree with the basic approach. The emphasis on personalised management by the owner(s) and lack of bureaucratic organisation have been repeatedly used in subsequent conceptualisations albeit with other elements added, such as close personal relations between employers and employees.

Having offered their ideal type, the Committee then found that due to a lack of data on 'the business population in terms of ownership, management, organisational structure and market shares' (Bolton Report, 1971:3) it was unable to offer any kind of national picture. It then switched to the kind of relatively crude quantitative definitional approaches which have been so widely used by government and researchers since 1971. The Committee had opted to study 9 sectors covering most of the economy, but excluding agriculture, professional and financial services, and solved its problem by adopting what it felt were suitable quantitative definitions for each. For instance, in manufacturing a 'small' business was one that employed 200 employees or less, in retailing it was a business with an annual turnover of £50,000 or less, in construction it was 25 employees or less. In some sectors, the quantitative indicator was very specific to the kind of economic activity in which businesses were engaged. In road transport, for example, the committee adopted the definition of a small business being one with '5 vehicles or less' (Bolton Report, 1971:3).

These quantitative definitions have either not survived very well or have been little used. The definition '200 or less' employees offered for manufacturing has been widely criticised as being too generous. Some argued that by the time a manufacturing firm employed 200 people many of the characteristics seen as typical of the small firm in the committee's qualitative ideal type, such as personalised management and minimal organisational structure, would be largely absent (Goss, 1991:30).

The definitions based on turnover measures have suffered from the impact of inflation and no simple upgrading compensates for this. Besides the doubtful utility of offering a single figure for a highly disparate range of economic activities, the 1989 equivalent figure in retailing, for example, £410,000 (Employment Department, 1989:9) was already absurdly high when set against the actual turnover distribution of UK businesses revealed by clearing bank data. The latter indicates that even 2 years later, in 1991, 89% of *all* accounts of business customers of the clearing banks had turnovers of less than £250,000 (Midland Bank, 1993a). In other words, the impact of inflation on business turnover since 1971 has been less than on prices generally rendering the definition less and less useful.

Other definitions generated by the Bolton Committee might be helpful but have not been used extensively. The road transport definition which categorised a small business as having '5 vehicles or less', for instance, has not been used in any research of which we are aware. The definition offered for catering, 'all excluding multiples and brewery managed pubs' seems unreasonably wide given the complex mix of types of enterprise which might be listed under 'catering' (Gabriel, 1988) and, unsurprisingly, appears not to have been used.

More recently, users of solely quantitative approaches have become increasingly *ad hoc* and cautious. The quantitative limits selected are often very explicitly described as selected for their simplicity and few claims for generalisability or still less universality are made:

> The study includes businesses employing up to 200 people. This does not, however, imply that we accept the Bolton Committee rationale that all businesses of this size are 'small'; rather we are agnostic about the size definition of small businesses, recognising that what counts as 'small' will vary according to many factors, including the labour market and the industrial sector in which they are located.
>
> (Atkinson and Meager, 1992:2)[3]

Clearly, simple quantitative conceptualizations have their uses. Where, for example, anything other than this approach is very difficult such as European-Community-wide statistics for economic units, they are better than nothing. Within a particular sector, simple quantitative definitions will also be appropriate since sectoral specificity in effect controls for many other aspects which often vary greatly from one sector to another.

It is the extreme variability in the characteristics of small enterprises which undermines attempts to apply simple quantitative definitions across the entire range of activities in which such enterprises engage:

> No simple definition of what constitutes a small firm can be useful for all purposes. A window cleaner with a ladder and a bucket; an independent shop with two employees; a farmer with 300 acres, one employee, a tractor and other equipment; a clothing manufacturer with fifty employees; all share some common problems which are essentially different from those of a multinational company. It is not necessary to agree upon a precise threshold point at which a small business becomes a large one, to make useful generalizations about small and large firms.
>
> (Bannock, 1991:2)

The examples offered above make the point succinctly even if many of those engaged in research and policy-making might regard the dismissal of the need for a solution as over-sanguine.

A QUALITATIVE APPROACH: GROUNDED DEFINITIONS OF THE SMALL ENTERPRISE

The alternative approach, developments of the qualitative definitions of which the Bolton Committee's initial ideal type is the progenitor, has been revived in recent years. They have often been combined with quantitative elements to add to their operational utility. It is this kind of approach which has been adopted in this study since it met our aim of coming as close as possible to the key people involved in the kinds of economic activities we proposed to research, that is both small business owners and others contributing to a particular kind of economic activity.

We call our approach a 'grounded definition' of the small enterprise. It stems from theoretical developments in conceptualisation by Curran and Stanworth (1986) and Burrows and Curran (1989). Essentially, the key difference in the approach is to shift the problem of defining the characteristics – qualitative and quantitative – from the researcher to those most involved in the kinds of economic activities selected for study. Thus, for one of our selected activities, small garages and vehicle repairers,[4] we approached a range of sources of information including trade association representatives, owner-managers and executives in various parts of the motor vehicle sector, academic sources and official statistics.

The basic question we put to these sources either directly or by interpreting documentary materials, was what constitutes 'small', 'medium' and 'large' businesses in this kind of economic activity? Every kind of economic activity which has been in existence for any period of time develops a culture, ways of thinking, assumptions, beliefs and values expressed in behavioural forms. For instance, many kinds of economic activity have their own language, technical terms or other linguistic usages which those involved find useful or necessary to conducting their economic activity and engaging in transactions with others. These are accompanied by other behavioural forms such as ways of making an agreement with others, payment practices and production methods. Economic cultures of these kinds are found in middle-class activities such as the Stock Market through to printing and street market traders. In short, the culture of any economic activity is the meanings and behavioural outcomes generated around that activity in the everyday practical accomplishment of the production of goods and services.[5]

One common aspect of economic cultures, as our preliminary investigation demonstrated, is the assessment of other enterprises engaged in the same kinds of activities on various kinds of ranking criteria. For instance, in almost all kinds of economic activities some of those involved will be seen as 'cowboys' by others often those who have been in the area for a long period. 'Cowboys' are seen as offering poor quality goods or services, often at prices lower than other firms who operate to higher standards, and who may hoodwink less well informed consumers and provide what is seen as 'unfair' competition by most other firms in the area.

One common way of ranking other firms is size measured in some way which those in the area agree is appropriate. Often, as we discovered, the criteria used are a mix of qualitative and quantitative elements. What we also found was that while there was no exact agreement among those we talked to on the precise boundaries of 'small', 'medium' and 'large', there was nevertheless sufficient consensus for us to be able to adopt a definition of a 'small firm' in our selected areas of economic activity which reflected reasonably accurately the ideas of those most directly involved.

NINE TYPES OF ECONOMIC ACTIVITIES

There are a very large number of different kinds of economic activities, the heterogeneity which marks any complex economy and is reflected in the UK in the Standard Industrial Classification (SIC) which has up to 6 digits to cover all sectors. To cover them all would be both impractical and beyond the resources available even to well funded researchers. Very roughly, economic activities can be divided into production industries (SIC 1–4) (manufacturing plus mineral extraction and public utilities) and construction (SIC 5) and services (SIC 6–9). In the UK of the 1990s, according to VAT data, manufacturing industries (SIC 1980 2–4) constitute around 10% of businesses, services (SIC 1980, 6–9) 66% and construction (SIC 1980, 5) 15% (Business Monitor 1992). The selection of the kinds of economic activities to be studied had to take into account this weighting. In order to allow a comparison to be made an 80–20 division was adopted between services and manufacturing. This allowed a sufficient number of manufacturing firms to be included for comparison.

The two main samples from which data are presented were constructed for two different research projects. One was concerned with small firm–large firm relations in two contrasting local economies (the characteristics of these are described below) and the second with small service sector firms in 5 other localities, also chosen to contrast with each other. Although the projects were separate, they were led by the same researchers and employed similar methodological approaches and initial thinking. The data collection and fieldwork of the two projects overlapped chronologically. In part, this book was inspired by the similarities in findings from the two studies prompting the development of a wider interpretation. For all these reasons, while there are differences between the projects, it is felt that combining them produces mutually supporting data sets which contribute to the development of much more powerful analysis than a single project would offer.

To control for the heterogeneity of manufacturing, some selection of kinds of economic activity was required. For various reasons small firms in two sectors were chosen: printing and electronics. Printing is usually classified as 'manufacturing' (see for instance The Census of Production) though it shares many of the characteristics of producer services businesses since it mainly provides a service to other businesses. Most smaller businesses in the sector are involved in general printing (though specialisation is on the increase) with links with a wide range of other businesses: customers can literally come from any other sector of the economy.[6] In terms of the specific focus of this book – the importance of local economies and business-to-business relations, small general printing firms should be ideal for examining such spatial clustering and business linkages. They should provide clear examples of businesses which help generate local economic networks.

The electronics industry was also selected, in part, because of its favourability to theoretical interpretations which stress local economic relations and close business-to-business relations. 'Electronics' is difficult to define precisely in terms of the kinds of activities which can be so labelled since there is such a great diversity of electronics applications. So many products used in the home and business now contain electronic components and there is such a high rate of technological change that boundaries are difficult to draw. We have followed the categorisation of the National Economic Development Office (NEDO) (1991a). As several observers, such as Thorburn and Takashima (1992) whose work was discussed in the previous chapter point out, there are extensive vertical and horizontal relations in this industry with subcontracting and other kinds of inter-firm relations being common not only between firms in the sector itself but with businesses in many other sectors. Together the electronics and printing industries samples totalled 60 businesses.

The approach adopted to provide a rationale for the selection of small service sector enterprises and to ensure representativeness was necessarily rather more complex than the judgemental approach adopted in choosing the types of manufacturing enterprise. It was decided to locate the kinds of enterprise on two criteria:

i)   A continuum with traditional services at one pole and recently emerging services at the other.
ii)   A continuum with services meeting the needs of other businesses at one pole (producer services); services meeting the needs of other services and private consumers in the middle (mixed services); and services aimed at satisfying private consumers only at the other pole (consumer services).

In addition, subject to the above constraints, we felt there should be a bias towards more recently emerging forms of services activities, that is, the kinds of activities which are representative of the so-called 'services revolution' which was at the heart of economic restructuring in the UK in the 1980s (Graham et al., 1989). How these newer forms of services activities are related to localities and what kinds of business-to-business relations they typify is crucially important in saying something about trends in these phenomena.

The result of the above strategies was the selection of seven types of services activities:

i)   *Computer Services.* Firms involved in any or all of software development, system integration and installation; user support services; data processing; database management; facilities management.
ii)   *Vehicle Repairs and Servicing.* Firms principally engaged in routine servicing and repairs of private and commercial motor vehicles, but excluding franchised dealerships retailing new vehicles and franchised outlets of larger enterprises offering exhaust, battery and tyre replacement services or servicing.

iii) *Employment Agencies.* Businesses involved in finding people perma-
     nent or temporary employment with other employers; secretarial
     services such as report typing, copying and binding; training of
     people or employees of other businesses in word processing, com-
     puting, sales and other business skills.
iv) *Plant and Equipment Hire.* Firms whose main business is any of the
     following: the hiring of construction and DIY tools and plant, skips,
     business equipment and vehicles (but not car hire firms).
v)   *Advertising, Marketing and Design Agencies.* Businesses engaged in one
     or more of: marketing consultancy and research; advertising plan-
     ning and design origination, selection and purchase of media outlets
     for advertising; direct mail activities including list broking; the co-
     ordination of the above activities.
vi) *Video Hire, Health, Beauty and Leisure Clubs.* Businesses which trade
     exclusively as video hire outlets; keep fit facilities such as gymnasia;
     sports clubs, dance exercise studios and sun tanning/sauna services.
vii) *Free Houses, Wine Bars, Licensed Restaurants.* These include only single
     outlet 'free house' public houses, wine bars or restaurants with a
     licence to sell alcohol.

Again, there is a problem in placing clear boundaries around some of
these kinds of activities. In practice, though some businesses called for a
decision on whether they should be in the sector category or not, the great
majority of firms which were listed in the sampling frames presented few
ambiguities. As described earlier, a 'grounded definition' of the small enterprise was constructed by tapping the shared business cultures of those
involved in the seven different kinds of enterprise. The definitions finally
adopted are given in Figure 3.1. In total, this sample consisted of 350 businesses, approximately 70 of each of the seven types.

Data from two further subsamples are also included in the study. The
reasons for their selection were related to the specific aims of the two projects as originally designed but the data produced is directly relevant to the
thesis developed in the present book. The first of these subsamples consisted
of 16 large enterprises and organisations selected from the same two localities as the manufacturing small firms. These were engaged in a variety of
activities – manufacturing, retailing and the public sector – and were chosen
to represent the largest employers in each of the localities. Such enterprises
might be seen as dominant or highly influential in a locality and at the core
of any local economy.

The 16 enterprises or organisations – 8 in each of the two localities – were
selected from a list of the 20 largest employers in each area to ensure a
balance between manufacturing and services and the private and public
sectors. The specific aim of the original project required that the purchasing
policies and practices of each organisation be investigated to ascertain, first,
the extent to which they were linked to the locality and local firms and,

Manufacturing

Printing   Legally independent enterprises, managed directly by an owner-manager or managers engaged in general printing with not more than 20 full-time employees or part-time equivalents.

Electronics   Legally independent enterprises, managed directly by an owner-manager or managers engaged solely in some branch of manufacturing electronic equipment or components either as complete or part complete products (SIC 33 and 34). Normally the firm would not employ more than 30 full-time employees or part-time equivalents.

Services

Computer Services   Legally independent enterprises, managed directly by an owner-manager or managers involved in any or all of: software development; system integration and installation; user support services; data processing; data bank management and facilities management with not more than 20 full-time employees or part-time equivalents.

Vehicle Repairs and Servicing   Legally independent enterprises, managed directly by an owner-manager or managers principally engaged in routine servicing and repairs of commercial and private vehicles with up to ten full-time employees or part-time equivalent.

Employment Agencies   Legally independent enterprises managed directly by an owner-manager or managers and involved in providing employees for other businesses, secretarial services and training. Not more than ten full-time or part-time equivalent employees excluding people registered to be placed with other businesses.

Plant and Equipment Hire   Legally independent enterprises managed directly by an owner-manager or managers hiring construction tools and plant, skips, business equipment and vehicles with up to ten full-time employees or part-time equivalents.

Advertising, Marketing and Design   Legally independent enterprises managed directly by an owner-manager or managers engaged in marketing consultancy and research; advertising planning and origination; selection and purchase of media outlets for advertising; direct mail activities and the co-ordination of the above with not more than 25 full-time employees or part-time equivalents and not listed in Campaign's top 50 advertising agencies or top 30 agencies listed annually.

Video Hire, Health, Beauty and Leisure   Legally independent businesses directly managed by an owner-manager or managers. Video hire businesses must trade exclusively as such and not have more than three outlets. Others will provide health-enhancing, sports, dance exercise, sun tanning and sauna services through a single outlet and not have more than ten full-time or part-time equivalent employees.

Free Houses, Wine Bars and Restaurants   Legally independent businesses directly managed by an owner-manager or managers. A 'free house' is a single outlet, full on-licence business whose major defining consumable is beer though other drinks and food may be sold. Wine bars are similar with wine being the major consumable. Restaurants are single outlet businesses with a licence to sell alcohol on the premises. In none should there be more than ten full-time employees or part-time equivalents.

Note: In practice, the employment numbers listed were exceeded for some firms in the samples due to incomplete information at selection or changes in employment numbers subsequently. However, in no instance did this go with a failure to meet any of the other criteria listed.

Figure 3.1   Nine Types of Economic Activity and Seven Grounded Definitions of the Small Enterprise

second, the extent to which they purchased from small firms, directly or indirectly. These aims, therefore, fit closely with the aims of this book – to explore the relations between firms in specific localities and the extent of an integrated set of economic activities which might be labelled 'a local economy'.

The second subsample providing additional data was drawn from the larger sample of 350 small service sector enterprises introduced above. It consisted of 45 small businesses in all five localities who were selected randomly to participate in a critical incident study. In this the aim was to explore the ways in which owner-managers handled the problems produced by non-routine events or 'critical incidents' which can arise from time to time in any business. For instance, almost every small business loses an important customer at some time whose loss has potentially serious implications for the future of the business. Or, again, the reliance on owner-managers to provide the essential leadership and direction to the business means that a family issue – death or severe illness of a spouse or parent, or even a happy event such as a new addition to the family – can mean the business suffers from a lack of attention at the top.

What the critical incident study sought to determine was not only how the owner-manager(s) handled the problems caused within the business but also the extent to which they used outside contacts as sources of help and support. These could include other business owners, bank managers, accountants, family and friends, and it might be assumed that where this occurred these external links would be mainly local. In other words, the data from this study also provided information on the kinds of local connections (or their absence) which go to make up an integrated local economy and indication of the extent of 'embeddedness' of the economic in non-economic social relations with family, friends and others.

LOCALITIES AND THEIR SELECTION

At the time the research designs for the projects from which data is presented in the book were formulated (the late 1980s) there was an increasing concern with spatial aspects of the economy (Champion and Green, 1988; Massey and Allen, 1988; Cooke, 1989a). It was, therefore, highly appropriate to ensure that spatial variation would be incorporated into research designs of the projects. To this end, the 410 small businesses and 16 large enterprise/public sector organisations were drawn from seven contrasting localities.

The manufacturing businesses and large enterprises/public sector organisations were from two localities:

i)   *Kingston upon Thames* is part of the affluent, highly dynamic South East region which has enjoyed a high level of economic prosperity since the end of World War Two. It has never been a centre of heavy industry or traditional manufacturing. Its main manufacturing has been linked to aerospace activities with links with the aircraft industry going back to 1912.[7] One consequence of these links is a high concentration of electronics businesses. It is located adjacent to the M3, M4 and M25 motorways and Heathrow and Gatwick airports. Indeed, its communication links with other areas make it very difficult to say what 'Kingston upon Thames' is as a focus of economic activities. Many who live within the borough boundaries, for instance, work outside and especially in the centre of London. Many of those who work in the borough live outside its boundaries. Similarly, retailing outlets (including two large department stores, one of which now incorporates a modern 'mall' type shopping centre) attract customers from a wide area. The borough's official boundaries were drawn in the 1974 local government reorganisation to include Surbiton, New Malden, Tolworth and Chessington but it remains the smallest of the 32 London boroughs. The largest single employment sector is public administration (35% of the labour force in the borough itself) and services, overall, are responsible for over 70% of employment (Census of Employment, 1987). Although the area suffered in the recent recession, this should be kept in perspective since the decline started from a high level of activity: in March 1991 the official unemployment rate for Kingston Borough was 3.9% (Kingston Borough Council, 1993, see Table 3.1). In April 1993, this had increased to 8.4% but was still relatively low in national terms (Kingston Borough Council, 1993).

ii)   *Sheffield*, in strong contrast to Kingston, has had a very troubled economic history over the last two decades because of the decline of heavy industry, steel making especially, and manufacturing. It is a much more geographically focused economy than Kingston Upon Thames. Although it is part of the Yorkshire and Humberside region it is also demographically, politically and culturally much more of a centre with which the half a million people who live in the area can identify. Besides steel making and steel products, especially cutlery and other products made with the special alloy 'stainless' steel, a trademark exclusive to the city since 1924, Sheffield also had a strongly developed manufacturing sector more generally.

Measures of the decline of manufacturing economic activities in the area are plentiful. For instance, the 1987 Census of Employment found that employment in the steel industry fell from 45,000 in 1971 to 13,000 in 1987 (DEED, 1989b). In the locality prosperity index constructed by Champion and Green (1988) Sheffield scored 262 out of 280[8] indicating that only 18 other localities were ranked as less prosperous in Britain. In other words, the decline in steel making and manufacturing has not been offset by an expansion in services and knowledge-based industries, though services now provides more jobs than any other type of economic activity. In March 1991, in the middle of the data collection period for the study, unemployment was 11.3% against a national level of 7.5% (Sheffield City Council, 1991).

The 350 service sector small businesses were drawn from five localities selected again to ensure that any spatial contrasts would be revealed. The localities were:

iii) *Guildford*, chosen to represent a highly affluent, low unemployment locality in the South East. On the Champion-Green prosperity index, for instance, Guildford ranked as the 15th most prosperous local labour market area in Britain. Although not geographically distant from Kingston upon Thames, it is more representative of the region's economic characteristics since Kingston, is very much a locality on the margin of Greater London (usually treated as a separate 'region' by government and economic geographers) and the South East region proper. However, like Kingston it is difficult to draw clear boundaries around what might be called the 'Guildford local economy'. Although Guildford is the main county town, it is not a focus for economic activities in the same way as, for example, Sheffield but is much more part of a wider area which includes towns such as Woking, Farnham, Dorking and Aldershot. In turn, these connect with other towns in the region such as Reading and Basingstoke to produce an almost seamless pattern of economic activities. This effect is, in part, produced by good road links with the M3 and M25 both less than 10 miles from Guildford. Gatwick Airport is also close with Heathrow Airport within reasonable travelling distance using the motorway connections.

Economic activities in the area are dominated by services. For example, by the mid-1980s, almost 8 out of every 10 jobs in Guildford were in services and less than 12% in manufacturing (Census of Employment, 1987). Much of the manufacturing is in electronics and other high tech areas rather than in older style manufacturing such as motor vehicle construction. Primary industry has never had a strong representation in the area and provided jobs for fewer than 5% of the local labour force in 1987. In other words, this locality's economic activities were already 'restructured' by the mid-1980s, that is, they were already the economic mix that has been argued to be the kind to which the whole UK economy is shifting as it becomes a post-industrial economy. The relative prosperity of Guildford is shown in its very low unemployment rates. In March 1991, the unemployment rate for the District was 3.2% (Guildford Borough Council, 1993).

iv) *Doncaster* was selected to offer an example of a Northern locality, which, like Sheffield, displayed the characteristics of economic decline in primary industry, coal mining especially, and old manufacturing industries such as railway engineering – both the 'Flying Scotsman' and 'Mallard' class locomotives were built in Doncaster. Like Sheffield also, the decline in these older sectors has not been compensated for by an expansion in areas such as services. Doncaster, on the Champion-Green index, does even worse than Sheffield since it is rated 274, that is, only 6 other localities in Britain managed a lower score.

Spatially, Doncaster consists of a Metropolitan borough area surrounded by other nearby economic clusters such as Mexborough,

Thorne and Rossington with Barnsley and Rotherham nearby. Although primary industries and manufacturing have declined, at the end of the 1980s they were still responsible for a third of the jobs in the Metropolitan borough while services provided just under 60% of jobs (Doncaster Metropolitan Borough Council/NOMIS, 1989). In 1989, the Doncaster, Barnsley, Rotherham and Mexborough areas averaged over 12% unemployment compared with a national level of 6.9% (Labour Market and Skills Assessment, 1990/91:20). In the Doncaster travel-to-work area in March 1991, the unemployment rate was 11.1% (Employment Gazette, 1991).

A further indicator of the problems faced in this area is the range of assistance available to promote more economic activity. Besides government regional assistance, British Coal Enterprise and several varieties of European Community funding (eg European Regional Development Fund, the European Coal and Steel Community Assistance and European Social Fund) were also available.[9] During the period of the fieldwork for the study, there was considerable local optimism that the level of economic activity would rise, for example, through a proposed road-rail interchange to make Doncaster a major terminal for rail traffic resulting from the opening of the Channel Tunnel.

v) *Islington* was selected to represent an inner city local area with a very mixed set of economic activities. London boroughs were not included in the Champion-Green index but Islington was subjected to a preliminary study to ensure that it provided a wide range of poor and affluent areas and populations. It offers examples of the decline of long established, inner city manufacturing activities as firms disappear or relocate in areas offering better accommodation and a better transport infrastructure. But parts of Islington are also spatially close to the City. This has attracted many small businesses since they can serve the markets created by City activities without having to pay City rents. At the other end of the borough, it borders on boroughs such as Hackney and Waltham Forest, among the poorest in London.

Islington also contains a very mixed population. Like most inner London boroughs it has a substantial ethnic minority population with a long established Greek-Cypriot community being especially prominent. Because many of the businesses have located in Islington to be near the City, their owners and many of their employees do not live in the borough. Unemployment varies and is not easy to establish because the workforce is geographically mobile so that an increase in the number of jobs in the borough, for instance, may have no impact on the level of unemployment among the borough's residents. Unemployment in the location was relatively high at 14.2% in March 1991 (Islington Borough Council, 1993) although it should be borne in mind that a good deal of economic activity and employment involves commuting from outside the area.

The actual area covered by the study was slightly larger than the local authority's boundaries. The reason for this was that in order to recruit sufficient numbers of the 7 types of economic enterprises listed earlier, the geographical areas of the sampling frames had to be extended. This was done in a way which ensured that the areas beyond the local authority boundaries were immediately adjacent to, and of a character with, the nearby areas inside Islington.

vi) *Nottingham* was chosen to represent a Midlands economy. It was also at the mid-point of the Champion-Green index being ranked 141 out of the 280 localities listed. Like many other areas in the Midlands, Nottingham suffered from the decline in manufacturing in the early 1980s. However, some major national manufacturers still operate, notably T I Raleigh. The city also has a very long-established clothing and knitwear industry. Where Nottingham seems to have been more fortunate is in generating new activities in the 1980s so that the economy recovered faster than many other similar areas though not at a sufficient rate to put it among more prosperous areas such as Guildford.

Unemployment was very unevenly distributed throughout the area. Overall, it reached 20% in 1985 with some inner city wards recording levels as high as 36% even as late as 1988 when unemployment generally was falling in the UK. Other areas abutting the city have unemployment levels well below national levels reproducing an effect found in many parts of Britain where inner city decline has gone with higher prosperity and employment levels in the areas away from the centre, due in part to economic activities relocating. In March 1991, unemployment was 8.2% in the city overall (Employment Gazette, 1991).

vii) *North East Suffolk*. The final area selected for study was a rural locality. Rural localities have been neglected until recently but are now receiving attention as their declining agricultural activities are being replaced by new non-agricultural activities seen as part of a process of urban–rural shift (Keeble et al., 1992). The core of the area chosen was the Rural Development Area (RDA) designated in 1984 extended to include an area of Suffolk to the north of the RDA plus a part of Norfolk just over the Suffolk boundary, Lowestoft and the coastal area up to Great Yarmouth. The RDA was selected after discussion with the Rural Development Commission, one of the sponsors of the research programme, and the wider area was included because the area is so thinly populated that it would otherwise have been impossible to obtain a full sample of each of the seven types of service enterprise required by the research design.

East Anglia, of which North East Suffolk and the RDA is part, has been widely described as one of the boom areas of the 1980s with

Table 3.1　Unemployment Levels and Prosperity Index Rankings for the Seven Localities

	Unemployment March 1991 %	Index of prosperity*
Kingston upon Thames	3.9	N/A
Sheffield	11.3	262
Guildford	3.2	15
Doncaster	11.1**	274
Islington	14.2	N/A
Nottingham	8.2**	141
Lowestoft	8.9	213

Notes: * Based on Champion and Green's amalgamated index (1988). The index ranks the most prosperous as 1 and the least prosperous as 280 (see Note 8 for a brief description). No index values are available for London boroughs.
** Travel-to-work area. Unemployment data from the Employment Gazette (1991) except Guildford (Guildford Borough Council, 1993), Kingston (Kingston Borough Council, 1993) and Islington (Islington Borough Council, 1993). No composite unemployment figures are available for North East Suffolk.

official statistics showing that it was the fastest growing region economically in the UK with the exception of the South East (Dickens, 1988; Daly, 1990). However, the area selected for this study did not share this rapid increase in prosperity: it was mainly the southern half of Suffolk which benefited.

As might be expected, the RDA is strongly agricultural with up to 30% of the workforce in this and related activities such as food processing in some areas (Rural Development Commission, 1988). Agriculture has, however, been steadily losing jobs since the mid-1970s. Unemployment peaked in 1986 but then declined for the rest of the decade due to expansion in food processing, an increase in services and the Sizewell B nuclear power station construction work. The locality remains remote from larger centres of employment and is poorly served by major roads and transport. Although the population grew in the 1980s, this was mainly due to inward migration of commuters and retired people plus some newcomers bringing in new businesses often craft-based or connected with other leisure activities.

Lowestoft and the Waveney area to the north of the RDA are rather more urban though far from prosperous for much of the 1980s. Lowestoft, for example, suffered severe recession for most of the 1980s due to the decline in tourism and fishing, with unemployment reaching 17% in 1987 and only recovered when additional jobs in food processing and manufacturing were generated. In the late 1980s plants opened by several major companies such as Birds Eye, Sanyo and Shell (off-shore activities) created new jobs and helped bring unemployment down but other major activities in the area such as tourism and fishing struggled and Lowestoft could not compete with Felixstowe in the south of the region as a port. In March 1991 the unemployment rate for Lowestoft was 8.9% (Employment Gazette, 1991). Lowestoft ranked 213 on the index developed by Champion and Green (1988).

Together the 7 localities offer a cross-section of the UK economy at the beginning of the 1990s. They include prosperous and economically deprived areas, areas representative of the North–South divide and urban and rural localities. While no claim can be made that the localities offer a total coverage of the UK economy – they do not include localities outside England, for instance – they still offer a spectrum of localities from which a good deal of generalisation about the levels of integration and small firm–large firm relations typically found in Britain can be made with some confidence.

SAMPLING FRAMES AND SAMPLES

A problem which bedevils any kind of locality research on economic activities is constructing representative samples of businesses. In most localities, however defined (local authority areas, travel-to-work areas or the more recent TEC 'local economies', for instance) there will be a handful of large employers, those employing, say, more than 500 people, of which several will be in the public sector rather than the private sector. In Sheffield, for instance, half of the largest 10 employers are in the public sector. The rest of a locality's economic activities will be carried out by a large number of small businesses, most employing fewer than 5 people.

For the two localities – Kingston Upon Thames and Sheffield – where large firms and organisations were interviewed, the selection of these larger bodies was relatively easy. Having compiled lists of the largest employers, it was then decided to interview representatives of 8 organisations in each of the localities with a reasonable balance between the private and public sectors. In the Kingston locality the smallest of the 10 largest organisations employed 400 people but in Sheffield the smallest employed almost 2,000 people. This difference reflected a large size difference among organisations in the two areas. For example, at the time of the research Kingston's largest employer had 2,000 employees while in Sheffield, eight of the top ten employers had workforces of over 2,000. As might be expected, co-operation from the large organisations invited to participate in the research was excellent and a response rate of 88.9% was achieved.

While it is relatively easy to locate the larger employers in any locality, it is very difficult to find any up-to-date, complete lists of smaller businesses from which representative samples might be drawn. A major reason for this difficulty is that any lists date very quickly because of the high level of 'churning' in the small business population, that is, high rates of births and deaths. For instance, VAT data for 1990 shows that there were around 235,000 'births' (new registrations) which were offset by 185,000 deregistrations producing a net increase of 50,000 for the year to an overall total of 1.7

million (Daly, 1991:580). As pointed out, earlier, VAT data covers only a proportion of mainly larger 'small' businesses and it may be that businesses not covered, that is, not registered for VAT, have even higher levels of 'churning'. There is also the point that there are substantial locality variations in churning levels and losses and gains: Daly (1991:582) estimates that the net change over the period 1980–1990 in Surrey, for instance, was a 62% increase in registrations while in Suffolk it was 34%.

For this study there was an additional problem related to the use of grounded definitions for the 9 kinds of economic activities covered. Published lists of any kind – local authority business directories, *Yellow Pages* etc – would not provide sufficiently detailed information to be able to construct a complete sampling frame, that is, a list of businesses which met the criteria adopted and excluded other businesses for each of the selected localities. The only methodologically acceptable alternative was to construct our own up-to-date sampling frames for each type of enterprise in each locality.

This very laborious task took several months to complete in the 5 localities from which the services small businesses were recruited. The research team carried out initial studies in each area collecting as much information as possible in the form of local trade and business directories and any similar information. From these, together with *Yellow Pages*, lists of firms were compiled excluding any that were easily established as large or branches of large firms. For instance, the ownership of licensed premises can be established by inspecting local licensing registers. Garages which are franchised suppliers of new cars (excluded by the grounded definition) usually make this clear in local directories and advertising. In some instances, these sources did not produce very many examples of particular kinds of enterprise or it was suspected some businesses were being missed because lists, including *Yellow Pages*, were not up to date or complete.

Video hire outlets were the most difficult to locate and this was solved partly by street searches conducted while the interviews with other types of enterprise were being carried out. This direct observation method was also used to ensure that sampling frames for other types of enterprise were complete. In the other two localities where only printing and electronics firms were recruited, available lists, *Yellow Pages* and previous experience in researching small businesses in these two activities proved adequate.

After each list of each type of service enterprise in each locality was compiled it was accepted that they would still contain businesses which failed to meet the grounded definition criteria but it was decided that no bias would be introduced into the samples if this was ignored at this stage. For each type of enterprise in each locality, a suitable sampling fraction was adopted to produce the desired sample of 10 firms. The sampling fraction was, of course, dependent on the number of firms on the list and was sectorally highly variable. For example, in Doncaster the original compilation produced a total of 144 garage and vehicle repairers but only 33 advertising, marketing and design businesses.

In the two localities where manufacturing businesses were recruited, it was decided that 30 businesses (15 printing and 15 electronics firms) from each locality would be sufficient for the aims of the study. Here, instead of using a sampling fraction, it was decided to recruit firms from the available lists serially until the sample reached the desired size. Again, it was accepted that the lists might contain firms which would not be 'small' or whose activities fell outside the definitions adopted. Again, also, it was believed that suitable filters introduced at later stages in sample selection, would eliminate these without bias resulting.

Some of the filters to eliminate unsuitable businesses were introduced at the next stage. All selected businesses (either through using the sampling fraction for services businesses or manufacturing firm lists) were contacted by telephone with researchers asking the name of the owner-manager or a senior director and any other information on size measured by number of employees, its products or services and whether the firm was a branch of a larger firm. The aim here was to eliminate unsuitable firms and replace them with suitable firms. However, it was sometimes not possible to elicit all the information required in a preliminary telephone call. Representatives of firms were often suspicious of the motives of the enquirer despite being told it was for an academic research programme.[10]

The next stage was to send a letter to the owner-manager of the selected firm together with a brief explanation of the research project, inviting them to participate. Each letter was followed up a few days later by a telephone call to the owner-manager asking if they had received the letter and explanation and if they had any queries about the research. This call was also used as a further filter to exclude unsuitable firms. Previous information on the firm was confirmed and any additional information needed was sought to ensure it met the grounded definition criteria. If the business was suitable, the respondent was invited again to participate and an interview arranged where possible. Some respondents were willing to participate but asked to be contacted again later to arrange a convenient date and time.

Overall, by the above stage of sample construction a substantial number of businesses were eliminated as unsuitable. For instance, in the sample selection processes for the small service sector businesses, over 300 businesses were eliminated. A further 277 refused to be interviewed and these were treated as non-respondents though in many cases it was impossible to determine whether they fitted the relevant grounded definition. In all, over 1,200 letters were sent out although, as the quota for each type of enterprise in each locality was reached, any outstanding letters were followed up.[11]

Table 3.2 provides details of the overall response rate and response rates achieved for each type of enterprise and in each locality. The overall response rate is 58.6% though this masks substantial variations between the types of enterprise and localities. For instance, the response rate in computer services is almost 80 per cent while for garage and vehicle repairers it is half that at 40%. Similarly, in the two localities from which the manufacturing

Table 3.2 Initial Sample Response Rates for Types of Small Businesses and Localities

	King-ston	Shef-field	Notting-ham	Guild-ford	NE Suffolk	Don-caster	Isling-ton	All	N
Printing	78.9	83.3	–	–	–	–	–	81.1	30
Electronics	78.9	88.2	–	–	–	–	–	83.3	30
Advertising Marketing & Design	–	–	84.6	75.0	62.5	75.0	76.9	74.3	52
Computer Services	–	–	100.0	73.0	76.9	76.9	62.5	78.5	51
Employment Agencies	–	–	75.0	83.3	90.9	62.5	76.9	77.8	49
Free Houses, Wine Bar and Restaurant	–	–	58.8	52.6	62.5	45.5	50.0	53.8	50
Garage Repairers	–	–	34.6	57.9	37.0	27.8	50.0	40.0	50
Plant and Equipment Hire	–	–	66.7	53.3	45.8	46.2	50.0	51.0	49
Video and Leisure	–	–	52.6	55.6	43.5	35.7	34.6	43.8	49
Overall Response Rate	78.9	85.7	61.9	63.7	54.6	48.9	53.9	58.6	410
Completed Interviews	30	30	69	72	71	69	69	410	

Note: Details of the sample of large organisations and response rates are given in the text.

samples were drawn – Kingston upon Thames and Sheffield – the response rate is around 80% while in Doncaster the response rate is just under 49%.

Some of the reasons for these variations emerged clearly in the fieldwork. For instance, among garage and motor vehicle repairers it quickly emerged that one reason for the relatively low response rate was the character of the business itself. As most motorists themselves know, motor vehicle repairs and servicing operate on a tight 'just-in-time' basis. Owner-managers are often struggling to get vehicles back to their owners as quickly as possible and the research team found it difficult to get them to agree to a time to be interviewed or, having agreed a time, the interviewer arrived to find the owner-manager unable to give the interview because of pressure of work. Video hire outlets, another low response rate sector, were often owned by absentee owners with day-to-day running left to an employee. This sometimes made it difficult to contact the owner-manager or get them to agree to a time and place where the interview could take place.[12]

The locality differences in response rates are more difficult to explain. The higher rates achieved in Kingston and Sheffield may well result from the ability of the research team to focus on only two kinds of enterprise and, hence, give more attention to each firm. It may also be a reflection of the type of enterprise. On average, manufacturing businesses are larger than services businesses and, as much previous research has shown, response rates are generally higher for larger firms even within samples of 'small' firms. In North East Suffolk, the large geographical area to be covered made for problems and in Islington there was a markedly higher reluctance to have contacts with others outside the enterprise, regardless of who they were (see Chapter 4). Doncaster proved much more difficult than expected but there was no obvious reason why the response rate should be lower than in any other of the localities.

It is worth emphasising that the overall response rate of 58.6% was high by small business research standards. The most commonly adopted research strategy in small business research is mail questionnaires whose response rates are generally very poor compared to the rates achieved in the present studies. For instance, the recent Department of the Environment-sponsored study of small businesses in urban and rural localities carried out by Cambridge University researchers attempted to contact 7,500 urban firms and 3,500 rural firms but managed to achieve response rates of only 7% for the urban firms and 13% for the rural firms (Keeble et al., 1992:51).[13] Although these are generally lower rates than achieved by other researchers using mail questionnaires, they do illustrate the methodological weakness of the strategy, a weakness amplified by the accompanying response bias which results from larger small firms being more likely to respond to mail questionnaires than 'small' small firms.

INTERVIEWING AND INTERVIEW SCHEDULES

Owning and managing a small enterprise is a highly complex role and the enterprise as a social grouping – defined in terms of owners, employees and others with some link with the business such as owner-managers' spouses – is equally complex. Experience shows that in complex situations of this kind, face-to-face interviews using semi-structured or unstructured interview schedules are the most effective strategies for collecting relevant data. The more commonly used mail questionnaire not only suffers from the poorer response rates noted above but is also much more restricted in terms of the kinds of questions that can be asked and in its potential for exploring the complexities of the small enterprise.

In the present studies all main interviews were face to face using semi-structured or unstructured schedules and all interviews were tape recorded.[14] This allowed not only quantitative data to be collected in the 410 interviews but also very substantial amounts of qualitative data. In recent years, there has been considerable debate on the epistemological issues surrounding the use of quantitative and qualitative research strategies in the social sciences and small business research (Hughes, 1990; Burrows and Curran, 1989). Although variable-centred approaches have dominated small business research in the past, it is easy to argue that the complexities of owner-managers' motivations and behaviour and the small enterprise as an economic and social unit with complex links with the wider environment, are less than favourable to straightforward quantitative approaches. To these points might be added a reminder of the heterogeneity of the small business population which makes it even less amenable to conventional, positivist analyses.

The interviews with the representatives of the large private firms and public sector organisations employed the same face-to-face, semi-structured approach as that used in the small firm interviews. This minimised problems which might arise if the two kinds of bodies – small and large firms and organisations – had been approached in different ways. The main problem was ensuring that the large firm/large organisation representative to be interviewed was the most suitable person to answer questions on the firm or organisation's purchasing strategies and relations with other firms. Considerable efforts were devoted to identifying the right person and we believe that in all cases these efforts were successful. Many were also able to supply supporting documentary materials on their firm's or organisation's policies.

In the following chapters, the value of the highly labour intensive interviewing strategies in exploring in depth the complexities and subtleties of owner-manager motivation, strategies and relations with the wider economy and society is demonstrated. At the same time the size of the samples totalling 410 small firms engaged in nine varieties of economic activities in five localities allows some quantitative analysis to be presented where appropriate and especially to offer a context for the qualitative interpretations developed.

CONCLUSIONS

This chapter has concentrated on the methodological strategies and characteristics of the samples of owner-managers who participated in the studies to produce data that is analysed in the next three chapters. This background information has been presented in some detail for a number of reasons. First, in the earlier chapters we were highly critical of much of the research to date on localities and local economic activities on methodological grounds. We argued that is was generally 'top down' in approach and very dependent on aggregate data taken from national data sets. In addition, a great deal of the data is 'simple numbers', that is, data collected from official returns or very straightforward mail questionnaires. In other words, we feel that much of the existing literature was failing to focus sufficiently closely on localities' economic activities and that, methodologically, the majority of studies upon which so much theorising is based has in-built weaknesses which are partly responsible for the flawed interpretations we believe are offered.

The common alternative methodological approach of the three studies which are the basis for the main arguments in the following chapters, is, as this chapter has shown, very different to that commonly adopted in other studies. It is very much 'a view from the ground', which develops its interpretations of the internal and external strategies of small and large firms in relation to locality from data collected from those most directly involved in making these strategies happen. These are the small business owner-managers and large enterprise executives responsible for key aspects of the organisations' relations with the wider economy and community.

This data-driven, 'view from the ground' based on the methodological strategies described, is used to produce an alternative interpretation to counter currently dominant views of relations between economic activities and localities. In the next three chapters this alternative view is presented as a contribution to developing a deeper understanding of some of the basic elements in the restructuring of the UK economy and social institutions and the links between them which have been central to economic and social change in the 1980s and 1990s.

Notes

1. Support for this estimate is provided by VAT data itself. In 1991, for instance, the Central Statistical Office reported that the number of UK businesses, based on VAT registrations, was 1,795,360 (CSO Bulletin, 58/91). It pointed out that the register was incomplete for businesses whose main activity was exempt from VAT (eg insurance). The total may be compared with the estimate offered by Daly and McCann (1992) of 2,988,000 UK businesses at the end of 1989 although this total included the self-employed without employees, the so-called 'one person businesses'. It suggests that, if anything, Jennings' estimate understates the proportion of businesses not registered for VAT. The sharp increase in the minimum turnover threshold in 1991 from £25,400 to £35,000 (raised in 1992 to £36,600 and in 1993 to £37,600) will almost certainly have increased the proportion not registered. For a recent discussion of estimates of the total number of businesses in the UK and their size distribution see McCann (1993).
2. Strictly, the Census of Production data unit is 'the establishment' not the enterprise. An establishment may be a branch of an enterprise or a business with several branches. Distortions introduced by this difference will be less in relation to small businesses since they are more likely to have only a single outlet. It is the lower likelihood of data being collected on small units at all which renders this source inadequate.
3. The quote might be taken to imply that the study by Atkinson and Meager is of manufacturing small businesses (since this was the only kind of small business for which the Bolton Committee offered this definition) but, in fact, their study covered businesses in agriculture, construction and services also. No reference is made to other Bolton Committee definitions applicable to some of these areas.
4. The reasons for the selection of particular kinds of activities and a full list of the activities are given later in the chapter.
5. As Holton (1992:182–185) has recently argued, 'culture-in-action' in the sense used here has been neglected to a great extent in the analysis of economic activities because of an over-emphasis on instrumental reasoning and rationality in economics and the market ideologies which have increasingly dominated political discussion of the economy. In practice, as economists and those committed to market ideologies admit, albeit reluctantly, real people do not

adhere to either model but inject all kinds of non-economic meanings and non-instrumental behaviour into economic activities. These represent, in part, the links between economic and non-economic areas of social life discussed in Chapter 1.

6. Background statistics on the industry are regularly provided by the British Printing Industries Federation (see eg BPIF, 1991) and other sources provide convenient overviews (see eg the *Times*, December 1990). BPIF data was a major source of information on what was regarded as a 'small' business in the industry though the staff of the Small Business Research Centre also relied on their long-standing links with the industry, which date back to the early 1970s, involving several research projects.

7. A link that ended with the closure of the British Aerospace plant at the end of 1992 though there remain many other indirect connections with the aircraft industry. For instance, Racal Defence and Plessey Radar have local plants.

8. The Champion-Green index of local prosperity was used to select several of the localities studied to ensure sufficiently strong economic contrasts between them in order to maximise the likelihood of spatial differences being revealed. The index divides Britain (England, Scotland and Wales) into 280 Local Labour Market Areas (LLMAs) and ranks each from the most prosperous, 1, to the least prosperous, 280. London Boroughs are not covered by the index so there is no ranking for Kingston upon Thames (or Islington, the other London locality selected for study discussed below). The use of the index to aid initial locality selection should not be taken as indicating any acceptance that LLMAs coincide with any equivalent of a 'local economy'.

9 .Over the last year or so, much has been made of the greater impact of the current recession in areas such as the South East. However, what is often forgotten is the huge initial differential in levels of prosperity between, for example, areas such as Guildford and Doncaster at the start of the recession. A visitor to the localities in the early 1990s would be in no doubt about which was the most prosperous and which was having to struggle the most to counter the effects of economic deprivation.

10. Small businesses receive many unsolicited telephone calls from people trying to sell all kinds of products or services. Callers sometimes introduce their sales talk by claiming to be conducting 'research'. Owner-managers are therefore often suspicious of those saying they are researchers even where the research aims are genuine.

11. Some firms were contacted to explain that the quota of firms in their sector of the economy had been reached and their help was no longer required. Some firms contacted the centre themselves to offer their further co-operation and were again told that the quota had been filled.

12. It will be noted that although the total sample sizes for each locality reaches the target size adopted overall – 60 manufacturing enterprises and 350 service sector enterprise – there are small variations between totals for types of enterprises and localities – in the larger sample. These differences reflect the problems which inevitably arise when a research design calls for quotas for a range of types of enterprise. It is difficult under these circumstances for a research team to hit the exact target number of firms in seven categories. However, the variations are small and unlikely to bias the overall results.

13. The survey also included face-to-face interviews in 285 firms but no response rate is reported for this sample.

14. Telephone interviews were also conducted with surviving firms in the small service sector firm study in March 1992 and March 1993. These were brief interviews to collect data on how the business has been faring during the previous 12 months – a period of severe recession – and to ask questions on

awareness and usage of TECs, the budget and some other current issues. In both studies, response rates of over 90% were achieved for the firms remaining in business. For further reports on the findings see Curran and Blackburn, 1992 and Woods et al., 1993. Findings on awareness and usage of TECs from these studies are reported in Chapter 4.

4

SMALL FIRMS, THEIR OWNERS AND RELATIONS WITH LOCALITIES

INTRODUCTION

This chapter presents evidence from the 410 small businesses utilising the variety of data collection methods described in Chapter 3. It seeks to identify the extent and nature of the linkages small businesses have with their environments. Many current models of business interaction emphasise the importance of small and large firms working together within delimited spatial boundaries. The social science literature is full of references to the 'flexible firm', Post-Fordism, just-in-time (JIT) relations and so on, within which the small supplier firm and locality are often given prominence. Many of the arguments make assumptions about the small business, often drawing from international examples and poorly substantiated ideal types as Chapter 1 showed. These fail to take into consideration the different cultural, social, economic and political contexts of businesses in Britain and, as a result, have reinforced misconceptions about how small businesses function in the UK.

It is a main contention in this chapter that newer types of small business, which are increasing in numbers, are less connected with their immediate locality than older kinds. This diminishes the relations between small businesses and locality. There needs to be a re-evaluation of the ways in which businesses articulate with their environments and there is a need to focus on *substantive*[1] economic relations and the latter's links with non-economic relations. Only by assessing the level of embeddedness of small businesses in their locality, that is, the extent of business owners' *non*-economic relations with others outside the immediate family, can we understand and assess fully their role in the local community and economy. The results will be significant for our knowledge of small businesses and our understanding of the links between economic activities and locality. Equally notable in this context is the actual nature of large firm–small firm links discussed in the next chapter.

This chapter begins with an analysis of the different business linkages in which small firms are engaged, focusing on their trading patterns, market relations and connections with large firms. Then an analysis of their network participation is undertaken with an emphasis on the extent to which small businesses are embedded in a local economy and community. These findings will be complemented by the investigation of large organisations in Chapter 5, to provide a comprehensive study of large firm–small firm relations and locality.

TRADING PATTERNS AND SMALL FIRMS

One conventional theme in discussions of small business trading patterns is their close relations with other local businesses and local economic activities. Indeed, since the majority of enterprises are small, the 'local economy', however defined, will contain a large number of smaller businesses. This applies to businesses in manufacturing as well as consumer and producer services. Evidence on the actual role of small businesses in local economic activities, on the other hand, in terms of sales and purchases, is scarce. Through their ability to respond to local demands, close knowledge of local conditions and their immediate physical access to the local market, it is assumed that they can operate more effectively than larger enterprises based inside or outside the locality. This point was argued long ago in the Bolton Report:

> the role of small firms is to carry out functions which they can perform more efficiently than larger firms . . . Obvious examples of such activities are the village shop or the launderette around the corner which are small because they serve a limited local market – a large establishment set up in such a location would not be fully utilised.
>
> (Bolton Report, 1971: 28)

Such views have received a considerable fillip from the proponents of the industrial district thesis discussed in Chapter 2 integral to which is its strong local component.

Evidence from the studies carried out in the research programmes we draw upon offers significant findings on the above issues. In aggregate, the businesses showed a high degree of local dependence for their sales (Table 4.1). On average, businesses sold almost two-thirds of their output locally, that is, within a radius of 10 miles, although this was lower in manufacturing (56.4%) than services (67.3%). Conversely, almost a third of the firms' sales went outside the locality and just under 3% was exported outside the UK.[2]

What is most striking in these findings is the vast sector differences in the geographical distribution of sales highlighting the heterogeneity of small-scale activities. Firms in consumer services, such as video hire, health studios and clubs, free houses, wine bars and restaurants, were, as expected, tied very closely to local markets. Many consumer services are consumed at

Table 4.1   Geographical Sales Patterns and Type of Enterprise

	Average local sales	Average sales rest of UK	Average export sales
Printing	79.6	20.2	0.2
Electronics	32.9	56.2	11.0
Manufacturing Sector	*56.6*	*37.9*	*5.5*
Advertising, Marketing and Design	37.8	58.5	3.7
Computer services	37.5	57.7	4.8
Employment Agencies	61.6	32.8	5.7
Free Houses, Wine Bars and Restaurants	79.8	20.2	0.0
Garages	82.4	17.4	0.2
Plant and Equipment Hire	81.9	18.0	0.2
Video and Leisure	93.9	6.1	0.0
Service Sector	*67.3*	*30.6*	*0.0*
All	**65.7**	**31.7**	**2.6**

Note: Figures relate to mean sales. N = 405. Five firms were unable to provide approximate sales figures. A local market is defined by the respondent. Where guidance was requested it was defined as encompassing a 10-mile radius. Percentages may not add to 100 due to rounding.

the point of purchase and by implication are not transportable, although, as is pointed out below, even businesses in the same consumer sectors had different geographical market 'shapes'.

Firms in business services, such as advertising, marketing and design; employment, secretarial and training agencies; and computer services, showed a much lower level of local sales. Of these, advertising, marketing and design showed the lowest level with over 60% of sales deriving from business with clients outside the locality. This finding is similar to that of a study of small management consultancy and market research firms which reported that over 70% of sales were outside the locality (Keeble et al., 1991).[3]

In the two sectors classified as 'manufacturing', electronics businesses operated over a much wider geographical area than printing (Table 4.1). Printing firms had more in common with consumer service firms, drawing a majority of their customers from within the local area. The internationalisation of electronics is well documented elsewhere and is best illustrated by the high levels of international purchases and sales (NEDO, 1991a). What these findings reveal is that small electronics firms reflect this trend, although 'export' in the context of this study is more likely to mean sales outside the locality rather than the conventional trans-national definition.

In sum, the findings highlight the unevenness between sectors in their non-local orientation or, conversely, local dependency. Thus, the substantive relations of the businesses, that is, the actual or real relations that exist between businesses and their customers, vary enormously between sector.

Even with the above detailed data, *intra-sector* differences between businesses are masked. This is especially important in consumer services where consumption can take place at the point of purchase and the consumer travels to the business for that service. A 'local market' in this context is far from a simple notion. For example, the 'local market' of a free house in a suburb may be confined to a few streets over a mile or less but in a city centre the market may be very wide, with consumers travelling into the area from a wide range of initial points. Thus, although ostensibly consumer services are much more locally dependent than business services, this may be mitigated by the willingness of consumers to travel considerable distances to buy goods and services so that the market 'shapes' of firms in the same sector may vary tremendously.

A major factor influencing the extent of local sales both between sectors and within sectors appears to be the level of specialisation of the business. 'Specialists' attempt to create a market niche for the firm by concentrating on a narrow range of services or products while 'generalists' take the view that the firm should take whatever orders come along. One important ramification of this is that the more a firm specialises, the less likely it is that the local market can provide sufficient demand for its output, other things being equal. This sometimes is not so much a result of the choices of owner-managers as a reflection of the character of the industry in which the firm operates and its markets. For example, historically, most printers have been 'jobbing' or 'general' printers where owner-managers are prepared to undertake most jobs. But, as in other industries, specialisation has increased in the last decade or more as a result of changes in technology, capital costs and labour skills. This means that some printers can no longer depend on local markets and customers with specialist requirements are aware they will often have to go outside the locality. However, the relatively large proportion of sales to local customers by printers is a reflection of the general character of the market for their outputs.

In contrast, the electronics sector contained many more specialists who had developed niche markets which could not be sustained by local markets. In some ways this sector was similar to computer services where, again, the level of specialisation and therefore geographical dispersal of sales, was relatively high. These sectors and especially information-based services have shown a rapid growth in the last decade (Keeble et al., 1991 and 1993). Thus, the most salient finding is that the new, emerging sectors of the economy appear to be *less* locally based.

One further theme in the analysis of local sales is the positive relationship between market dispersal and age of the business. Newer businesses are more likely to begin by serving local customers but as they develop a market niche, they will begin to sell over a wider area. This is borne out in the data. Older businesses were more likely to have developed a wider geographical customer base although, again, this is strongly contingent on sector. One finding illustrating this point was the more extensive trading patterns by the electronics firms in Kingston compared with those in Sheffield. This is explained by the level of development of the electronics firms in the Kingston area, which were older and larger, on average, than those in Sheffield (see Appendix: Table A4). In Kingston the electronics firms have developed a higher level of specialisation and market confidence. The result is that their customers are drawn from a much wider geographical area than the electronics firms in Sheffield.

PURCHASES, LINKAGES AND LOCALITY: EVIDENCE FROM PRINTING AND ELECTRONICS

An analysis of the input or purchasing linkages of the manufacturing firms amplifies further the variety of ways in which small firms connect with the wider economy. In aggregate, almost two-thirds of the manufacturing businesses purchased less than 50% of their material and services inputs from within a 10-mile radius, as measured by value (Table 4.2). Again, there were considerable sector differences between printing and electronics firms, the former at first sight showing a much higher level of local integration.

Table 4.2 Percentage of Purchases from Within a 10-mile Radius

Percentage	Printing	Electronics	Total
None	15.0	38.5	28.3
1–49	20.0	50.0	37.0
50–100	65.0	11.5	34.8
N =	**20**	**26**	**46**

Note: Figures may not add to 100 due to rounding.

The wider spatial purchasing patterns in electronics echo those of other studies of high technology firms.[4] For example, Gripaios et al. (1989) in their Plymouth study found that local suppliers were of little importance to independent, high-tech firms in the locality and the latter sold less than 25% of their output to local firms. The findings do, however, counter those of Oakey and Cooper (1989) who found evidence of local purchasing linkages amongst high technology based firms (although these were weaker in the South East of England and Scotland than in the Bay Area of San Francisco). One probable reason for these differences is the looser definition of 'local' in the Oakey and Cooper study: they opted for a 30-mile radius as opposed to the 10-mile radius in the current study. A 30-mile radius, might be argued to be a very generous definition of 'local' for the UK. Culturally, a 30-mile radius definition of 'local' may be acceptable for the United States but in Britain few would consider 'local' to cover such a wide area.

One possible reason for the relatively lower level of local integration of electronics firms is the higher unit value, weight-for-weight, of components compared with printing materials. This makes the transport of components more economic. However, such an analysis is not without its methodological complexities for although printers have a stronger local supplier orientation, these are usually local branches or distributors of national or even international suppliers of paper, ink and other consumables. Care should be taken therefore not to misconstrue these superficially local supply linkages as any indications of an industrial district or similar industrial agglomeration.

There is no reason to suggest that service sector supply linkages were stronger than in the electronics sector. Although data was not collected from the service sector firms directly on supply purchasers, several of these sectors also clearly had mainly non-local suppliers including computer services, free houses and small garages, although the latter may deal with local factors.

These findings on sales and supplies linkages are important in relation to the consideration of locality in the analysis of economic activities. Small firms have been shown to have varying levels of economic integration with their locality. There is *no* common market they share which can be delimited spatially and even those service firms trading over limited geographical areas often had substantially different market 'shapes'. Moreover, newer types of small business have much lower levels of local economic relations and, as a result, the link between small-scale economic activities and locality becomes further attenuated.

TYPES OF BUSINESS RELATIONS BETWEEN FIRMS

The types of relationship small businesses have with their customers has been the subject of much speculation but has received limited rigorous investigation. This lack of empirical evidence is peculiar given that most of the currently influential theories of inter-firm relations have something to say about small firms and their links with customer firms. For example, the theories of the regulationist (Aglietta, 1979) and institutionalist (Hirst and Zeitlin, 1989) schools all have implications for the role of small firms in the economy and the level of autonomy which they have over their internal decision making. These models also have strong spatial dimensions.

Although the sales and purchasing patterns of the businesses have been discussed, so far there has been little examination of the nature of the relations between businesses. This is particularly important not merely from the point of view of subcontracting, that is, a formal business relationship extending over time and usually involving more than one order, and whether it is on the increase, but also its role in the development of local economies. Moreover, there is a need to unpack the nature of relations between small firms and their customers to provide evidence on power relationships between suppliers and customers.

As indicated in Chapter 2, much of the evidence to date has been based on argument by illustration or drawn from single sector manufacturing studies which are insufficient to provide a secure validation of the grander theories.

Printing	Business
Electronics	Business
Advertising, Marketing and Design	Business
Computer Services	Business
Employment Agencies	Business
Free Houses, Wine Bars and Restaurants	Consumer
Garages and Vehicle Repairers	Consumer
Plant and Equipment Hire	Business
Video Shops/Leisure Businesses	Consumer

Note: Allocation to one or othe type is defined by having more than 50% of their customers from this type.[5]

Figure 4.1   Main Customer by Sector Type

Finally, many studies in this area suffer from a 'top-down' approach, for example, reporting that large firms are subcontracting work and then assuming that this is undertaken mainly by smaller businesses.[6] Further, there is little investigation of whether firms receiving the orders are aware that this is a long-run contract or that the relationship is secure, that is, the purchaser will not switch opportunistically to other suppliers.

Data from the research programme showed that in three of the nine sectors studied, the prime customers were private consumers (Figure 4.1). These firms normally rely on a large number of consumers although, as described above, their market 'shapes' often vary even within the same sector. Their relations with other businesses therefore provide little evidence for theories of subcontracting. A very substantial proportion of small businesses are of this kind.

SMALL FIRM TRADING AND CUSTOMER SIZE: EVIDENCE FROM PRINTING AND ELECTRONICS

The role of small businesses as contractors and the size of their customers were two major areas of investigation in the study of printing and electronics. One of the main aims of the electronics and printing study was to assess the extent of large firm–small firm business linkages in a local economic context. One way in which data was collected involved asking business owners if they had *ever* undertaken any work for large local firms or public sector organisations.[7]

Two-thirds of the owner-managers claimed to have undertaken some business with local, larger firms and public organisations (Table 4.3). But this was often indirect, that is, they worked through another firm, in effect operating as sub-subcontractors. Printers in particular were more likely to have undertaken work with the local, large firms and organisations listed.

Table 4.3 Small Firms Reporting Trade with Large Public and Private Organisations in Their Local Economy

	Kingston		Sheffield		
	Printers %	Electronics %	Printers %	Electronics %	All
Never Traded with Any of Ten Listed Large Organisations	20.0	64.3	13.3	33.3	32.2
Proportion of Small Firms Reported Having Traded with Local Large Organisations	80.0	35.7	86.7	66.7	67.8
All	**15**	**14**	**15**	**15**	**100**

Note: Respondents in each local economy were shown a list of ten large local public and private enterprises and asked whether they had ever had any business dealings with any of those listed. Eight of these large local and public organisations were then interviewed in each locality. (The findings are reported in Chapter 5).

However, it must be borne in mind that this question asks if they had *ever* undertaken work for the firms and organisations listed: very few of the firms were currently involved directly in such trade. It was also uncommon for small firms to report continuing relationships with the larger organisations, instead most of the trading involved carrying out small or one-off orders.

Spatial differences in the relations of the electronics businesses with large local businesses and public sector organisations add a further dimension to the analysis. A third of the electronics businesses in Kingston claimed to have performed work for the large local organisations listed compared with two-thirds of the electronics firms in Sheffield. One possible explanation for this difference in trading patterns is the age and size characteristics of the two subsamples. The electronics businesses in Kingston were older and larger than those in Sheffield allowing them to develop markets beyond their immediate locality. This is reinforced by the location of the electronics and related industries in the South East. Kingston is adjacent to the concentration of electronics firms and defence contractors along the M4 corridor which provide extensive markets for specialised electronics products.

Links with larger firms, where they occurred, were intermittent rather than continuous. In some cases, respondents explained that these linkages were indirect, or had taken place a long time ago. Thus, Table 4.3 over-states the links between small and large firms in the localities and should not be interpreted as evidence of permanent horizontal or vertical linkages.

These results are mirrored in the analysis of the amount of trade the printing and electronics firms did with other small and medium sized firms. Printing firms undertook the bulk of their trade with other small or medium sized enterprises, whereas electronics businesses sales had a greater large firm bias, particularly in Kingston (Table 4.4).

Table 4.4   Percentage of Trade with other Small or Medium Sized Firms

	Kingston		Sheffield		
Percentage Business	Printers %	Electronics %	Printers %	Electronics %	All
0–24	6.7	61.5	0	40.0	26.3
25–49	6.7	15.4	7.1	20.0	12.3
50–74	26.7	15.4	50.0	13.1	26.3
75+	60.0	7.7	42.9	26.7	35.1
N	**15**	**13**	**14**	**15**	**100**

Note: Two firms were unable to provide information.

SMALL FIRM-LARGE FIRM RELATIONSHIPS

Small business owners commonly adopted a strategy of attempting to personalise relations with customers generally as a way of ensuring that the customer believed they always received priority or that they were dealing with the key staff of the smaller business. In other words, they sought to tie the customer to their business as closely as possible. This confirms findings from other studies (Curran, 1987). But where the customer is a large firm it suggests how fragile such relations can be, especially if the key contact in the large firm moves or leaves the organisation.

The bulk of the literature on relations between large and small businesses is situated in the discussion of sub-contracting (see Chapter 2). Results from the printing and electronics businesses revealed that this kind of relationship was not seen as the norm. The language of 'contract work' or 'sub-contracting' was often alien to the majority of business owners interviewed or they rejected it as a way of describing relations with other businesses: it

Table 4.5   Contract Work Undertaken by the Manufacturing Firms

	Kingston		Sheffield		
	Printers %	Electronics %	Printers %	Electronics %	All
Percentage of output based on contracts					
0–24	63.6	69.2	78.6	66.7	69.8
25–49	18.2	0	7.1	6.7	7.5
50–74	9.1	15.4	14.3	13.3	13.2
75+	9.1	15.4	0	13.3	9.4
Total N =	**11**	**13**	**14**	**15**	**100**

Note: 'Contract' here refers to a formal business relationship extending over time and usually involving more than one order. See Chapter 2 for a fuller definition. Figures may not add to 100 due to rounding.

was not the way they did business. One key finding here was that less than a quarter of businesses undertook work on sub-contracting as we have defined it in Chapter 2 (Table 4.5).

For the electronics businesses, sub-contracting relations were more common, in some cases accounting for up to 30% of sales. Links between printers and their customers were, however, normally intermittent: market relations rather than subcontracting relations. A main reason for this was that product orders and requirements were relatively straightforward, the kind which any competent 'jobbing' printer could perform. The printer expected future orders and usually received them, but they were not guaranteed or the subject of a continuing contract relationship as we have defined it. The printers tried to maintain close continuing links at a personal level to ensure a long-term relationship but there was nothing formal to guarantee it.

Even when formal contracts existed or there was a continuing relationship, this did not necessarily lead to the small firm being dominated by a large customer. Analysis of the qualitative data revealed that most printers considered themselves to be offering a service based on their technical expertise, often at short notice, and as a result did not see themselves in an unequal power relationship as some of the studies of manufacturing small firms, and especially engineering, have suggested is typical.

One printer discussed his relationship with a large firm customer in candid but revealing terms:[8]

> Its too technical for them to understand. They tend to come [only] for a nosey at Christmas time to get on the bottles list. Very occasionally they will come in if the work is not to be returned to them but to a third party. There is no control of our process.
>> (Owner-manager, small print firm, Kingston)

This view was echoed by owners of other printing businesses:

> They exercise control over how they want it to appear, not how we actually produce it.
>> (Owner-manager, small print firm, Sheffield)

Customers of printers exercised their power through *ex-post facto* inspection rather than through how the production process was conducted:

> They see proofs of work, some provide their own artwork, negatives.
>> (Owner-manager, small print firm, Sheffield)

> They insist on seeing regular proofs and insist on the house style being matched and if the quality is not right, they will reject the job.
>> (Owner-manager, small print firm, Sheffield)

The electronics businesses provided examples of more varied and more complex types of inter-firm relationships. We found evidence of a variety of relations ranging from very close working relationships with clients, through to 'hands-off' linkages. In some cases, connections between client and small firm supplier were close during the design, prototype and production phase. Indeed, in a few cases there was evidence of customers visiting small electronics firms to check on equipment, working conditions and the overall credibility of the business.

Again these different inter-firm relationships are highlighted by the business owners themselves:

> They require background information on our techniques and sub-contractors. They keep an eye on the progress of the equipment as it is going through the manufacturing stages.
>
> (Owner-manager, small electronics firm, Sheffield)

> We have inspections as quality is tested . . . get a visit every time there is an order, everybody is geared up to this BS 5750 quality assurance procedure.
>
> (Owner-manager, small electronics firm, Kingston)

These businesses were often working with their clients in developing an end product rather than being in a clear subordinate role, although the purchasing firm required information about the standards and working practices in the small firm.

There were, however, other kinds of relationships between electronics firms and their customers. In some cases the electronics firm was entirely responsible for its own design and development and its own products. In others, the work was routine, involving little except receiving the order with simple specifications.

The distribution of technological know-how between supplying firm and purchasing firm influences heavily the extent to which small firms and their customers interact. For example, one business interviewed is a leader in the manufacture of electronics measuring equipment for the food industry and claimed there were only two, or maybe three, competitors. Although its clients are often large national or international businesses, this smaller business has a considerable product knowledge advantage. It sells business solutions based on its technological know-how and this involves discussion initially with the client over requirements after which the smaller business has relative autonomy over the design, technological specification and production process.

The range of relationships was further illustrated by the computer services sector firms, which surprisingly were often similar to the printing firms.[9] The client describes a requirement usually in non-technical terms for a product such as software, but the relationship between the supplier and the customer is relatively unequal since the client is unlikely to understand fully the technical complexities involved. As a result, the supplier is empowered to decide the specifications, equipment and software. The supplier will devise a specification for the purchasing business and present it for further consideration and discussion. Only then are delivery times and the overall price for the job agreed.[10]

In other less common cases, the client provides a technical specification. This is likely to occur if the supplier is dealing with another software or high technology business and this leads to a more equal relationship since the client can influence the technical specifications of the product. These patterns of inter-firm relations are far from the models of dependency drawn from studies of older engineering sectors (eg Thorburn and Takashima, 1992) and their variability makes it difficult to separate the businesses in a particular sector into any typology of inter-firm relationships of the kind discussed in Chapter 2.

In summary, the nature of the relations between small firms and their customers was extremely variable from sector to sector. Printing businesses were probably the most autonomous, although control was exercised through inspection of the final product. For the electronics firms, it was more variable and depended on whether the firm was undertaking specialist or routine activities and the knowledge of the customer in relation to that of the supplier.

SMALL BUSINESS OWNERS' VIEWS ON WORKING WITH LARGE FIRMS

Results presented earlier, in Tables 4.3, 4.4 and 4.5, show that the majority of the business carried out by the printing and electronics firms is with other small or medium enterprises and although many had done work for large firms and organisations in the past, this was mainly on an intermittent basis and indirect. This bias towards dealing with small firms is not surprising in the light of the size distribution of British businesses where firms employing up to 20 people account for over 96% of all businesses (McCann, 1993).

The qualitative data revealed an ambivalence on the part of small business owners in printing and electronics about whether they wanted to do business with large organisations. One problem in carrying out work for large firms or organisations was the perception that they were slow to pay:

> I wouldn't touch them. Take [a large aircraft manufacturer], they can take anything up to nine months to pay. [A large prime defence contractor] are the same.
>
> (Owner-manager, small print firm, Kingston)

> We nearly got involved with [a large electrical tools and equipment manufacturer], a several million pound contract . . . but they were putting people out of business by not paying.
>
> (Owner-manager, small electronics firm, Kingston)

Late payment is regarded as a problem in the UK and has received widespread attention in a number of recent surveys (eg Cork Gully/CBI, 1991; Nash 1991). The problem of late payment was mentioned by numerous respondents although, like other beliefs, might be based on limited or no experience of actual dealings with large firms.

Around half of the small printing and electronics businesses believed that large organisations had some sort of policy on doing business with small firms. Several were willing to express these beliefs in detail[11]

They are not averse to us I think, it is more a positive policy than a negative policy. I have found large companies to be very positive in attitude and willing to listen to you. Different companies treat you very differently.

This was the case when I worked with BP [where] the computers are set up to provide a supplier with a cheque so it would arrive without postage delays, 30 days from invoice. It was all built into the system. Plessey are set up never to pay anyone at all unless you apply very large and very painful twists to various parts of their anatomy. BAC Group have a policy not to pay anyone inside three months.

(Owner-manager, small electronics firm, Kingston)

Other small business owners believed that larger enterprises were indifferent to small business. Others believed larger businesses would do business with smaller suppliers but other factors were more important. For example, when asked if he believed large firms had a policy towards small firms, one business owner said:

I don't think they do. I think large organisations will go where they will get the cheapest. [They have] no other policy other than that.

(Owner-manager, small print firm, Kingston)

Some respondents distinguished between the private and public sectors, feeling that the public sector was more likely to have policies specifying the minimum size of organisation to which an order might be given:

They [larger private sector enterprises] are quite happy to deal with small companies because they get a better service, as small companies value their companies [ie clients] more and provide a better after sales service in order to retain the business . . . If we have a product that will solve a problem they will buy it. The public sector are too bureaucratic. They have a minimum turnover [requirement], minimum number of employees etc.

(Owner-manager, small electronics firm, Kingston)

Despite the common beliefs and perceptions about large enterprise policies being negative or indifferent towards smaller businesses, a minority of owners saw advantages in dealing with large businesses. For example, when asked for a preference on size of customer one business owner explained:

[I would prefer] large firms. They've got more money to spend to update their equipment more regularly and they are more likely to require back-up service like maintenance and service contracts.

(Owner-manager, small electronics firm, Sheffield)

Those owners, a very limited number, who were undertaking work for larger enterprises had clear perceptions on why they had such linkages.

Overwhelmingly, the small business owners thought that the large customers traded with them because of their level of service and reliability. They believed this very much hinged on their ability to personalise their relations with customers and go beyond the bounds of conventional customer–supplier relationships. Two printers epitomised this quasi-personal relationship with customers when explaining why large customers did business with them:

> Service, we are a service industry, the fact we print is incidental, we don't think of ourselves as solely printers. We can solve people's problems for them, we deliver on time, we are neither cheap nor expensive but we charge the going rate . . . But our quality is good, but more importantly our service is excellent and because they get the work from us when they want it.
>
> (Owner-manager, small print firm, Kingston)

> We have a reputable name, you have to be competitive, you have to offer the service . . . Another point is that we have some pretty reasonable people here, we get on well with all our clients. The client is top as far as we are concerned. He or she must be.
>
> (Owner-manager, small print firm, Sheffield)

Evidence from the interviews with electronics owner-managers revealed a different emphasis centring on their technological know-how and specialist knowledge, which they believed combined to give them a market advantage:

> They know we are reliable. They know we are helpful. We will solve their problems for them. It is not necessarily the cheapest but the quality is there, always. They know they can rely on us.
>
> (Owner-manager, small electronics firm, Sheffield)

> Because we are one-off, not many companies actually do what we do . . . We give them exactly what they want. It's not the price or time . . . if they want the job doing, they will wait and pay for it.
>
> (Owner-manager, small electronics firm, Sheffield)

> Because of the technical skills of this firm. We can solve problems that they cannot solve for themselves.
>
> (Owner-manager, small electronics firm, Kingston)

The above findings refer mainly to the printing and electronics businesses but one reason expressed by both manufacturers and producer service business owners in explaining their low level of trade with large firms, was their fear of over-dependence on a single customer. Several explained that when they dealt with a large organisation they dealt with a particular person (a finding which further shows their quasi-personal marketing strategies). If that person moved or left the organisation, there was no guarantee that a successor would want to continue the link. There could also be difficulties in finding the right person when approaching a large firm for orders and problems in preparing tenders/specifications, which take time and money but may produce no orders.

Owner-managers were reluctant to use formalised 'text book' methods of marketing. For all the sectors covered, word of mouth was the dominant form of finding customers. This makes it less likely that they will have linkages with larger firms where customer relations are constructed much more formally using tendering procedures etc. Again sector differences prevailed in marketing and recruiting customers. For example, trade directories and exhibitions were significant for computer services and electronics firms, cold calling for advertising, marketing and design and employment agencies and local newspapers for consumer services, including free houses, garages and video shops.

But the prevailing picture was that small business owners were not connected to large firms and certainly not on a localised basis. The findings presented here suggest that not only are local small firm–large firm linkages underdeveloped but that many small business owners are reluctant to do work with large firms.[12]

BS 5750 AND SMALL FIRM–LARGE FIRM RELATIONS

Quality and quality standards have received increasing emphasis from government and business in an attempt to improve the performance of British industry (eg Department of Trade and Industry, 1991). As the next chapter and research by others (North et al., 1993) makes clear, this is having an impact on larger firms. Yet the adoption of BS 5750 has the potential to influence small firm–large firm relations primarily through large firms and organisations requesting or insisting that their suppliers become BS 5750 accredited.

The findings from this study indicate that small electronics firms are more aware of BS 5750 than those in printing and are aware of its role in the policies of large firms:

> Most large firms are working to BS 5750 procedures and because they're doing this, they're having to vet their suppliers and that will be having an impact on smaller firms. In a number of cases they will have to make allowances for the fact that many firms aren't BS 5750 approved. The policy may be to do certain assessments themselves to make sure of the fitness of that firm to supply them.
>
> (Owner-manager, small electronics firm, Sheffield)

This formalised quality procedure may drive a wedge between large and small firms in certain sectors especially where sub-contracting takes place, if small firms continue to be reluctant to BS 5750 and large firms increasingly insist on suppliers having BS 5750. This would weaken further the already underdeveloped linkages between large and small firms.

Other research supports the above assessment. For example, a Small Business Research Trust (SBRT) survey reported that only 10% of small firms had acquired BS 5750 accreditation and only a further 17% intended to do so (Small Business Research Trust, 1992). Generalising from this data, the SBRT estimated that under 2% of firms with less than 50 employees were registered.[13] One reason offered for this lack of enthusiasm is that BS 5750 was originated to serve the needs of large manufacturing firms and is, hence, less suited to small firms especially as such a high proportion are not in manufacturing (Bannock, 1991; North et al., 1993).

There may be exceptions to the above in some sectors, for example in electronics, where there are commonly more inter-firm relations and more dealings between larger and smaller firms. However, unless small firm owner-managers perceive BS 5750 as greatly improving the chances of doing business with larger firms, and assuming that they *want* to do more business with large firms, the incentives to adopt BS 5750 may not be great. In the longer term, of course, they may have to adopt BS 5750 if it becomes the norm in the sector but this will not help small firms do more business with large firms: it will merely ensure the status quo is maintained and the small firm is not marginalised further.

NETWORKING AND THE SMALL BUSINESS

'Networks' and 'networking' have become common notions in discussing how businesses connect with their environments. In small business research there have been quantitative approaches counting the contacts business owners have with other actors ranging from accountants, solicitors, to relatives and friends (Aldrich and Zimmer, 1986; Birley et al., 1989; Szarka, 1990). Using mainly mail questionnaires, these studies concluded that networking varies according to the geographical location and age of the owner-manager and business, among other factors (eg Aldrich and Zimmer, 1986; Birley et al., 1989). While such approaches have been useful in mapping the connections owner-managers have with others outside the enterprise, they are conceptually limited and based on somewhat insensitive research strategies.[14] For example, membership of an organisation has been taken to indicate a network connection but for many this may involve little more than paying a subscription and perusing a newsletter occasionally. Such nominal memberships are especially common where the person is a busy small business owner-manager.

The idea of the small business network as some definable entity comprising a finite, identifiable set of individuals has been questioned (Blackburn et al., 1990). Instead, networks might be better conceptualised as theorised constructs abstracting particular types of interaction which may occur between the owner-manager or other organisational representatives and the external environment of the enterprise. They may be active and hence observable at some moment in time, or latent, that is, become active only intermittently. Most micro-level studies of networks and networking have given little attention to the *meanings* associated with owner-managers' external contacts. What are the *motivations* for initiating and sustaining external contacts? It is argued here that networks are essentially cultural phenomena and focusing on purely business and other contacts using a variable centred methodological paradigm, is limited in its usefulness.

Of course there are some *a priori* reasons why small business owners' external connections and memberships may be important for material and information exchanges. For example, a lack of business expertise might cause the owner-manager to seek outside advice. Joining an organisation may provide an avenue for garnering information at critical points in the survival or development of any business or gaining further customers. Much of the more exhortative literature emphasises this aspect, and the local dimension is also often stressed (Bennett and McCoshan, 1993:Ch.15 *passim*; Business in the Community, 1990).

Yet in much of the network literature little emphasis is placed on the factors which mitigate *against* networking activities. One obvious negative influence is the time involved, which owner-managers may find difficult to find. Probably of more importance are the self definitions typical of many business owners. Numerous studies have reported the stress that owner-managers place on autonomy and independence (see eg Stanworth and Curran, 1973; Scase and Goffee, 1982 and 1987; Bevan et al., 1989). Network participation is often incompatible with such values and attitudes because it necessitates an open reliance on advice from others or other implicit admissions of dependence. In the 1980s, government devoted considerable resources to assisting small firms and setting up support networks for training and advice but the results in terms of take-up rates were generally disappointing.[15] One explanation for this is that participation in these networks is antithetical to owner-manager cultures (MacMillan et al., 1989). Thus, it is argued that the assumption in much of the more normative literature, that owner-managers are eager network participants, requires testing much more rigorously.

It is expected that there will be a wide variation in the way in which business owners interact with their local environments. Businesses operate within different industry sub-cultures and economic climates which may affect strongly the character and content of external connections. Spatial variations are a further factor which may affect networking. For example, an inner city economy will be very different to a rural economy in terms of potential networks and participants. Indeed, sectoral and spatial variations should be central to any study of local networks and local and sectoral economies for different local conditions will provide different opportunities and constraints for networking.

Small business owners' networks may be seen on a continuum. At one pole are all forms of compulsory participation in external relations axiomatic for the business to function at all (Figure 4.2). These include the purchase of supplies and resources and interaction with customers to sell their outputs. Contacts with the Inland Revenue are voluntary in a strict sense although in

Compulsory						Voluntary
Sales to customers	Purchase of resources	Government; Inland Revenue	Banks; Accountants; Solicitors	Marketing strategies	Advice seeking; Consultants; Government; Agencies	Memberships of organisations

Figure 4.2 Owner–Managers General Continuum of Business Networking Activities: Compulsory and Voluntary Aspects

practice the choice is nominal as are relations with banks, accountants and solicitors. There is, however, choice about the frequency and condition of such contacts. A marketing policy seeking further customers is even more voluntary and business owners often engage in proactive marketing strategies only intermittently (Hankinson, 1986; Blackburn et al., 1991). Other voluntary connections may be advice seeking from consultants or consultation with bodies such as TECs, which have been shown to be even more intermittent or even non-existent.

Further along the continuum still are activities which may be business-related or have some wider relevance to the owner-manager. These activities may include membership of pressure groups, political parties, trade associations or local social clubs. In some business sectors such connections will be regarded as essential by owner-managers since they may be an important source of custom: thus membership of organisations may be seen as crucial for some types of business and irrelevant for others. It is through an analysis of the content and meanings of external connections that we can extend our knowledge and theorising about how small business owners articulate with their wider social and political environments and the significance of these connections for economic linkages and local economies.

Although the extent of economic integration and business linkages, with accountants and so on, is an important dimension of how small businesses articulate with their wider environments, much of the discussion of linkages is uncoupled from other non-economic social relations and structures. More recent thinking has recognised that economic interactions between enterprises need to be related to non-economic connections (Granovetter, 1985). These contacts seen in terms of non-business contacts and 'networks' of one kind or another, add to the analysis of small businesses' links with localities and how these relate to economic activities. In other words, economic connections are embedded in social, political and cultural relations and structures. Indeed, strong political and social links are seen as especially critical for models of industrial development that have a strong local component (Pyke, 1992:9–10).

In the studies of the nine sectors, considerable attention was given on economic and non-economic linkages with the wider environment. The latter connections have two elements. First are those entered into that have an indirect but clear connection with their business. These include, for example, memberships of the local chamber of commerce, small business pressure groups and trade associations. The second element comprises those connections not related to business directly which reflect embedded relations such as owners' social relations, political party memberships, leisure activities and friendship and family relations. Although not entered into for business purposes, they may nevertheless have some relevance to economic activities.

In the studies reported here, all business owners were asked about their advice seeking from external parties such as enterprise agencies and TECs and their connections with external institutions such as memberships of clubs and associations and these are discussed in the next two sections. In order to understand in more depth the motivations for activating such connections and the role of social relations for business activities, a further study of three sectors using a more intensive 'critical incidents' method, was adopted.[16]

THE USE OF LOCAL ADVISORY BODIES AND AGENCIES: ACCOUNTANTS, SOLICITORS AND BANKS

Providers of advice and professional services, including banks, accountants, solicitors and public agencies, are often seen as key network facilitators providing support for business survival and development and provide another possible means through which businesses might be linked (eg Aldrich and Zimmer, 1986). What the findings of this research reveal is the rapid fall-off in contact with external support agencies according to the level of compulsion that the linkage entails.[17] Compulsory links are therefore not a very good measure of local business integration since they represent the essential external relations which would be required in any locality.

Accountants followed closely by solicitors are the most likely outsiders to be used as sources of advice by business owners (Table 4.6). Relationships with accountants were related mainly to financial advice rather than solving other business problems or linking business owners with an information and support network. All business owners have to make returns to the Inland Revenue which usually requires contact with an accountant for auditing or 'doing the books' and advice on tax matters over, for example, VAT and company cars. Advice, where received, was usually on a narrow range of issues and on an *ad hoc* basis rather than for the strategic planning of the business:

> If you ask the accountant a question they're happy to answer it . . . But we do not get a lot of advice coming from his end, saying that you should be doing this or that you should be doing that, we found.
> (Owner-manager, small electronics firm, Sheffield)

This emphasis on a narrow functional relationship with the accountant is shown by the reduction in the frequency of contact with the accountant once

Table 4.6 Sources of Help or Advice From Selected External Bodies on Solving Business Problems

Sector	Bank Manager	Accountant	Enterprise Agency	Educational Institution	Solicitor	Small Firms Service	All
			Percentage				
Printing	43.3	63.3	23.3	0	46.7	23.3	30
Electronics	60.0	63.3	23.3	10.0	33.3	30.0	30
Advertising, Marketing and Design	26.9	76.9	15.4	11.5	84.6	21.1	52
Computer Services	35.3	72.5	33.3	19.6	76.5	35.5	51
Employment, Secretarial and Training Agencies	40.8	75.5	24.5	12.2	71.4	22.4	49
Free Houses, Wine Bars and Restaurant	44.0	82.0	12.0	22.0	70.0	12.0	50
Garages and Vehicle Repairers	32.0	68.0	8.0	10.0	68.0	6.0	50
Plant and Equipment Hire	26.5	85.7	18.4	14.3	73.5	18.4	49
Video and Leisure	30.6	73.5	14.3	8.2	61.2	12.2	49
All	**36.3**	**74.4**	**18.8**	**12.7**	**67.6**	**19.5**	**410**

Note: Percentages do not add to 100 due to multiple responses.

the business has its own bookkeeper. An interview with two partners of a design business showed this:

How would you describe your relations with your accountant?

Female Respondent:

Yearly . . . (laughter). Once a year.

From your point of view, is that a good thing or a bad thing?

Very good I think . . . you know, it's fine. We do not see a lot of our accountant because we have a bookkeeper who is all but an accountant. So I mean they virtually do the most . . .

Male Respondent:

I think we've done very well with bookkeeping . . . brilliant. We've done half of the accounting work before we give it to him . . . we speak at the end of the year I suppose.

(Owner-managers, design partnership, Islington)

Overall, the business owners felt that accountants were not particularly knowledgeable about their business or industry. Thus, relations with accountants were considered to be satisfactory but restricted to a narrow range of advice and services. This confirms other studies which have found that business owners are unlikely to use standard financial and management techniques in their business (Hankinson, 1986). Therefore, although accountants are, on the whole, locally based, the scope for them acting as network

facilitators is limited. It was extremely rare for businesses to find customers through their accountant.

Similarly, contacts with solicitors were strictly limited to solving legal problems such as advice over premises or the drawing up a contract and used usually only very infrequently. Business owners in the service sector were less satisfied with solicitors than accountants on the service received.[18] Solicitors, therefore, were much less likely than even accountants to be able to act as network facilitators. One recurring theme was that owner-managers considered the cost of advice to be high, which tended to restrict the use of professionals both in frequency of contact and scope of business problems upon which they consulted these professionals.

This was also reiterated in the use of business consultants investigated in the study of service sector enterprises. Only 16% of the 350 service sector enterprise respondents had used a consultant, although those business owners that had tended to express satisfaction with the service received. This figure is somewhat lower than the 25% reported in a study by Smallbone et al. (1993: Table 1) although this is explained by the larger and older businesses in the latter study, as well as its focus on manufacturing firms.

Relations between the banks and small businesses have received a great deal of attention from government, the media and researchers. Banks are by far the biggest source of external funding for new and small business in Britain through the provision of loans and overdraft facilities (Wilson, 1979; Stanworth and Gray, 1991:Ch.4).[19] The bank–small business relationship has been reported as, at best, mixed and has recently been the subject of a Bank of England inquiry (Bank of England, 1993).

Just over a third of all the business owners had sought help or advice from their bank manager beyond routine cash transactions (Table 4.6).[20] It is noticeable, however, that electronics businesses have a much higher level of contact than other sectors. These businesses have larger capital bases (see Appendix 1) and a need for constant upgrading of capital equipment and product development, which will inevitably require more financial advice than other businesses experiencing slower rates of technological and market change.

The frequency of contacts between bank managers and business owners cannot, however, be taken as an indication of the quality of these relations. The survey of 350 service sector enterprises found relatively high levels of satisfaction of business owners with their bankers compared with the results from surveys by small business lobby groups (Curran et al., 1991:40–45).[21] One common point that emerged was that the quality of the relationship depended, in part, on the maturity of the business and the ability to build up a relationship, as indicated by one respondent:

> The bank manager of late is very good. In the early days he wasn't quite as enthusiastic. We were very close to changing banks. They were a bit shy of us because we were a new company and because of the type of

equipment that we sold. We had to start talking fairly large company figures straight away and they would rather see us build up more gradually which was an impossible thing to do. Once we got over the first couple of hurdles and they got a little bit more confidence in us, then everything seemed to settle out OK.

(Owner-manager, small electronics firm, Sheffield)

One main theme to emerge from business owners' comments was the poor knowledge they felt bank managers had about their business sectors. An owner-manager in the Kingston area, who was about to visit his bank manager, highlighted this and other views:

I'm not sure that the banks really understand the nature of my business. I think if we were selling Mars bars they could get to grips with it.

Interviewer:

Anything else you've noted about the quality of advice from the bank manager?

Respondent:

Well they vary don't they . . . you know, there was a bank manager for a short time that I found quite useful and had a good relationship and we could talk to each other and understand the situation.

(Owner-manager, electronics firm, Kingston)

The variation in the quality of advice from bank managers was a common theme found in the research. The view that the banks did not understand the nature of their business reinforces the owners' comments of the value on advice from accountants and solicitors and public and quasi-public agencies (see below).

A distinguishing feature of relations with banks is the difficulty in uncoupling the advice dimension from other contacts such as the bank's monitoring of the business and asking the business owner to come to the branch and see the manager or, rather less frequently, the manager visiting the business. As a result, business owners may find it difficult to approach their banks for advice on issues not related to their bank balance and, indeed, since many ideas or problems have financial implications, business owners were often deterred from approaching the bank. In other words, there was little evidence to suggest that bank managers could act as a hub for a local business network.

USING ADVISORY BODIES AND AGENCIES: PUBLIC AND QUASI-PUBLIC SOURCES OF ADVICE

As discussed earlier, all business owners have contacts with central and local government primarily through compulsory relations in the form of paying tax, VAT, PAYE and business rates. However, more recently, especially over the last 15 years or so, enormous energy has been put into small business support by government (Employment Department, 1992: Ch. 4).[22] Advice and information from the public sector takes a variety of different forms and derives from an array of sources. This is further complicated by the changing policies and agencies involved, some of which depend on local delivery (eg enterprise agencies, TECs, local authorities, colleges of further education and universities) while others are more geographically remote at a regional or national level (eg Department of Trade and Industry, the Enterprise Initiative, and the now defunct national Small Firms Service).

Our evidence suggests that government and quasi-government sources of advice and support have only a limited impact in terms of connecting with small businesses and that local points of provision do no better than more remote or national delivery points (Table 4.6). The former regionally based Small Firms Service was targeted at the kinds of businesses studied.[23] One in five of the businesses had used this service but there were considerable inter-sector differences. Electronics and computer services businesses showed a relatively high use of the service, a finding which probably reflects their owners' educational levels and needs for advice related to their involvement in new technology. The Small Firms Service, for instance, was often the first point of call for businesses seeking advice and assistance from the Department of Trade and Industry (DTI) on innovation.[24] These sectors contrast sharply with garages and vehicle repairers, video and leisure and free houses, wine bars and restaurants where the use of the Small Firms Service was one in ten businesses or less.

With regard to local linkages, the 400 or so enterprise agencies are among the longest established support bodies for small businesses and epitomise the notion of reaching businesses through a local outlet (Business in the Community, 1990). Over 300 agencies have received considerable support from Business in the Community in terms of their development and providing a model legal structure (Bennett and McCoshan, 1993:114–119). Their services vary from one agency to the next but, in general, they provide start-up help, business counselling, aftercare services and training, with a strong focus on those who want to become self-employed.

Overall, less than one in five businesses had used an enterprise agency. Computer service businesses were the most likely to have used their local enterprise agency but even among these only a third had done so. There were some locality differences although these were not as great as the sector differences (Curran et al., 1991:Table 35). The service sector businesses that had used their local enterprise agency had mixed views about the quality of the advice provided: there was a broad balance between those that rated the advice 'poor' and those that found it 'good' or 'satisfactory'.

Local educational institutions did less well than enterprise agencies as sources of advice, even though there is at least one and often several local institutions of further or higher education within each locality. The service sector businesses gave a higher rating to the advice received from educational institutions than from the enterprise agencies.

The use of local authority support and advice was investigated specifically in the study of the manufacturing firms (ie those in printing and electronics). The results further confirmed the low use of local sources of support and advice. Only 10% of the manufacturing firms had used their local authority for help or advice, despite these being local sources and despite these business types having higher than average levels of contact with outside organisations. Moreover, this study covered two contrasting local authorities in terms of the level of support for business with one being highly interventionist (Sheffield) in comparison to the other (Kingston). Surprisingly, there was little difference between the two localities in the use of local authority economic support. In Sheffield several respondents were actually critical of the local authorities policies especially in relation to its cost to the local population.[25] Such findings are not exclusive to this study. Low use was also found by Smallbone et al. (1993:289) who, in their study of mature small and medium enterprises, found that only 4% had sought assistance from their local authority.

As mentioned earlier, one feature of public sector support for small businesses has been its changing character and level of provision.[26] Probably the biggest institutional change that has occurred in this decade has been the establishment of 82 TECs in England in 1990–1991 and their equivalents, local enterprise councils (LECs) in Scotland. One of the major responsibilities of TECs is to support and develop small enterprise activities and this has involved, *inter alia*, acquiring control over the Enterprise Allowance Scheme (EAS), Enterprise Training and Business Growth Through Training as well as the Small Firms Service. These have often been renamed and repackaged by the TECs in their respective areas.

One dimension of the research on the service sector sample is longitudinal. Surviving service sector businesses were re-interviewed over the telephone in 1992 and 1993 and a key element of this survey was to assess their knowledge and experience of the TECs.[27] The results reveal that, in general, TECs are failing to reach small firms despite their local orientation and the enormous amount of publicity and effort devoted to repackaging the small business initiatives for which they are responsible (Table 4.7). In the survey undertaken in February–March 1992, 70% of business owners were aware of TECs but only just over 15% had approached their local TEC for help or advice. At the time of writing we commented:

> Although these are early days for the TECs, the question remains open on whether they will be any more successful than enterprise agencies as a local means of delivering management training and other support for the smaller business. The TECs are relatively new and they might improve their performance as they become better known.
>
> (Curran and Blackburn, 1992:28)

Other surveys conducted around the same time (eg Richardson et al., 1992) found even lower levels of awareness of TECs but a slightly higher

Table 4.7 Service Sector Businesses Approaching Local TECs for Help or Advice

	1992 %	1993 %
Advertising, Marketing and Design	10.0	25.0
Computer Services	12.2	24.2
Employment, Secretarial and Training Agencies	18.2	0
Free Houses, Wine Bars and Restaurants	15.8	13.6
Garages and Vehicle Repairers	4.5	0
Plant and Equipment Hire	6.8	8.0
Video and Leisure	8.8	9.1
All	**10.6**	**11.8**
N =	274	203

Note: Data is collected from service sector businesses in telephone surveys 1992 and 1993.

rate of use, although there are methodological and sample differences between the surveys.[28]

Even the levels of awareness reported may not be real since, as the surveys revealed, in some instances the acronym TEC may be interpreted as referring to the local technical college. This was also found by Richardson et al. (1992).

A further follow-up survey of the surviving service sector enterprises conducted in March 1993 revealed that our earlier views were optimistic. There was *no* significant increase in the use of TECs by the surviving businesses in 1993 compared with 1992 (Table 4.7). Again there are very strong sector differences with one in four advertising, marketing and design and computer services approaching their TEC but not a single firm from the garage and vehicle repairers and employment, secretarial and training agencies sectors. These more recent findings on the poor use and sometimes even poor awareness of TECs by small businesses, are supported by other research on small business owners. For example, research carried out in London covering the CILNTEC (City and Inner London North TEC) area in February 1993 found that 47.5% of small business respondents claimed to be aware of TECs in general but only 17.5% were aware of CILNTEC.[29]

One major aspect of TEC policy is that these new forms of support agencies should be local and run by local employers to serve the needs of local businesses. Yet one recurring argument in this chapter has been the lack of significance of the 'local economy' or 'local community' as a focus for small business activities. Although TEC areas tend to be coterminous with groups of local authority boundaries, the central point is that they are not coterminous with the substantive relations of businesses. The organisation and operation of TECs also contain a number of elements which militate against small business participation. TECs are managed by a board of up to 15 members, of whom two-thirds come from private sector businesses. However, these are drawn almost wholly from large-scale enterprise, especially in manufacturing (Emmerich and Peck, 1992:14). Others have pointed out that TECs:

> have a limited capacity to draw from local agents and business because of their external and appointed origin of boards – this limits their acceptance by other agents and restricts their capacity to transmit change, particularly to smaller firms.
>
> (Bennett and McCoshan, 1993:135)

The time demands on the busy small business owner make participation in TEC boards unlikely and it is difficult to see this changing.[30] The policies of the TECs towards small business are often top-down and it is not surprising, then, that 2 years after the formation of TECs, they still have low levels of contact with the owner-managers interviewed. Of course, as indicated earlier, and in other studies of public policy towards small firms (MacMillan et al., 1989) owner-managers are often reluctant to approach government or government-sponsored agencies for advice or support because government is seen as the tax collector, steeped in bureaucracy, and the (over)regulator of business. TEC's close association with government may have affected adversely their ability to reach small businesses.

In the light of the above and the relative insignificance of locality relative to sector for business owners, it is questionable whether the One-Stop-Shop (now renamed Business Link) initiative will alter fundamentally the historically poor level of government reaching small business through access points based on locality. It has been suggested elsewhere (Curran, 1993), and will be argued in Chapter 6, that a sector-based approach would provide a more relevant means of reaching owner-managers and acknowledge that small businesses cannot be treated as a homogenous group based on some spurious notion of local economic community or the effectiveness of across-the-board policies.

What the results from this section display is a lack of any marked affinity of business owners with locally based institutions. When looking for advice or support, owner-managers required advisers who had sector-specific knowledge and could respond rapidly. Locality or geographical proximity was secondary or even irrelevant. Sector differences in the use of outside advice were wider than locality differences, which suggests that different types of business have different advice levels and even different levels of need. It may also be suggested that some owner-managers, such as those in computer services and electronics, are more prepared to use outside sources of advice because their relatively higher educational levels may equip them to seek out help more readily and exploit the available sources.

OWNER-MANAGERS' MEMBERSHIP PATTERNS

One conventional, straightforward way of measuring relations business owners have with their environment is their links with third party institutions such as chambers of commerce, although this tells us nothing about the motivation or meanings of these links for the owner-manager. Yet the data is important in the context of this book from the perspectives of sector and location. For example, evidence of high levels of local institutional memberships offers indications of local economic integration whilst memberships of other non-business orientated bodies, such as political parties, may indicate the degree of embeddedness.

Evidence from the 9 sectors reveals the low levels of business owners connecting with outside economic organisations or bodies. Over four in ten of owner-managers in the surveys (42.9%) claimed to be members of no outside body whatsoever, local or national.[31] Overall, the strongest affiliation of the business owners was with their trade association. These are national rather than local bodies and are strongly rooted usually in an industry sub-culture.

Membership of national bodies including the National Federation of Small Business and the Forum of Private Business was also low at 9% of all respondents. The 'other business/professional grouping' in Tables 4.8 and 4.9 contains minor business grouping memberships but the figures are raised significantly by memberships of professional occupational bodies, such as the British Computer Society and the Institution of Electronics and Electrical Incorporated Engineers which are also nationally based. Owner-managers tended to belong to these organisations as individuals and there were statements about their occupation or sector identification rather than about business ownership. They also compensate for the low levels of trade association memberships in sectors with developed professional and occupational associations.

Table 4.8 Membership of Selected External Associations or Local Bodies

	Trade Association	Chamber of Commerce	Rotary Club/ Round Table	Local Political Party	National Small Business Association	Other Business/ Professional Grouping	N
Manufacturing							
Kingston	20.0	33.3	13.3	*	6.7	46.7	30
Sheffield	13.3	26.7	10.0	*	13.3	6.7	30
Services							
Nottingham	20.3	31.9	1.4	2.9	2.9	21.7	69
Guildford	40.3	37.5	1.4	5.6	16.7	22.2	72
North East Suffolk	33.8	18.3	7.0	11.3	18.5	19.7	71
Doncaster	24.6	20.3	1.4	0.0	5.8	17.4	69
Islington	26.1	10.0	1.4	5.8	2.9	21.1	69
All	**27.3**	**25.4**	**3.9**	**5.1***	**9.0**	**19.8**	**410**

Note: Percentages do not add to 100 due to multiple responses. See text for definition of 'other' grouping.
   * Covers service sectors only (350 firms)

Table 4.9   Membership of Selected External Associations or Bodies by Business Sector

	Trade Association	Chamber of Commerce	Rotary Club/ Round Table	Local Political Party	National Small Business Association	Other Business/ Professional Grouping	N
Printing	26.7	40.0	16.7	*	6.7	20.0	30
Electronics	6.7	30.0	6.7	*	16.7	33.3	30
Advertising, Marketing and Design	19.2	40.4	5.8	5.8	5.8	28.8	52
Computer Services	15.7	37.3	–	–	13.7	15.7	51
Employment, Secretarial and Training Agencies	18.4	44.9	–	8.2	8.2	34.7	49
Free Houses, Wine Bars and Restaurants	30.4	16.0	–	8.0	10.0	20.0	50
Garages and Vehicle Repairers	36.0	8.0	4.0	6.0	10.0	16.0	50
Plant and Equipment Hire	44.9	10.2	6.1	6.1	10.2	14.3	49
Video and Leisure	40.8	8.2	2.0	2.0	4.1	14.3	49
All	**27.3**	**25.4**	**3.9**	**5.1***	**9.0**	**19.8**	**410**

Notes: Percentages do not add to 100 because of multiple responses.
    * Covers service sectors only (350 firms)

Chamber of commerce membership was second highest: just over a quarter of the respondents were members (Table 4.8) but other locally based institutions including rotary clubs and political parties had much lower levels of membership and did not differ significantly between the localities. The overall picture therefore is one of a poor level of local integration in terms of memberships of these kinds of local groupings.

There were some interesting locality differences in levels of membership affiliations. Guildford had the highest levels of owner-managers joining outside bodies (72.2%) and Islington the lowest (47.8%). Guildford's business owners were strong joiners of institutions both nationally and locally: 40% were members of a trade association and 37.5% a chamber of commerce (Table 4.8). The wide differences in the strength and resources of chambers of commerce have been documented elsewhere (Bennett and McCoshan, 1993:119–125). One explanation for this may be that an energetically run chamber of commerce with which business owners can identify attracts more members.

Islington, like many London boroughs, is far from a single community but more of a variety of communities with a large commuter population who epitomise contemporary living patterns by having a clear spatial separation of home from work. Results from two focus groups[32] highlighted the especially low level of local networking of business owners in Islington. The high number of small business owners who, although having a business in Islington, lived elsewhere rendered community based business groupings difficult to develop and sustain.

One theme that has emerged strongly in the analysis of the economic linkages of the small business owners is the tremendous sector variations. Membership of outside organisations paralleled these findings revealing wider differences than those based on locality (Table 4.9). There were vast sector differences in the membership of locally and nationally based organisations. Overall, manufacturing firm owner-managers were more likely to join outside organisations than those owning service sector firms. Owner-managers of free houses, wine bars and restaurants were the least likely to be members of an outside institution while, in contrast, 70% of those running employment, secretarial and training businesses were members of some outside body.

Some of these sector disparities are to be expected. Those running employment, secretarial and training businesses need to maintain strong links with other – especially local – employers who are their potential customers. In contrast, those running free houses, wine bars and restaurants work extremely long hours, especially at the weekends, and have little spare time for joining outside organisations. Moreover, their customers are mainly individual consumers not other businesses. The low levels of memberships of garages and vehicle repairers are at first sight a surprise since they might be expected to join local associations. However, they also rely more on a private customer base than on other businesses and local business related memberships may not be important.

Other explanations for varying membership levels pivot on the differing educational levels of business owners. Storey et al. (1989) have shown that networking levels are related to education and social class. Parry et al. (1992:127) support this and argue on their findings that the *petit bourgeoisie* are not very active in politics or other forms of participation generally. This is reinforced by our data. Employment, secretarial and training and computer services owner-managers have a higher social class background than garage and vehicle repairers owner-managers, as indicated by their fathers' main occupation, and more external links of the above kinds.

There is a bi-modality in trade association membership with 4 of the sectors having fewer than 20% of owner-managers as members and a further 4 with more than 30% (Table 4.9). Membership was particularly strong among the plant and equipment hire owners and weakest among owners of the electronics firms. These differentials in membership appear mainly to reflect the industry sub-culture and cohesiveness of the sector. For example, the low level of trade association membership among the electronics' owner-managers might be expected since this is a fragmented industry with a broad, rapidly changing product base all working against a strong employers' collective identity. In contrast, plant and equipment hire is linked to a mature industry, construction, with distinctive products and services giving the sector a clear identity.

The low levels of predominantly local affiliations, such as rotary clubs, round table and political parties, do not vary significantly by sector. The low level of embeddedness locally, indicated by these low levels of memberships, contrasts sharply with the rather idyllic discussion of the importance of local business owners in the community in the Bolton Report (1971:26):

> Another major contribution of the local businessman (sic) to his community has been his willingness to contribute his experience to the service of the community in which he lives and works. Small business provides a valuable source of practical men to serve in local government, on the bench and in local, charitable and social organisations. These men are experienced in the organisation of activity on a small scale and have deep roots in the local community.

There was little or no evidence of this type of activity in the seven localities in our study.

In discussing owner-managers' external memberships and their patterns, it must be borne in mind that they are often nominal involving no or little real interaction with the body or institution. Only one in five of those who stated that they were members of an external body considered themselves to be an active member.[33] Again there were locality variations, the most striking being the low level of active members in Islington (11.6%) which further distinguishes this locality as having the lowest levels of connections through external memberships. Garages and vehicle repairers were the sector where owner-managers were least likely to consider themselves 'active' members of any organisations of which they were members.

In sum, the crucial finding is that business owners tend not to be active members of organisations. Locally based institutions did less well than national organisations in attracting small business owners. The low level of active membership of locally orientated, non-economic based institutions such as political parties, suggests that the level of embeddedness of small business owners in their community is weak. This finding is not surprising. Almost two out of three of the 350 service sector business owners reported working more than 50 hours a week. The average number of hours for the full-time self-employed, for example, has been estimated nationally at 47.3 hours a week in 1991 compared with 38.1 for all full-time employees (Labour Force Survey, 1993) and our sample reported even higher levels of working hours overall.

OWNER-MANAGERS NETWORKING: A CRITICAL INCIDENTS APPROACH

One limitation to the variable-centred approach of counting interactions between business owners and outside institutions as a way of assessing how business owners articulate with their environments, is the inability to explain why and how business owners activate a network. Thus, although the data is useful for counting connections between business owners and outside bodies it tells us little about the motivations, meaning and expectations of owner-managers in seeking outside advice or making other kinds of external contacts.

Although business owners may join bodies such as chambers of commerce for economic or social reasons, they may also have non-economic orientated links that are almost entirely social such as those with local sports clubs or friendships. These connections may indicate levels of embeddedness, that is, the extent to which their non-economic relations with others outside the economic sphere may also be a source of advice or other support for their business activities to complement or even act as alternatives to more formal, economic-based support institutions. The Bolton Report suggested embeddedness in this sense used to be extensive in the UK but our data suggests this is no longer the case.

As a way of overcoming the limitations of the variable centred approaches to discussing how businesses articulate with their environments, an alternative methodology adapted from Mitchell (1973) was used.[34] This *critical incidents* approach involved focusing on particular events as a means of exposing the character and content of the linkages between small business owners and others within the social and economic community. This was supplemented by two focus group discussions in Nottingham and Islington which added an element of data triangulation to ensure that findings and interpretations were not method-bound.

A sub-sample of 45 owner-managers was interviewed face to face on a range of 'critical incidents' that they had experienced over the previous 2 years. These owners were drawn from the 350 service sector businesses and were selected to cover the diversity of businesses studied in terms of their activities and level of external connections. The sectors covered were computer services; employment, secretarial and training agencies and garages and vehicle repairers. The firms were drawn from all 5 local economies in the service sector study.[35]

Five themes were selected as important to small businesses and their owners as a basis for exploring how they articulate with their environments: Customers and the market; Investment and finance; Co-directors and partners; Family and kinship; Local authority connections and involvements. Respondents were sent the list of potential themes for discussion before the interview. Each theme could produce a wide variety of critical incidents and respondents were asked to recall any that had happened to them and their businesses over the previous 2 years. The advance notice helped elicit more detailed narratives than might have been possible to bring to mind if the subjects were first raised in the interview itself.[36]

Each theme was introduced in general terms, with the interviewer providing a preamble. For example, in the case of gaining or losing a major customer, the preamble went:

Table 4.10   Selected External Contacts of Small Business Owners

	Research Programme Sample	Three Selected Types of Enterprise	Critical Incidents Sample
Local Enterprise Agency (1)	18.0	22.3	20.5
Chamber of Commerce (2)	23.7	30.0	28.9
Rotary Club/Round Table (2)	2.6	1.3	2.2
Business Consultant (1)	16.0	19.5	25.0
Small Firms Advisory Service (1)	18.3	21.5	25.0
Trade Associations (2)	29.1	23.3	35.6
Other Business Groups/ Associations/Bodies (2)	20.6	22.0	22.2
Proportion Who See Themselves Active Members of (2)	19.4	26.3	20.0
N=	**350**	**150**	**45**

Note: Percentages do not add up to 100 because respondents may belong to, or have used more than one of the above.

(1)   Data records whether respondent had *ever* approached the source for advice or help.
(2)   Data records respondent is a member of this body or group.

The Research Programme Sample consists of all 350 owner-managers in the main project. The Three Selected Types of Enterprise Sample consists of all 150 owners of the firms in computer services, employment, secretarial and training agencies and garages and vehicle repairers. The Critical Incidents Sample consists of the 45 owner-managers interviewed in depth on their critical incident experiences.

The success of any business greatly depends on its customers. Most businesses lose or gain a major customer from time to time and this can create problems – especially losing an important customer. We would like you to highlight any people who were involved, consulted or who helped you in this situation.

If the respondent had experienced an incident of this kind within the previous 2 years, the interviewer asked the owner-manager to 'talk me through what happened, how you coped with the situation and who you discussed it with'. Thus, the incidents were designed to allow us to investigate non-economic and economic linkages.

Customers or clients are critical to any business especially in producer services and manufacturing where each individual customer is probably more likely to be responsible for a significant proportion of the firm's turnover. Customers are formal economy connections though they may also be friendship, kinship or family contacts illustrating the possible linkages between the economic and non-economic areas.

Losing a major customer may lead the owner-managers to seek outside advice to help resolve the resulting problem. The owner-manager of an employment agency explained how he had lost a key, profitable contract to supply temporary employees to the local branch of a large national company. The contract was for 12 months and normally renewable. However, this status quo was shattered when the respondent was told that the contract would not be renewed:

> We were doing good business with them. We had . . . five or six people working at the company . . . it was all temporary work but it tended to be very long-term temporary work . . . I would say . . . 75% of the people we placed there were just place and forget . . . We've still got someone there now (on a different contract) who has been there three years on a temporary basis. It is good business.
> (Owner-manager, employment agency, Nottingham)

The client told the business owner that the contract was not renewed because his margins were too high. However, the respondent believed that it was because he had not maintained satisfactory personal relations with a key person in the client's personnel department:

> I was a bit disappointed. It meant obviously we had lost a fair chunk of turnover on the business and also a bit of prestige. Something which we thought was chugging along quite nicely. Nice business to have.
> (Owner-manager, employment agency, Nottingham)

Asked who he had discussed the loss of the account with, the owner-manager said nobody. Within the firm, there was nobody senior enough. He felt he could not discuss it with other business contacts outside the firm because it would damage the firm's image further. Nor had he been prepared to discuss it with the bank because he felt the manager would have been unsympathetic.

Family and friends are often perceived as sources of support and advice but again, this owner-manager mentioned it to them only 'in passing' and certainly not to seek advice. Instead, he had chosen to deal with the problem himself without outside help even though he admitted this contributed to the stress he felt over the matter. This was not an isolated case and also illustrates the point that family are often used to relieve stress rather than as a source of advice.

In a further case, a director of a garage in Islington described how the firm had lost an account worth approximately £1,000 a month, a substantial sum for the business. The client was a baker with several vehicles with whom the garage had built up a close relationship over time. However, the baker had stopped paying his account and this debt had increased despite repeated requests:

> We are having problems getting money from them. They were . . . You [can] delay payment to a certain extent but they always said they had got queries but they never write back to you within a certain [reasonable] time. It's always months afterwards when you're sending them threatening letters. So now we've put a stop on them.

Refusing to undertake further work for the client was not an easy decision. The same respondent cited a similar case and in both instances she had hopes of recovering some of the money owed. These non-paying clients were discussed with the firm's other directors but it was agreed that the respondent director should handle the problem, making whatever decisions she thought fit. There was no discussion with outside bodies, friends, relatives or other business owners. Losing customers, however big, was a problem you had to deal with in running a business. The respondent pointed out that if losing a customer resulted in a serious cash flow problem 'then you would have to go to the bank' but this had not been necessary in the cases discussed and would only be done very reluctantly.

Both the above examples highlight the restricted character of the networks and networking activities of business owners. Business owners were very reluctant to seek external advice to help them resolve the problem they faced. Losing customers is often a serious problem but is regarded as something that happens to a business. Yet it is also, in a sense, an indication of failure at least in the minds of many owner-managers. You do not discuss this 'failure' with outsiders, that is, bank managers, other business owners, accountants and so on, unless it is absolutely necessary. Close, non-business related friends and family may be told but in a way that shows the owner-manager's fortitude in adversity rather than as an aid to problem resolution.

All businesses require assets and some of the biggest items of expenditure are on capital equipment. Often this involves the owner-manager in decisions well outside their normal routine activities and might provide examples of how business owners connect into a network for information and advice. One common purchase many business owners have undertaken recently is a computer for administration. Most owner-managers are not computer literate and installing a system new to the business requires care, adaptation and training of staff. The purchase can therefore be a major investment for the firm which could or should be based on specialist advice from outside the business.

Employment agencies hiring out temporary staff often have complex payrolls to prepare every week and need to maintain information on their staff as they move from one placement to another. As an owner explained, in preparing wages:

> It is normally done in the evenings which is, if you like, dead time. You don't have the phone ringing . . . during the day you can get on with . . . the business. In the evenings it's quiet, you can do . . . the noddy jobs so it means you're doing the wages in the evening . . . late. Number crunching, makes you tired . . . gives you a headache.
> (Owner manager, employment agency, Nottingham)

The idea of computerising the payroll was one which the owner had thought of for some time but he had deferred doing so because of what he saw as the potential difficulties. A salesman cold-called and suggested a computerised system and, after some negotiation, the owner-manager eventually bought an ex-demonstration machine, plus software, training and support for just over £3,000.

This case was particularly significant. When pressed by the interviewer it transpired that the owner-manager had not approached other suppliers for quotes or sought advice beyond the sales representative with one exception, the owner of a business to which he supplied staff. This client was very enthusiastic about his computerised system and invited the owner-manager to view the system. The respondent decided not to visit his client but to take his word for it. The respondent's accountants and bank manager were not contacted as the supplier's sales representative had arranged finance which the respondent felt was attractive. Other than the telephone call to a fellow business owner, therefore, the owner-manager had acquired an expensive and complex piece of equipment without resorting to networking.

One explanation proffered by the owner-manager for this lack of seeking external advice was pressures on his time. Finding other suppliers to quote a price could, for example, lead to:

> the hassle of having maybe two other people come in and set up . . . machines . . . You are talking about an afternoon demonstration showing you how wonderful the thing is. The company we finally got the machine from is a multi-branch company. They seemed quite secure and everything and the service was reasonably good so we just went for it.

This finding was reiterated in numerous interviews regarding the purchase or leasing of equipment. What emerged was a general lack of any detailed, systematic evaluation when acquiring an expensive asset. Business owners often acquired assets on imperfect information and there was a reluctance to seek outside advice even from the firm's accountant or bank manager. Even when there was some contact with outside bodies, this was kept to a minimum and could hardly be described as extensive 'networking'.

CRITICAL INCIDENTS INSIDE THE BUSINESS

Business success depends ultimately on the ability of the owner-managers to work together and become an effective team where more than one owner is involved in the business. A high proportion of the owner-managers interviewed had problems in maintaining successful relations with partners and directors, often resulting in a radical change in relationships and, in several instances, a partner/director leaving the business. This may provoke business owners to seek outside advice or discuss the matter with outside parties.

A garage owner described an event which illustrates such a development but further reveals minimal networking, even in a crisis situation. The business had been running for 14 years and the founder then invited the respondent plus two others to join as directors because of their complementary skills.

After about a year, one director had to leave when he was found to be 'fiddling' the books. However, a more serious situation occurred after 7 years when the wife of the founder wanted to become a director and became very assertive in the running of the business. Both the respondent and fellow director objected strongly and this led to a dispute which lasted 3 years.

The respondent and his fellow director called an extraordinary general meeting of the company's board and voted the founder and his wife off the board:

> We voted them out. We only asked her to go but he said if she goes I go . . . Our shares were greater than his. One of those things . . . a bit like *Dallas* . . . It wasn't settled for three years, very expensive . . . We agreed figures in the first year and he wouldn't agree. He changed accountant three times, his solicitor three times, in the end it was settled out of court.
>
> (Owner-manager, garage and vehicle repairer, Guildford)

When asked who had been consulted during the event, the respondent said a solicitor and a bank but these contacts were purely functional: one for legal advice, the other to raise money to buy out the original founder. Although a solicitor and accountant were used at the time of the crisis, these connections were minimised because, in the respondent's view, they were 'expensive'.

The owner-manager had also discussed the problem with other business owners, mainly in the motor trade, and was surprised to find that disputes between directors were common. These contacts were not considered close friends, just 'people he knew in the trade', and were not continuing connections. His wife and that of his fellow director had also taken a lot of the strain, but other family and friends had not been involved except to hear the story, in *Dallas* fashion, as he put it.

What is revealing about this incident and others is that external contacts can be activated but many are one-offs and are particular to a specific event only. After the incident these contacts may become minimal or entirely latent. Contacts with family and kinship groups were one-sided in the form of 'stress relievers' rather than seeking information and advice.

CRITICAL INCIDENTS AND FAMILY LIFE

The level of commitment required for running a successful small business is unquestionably enormous and inevitably owners have difficulty disconnecting family from business and vice versa. The most common likely events in family life which may affect the business are the break-up of a marriage or long-term relationship or a death in the family.[37] Some owner-managers felt that they were neglecting family commitments because of the long hours they worked. Female owner-managers may be expected to be particularly prone to feeling family pressures given that the dominant culture stresses female commitment to home and children despite more opportunities for them in the formal economy.

A female owner-manager offered several examples illustrating these conflicting pressures, but one was particularly telling. She explained how she worked up to the last possible moment before she went into labour for the birth of one of her children:

> I was doing someone's wages when I went into labour and this poor man kept looking at me and saying 'Don't you think you'd better go now?' and I said 'No it's all right, I'll just finish the wages . . . Oh dear! Hang on a minute' [indicating a response to a pain contraction].
> (Owner-manager, employment agency, Suffolk)

After the birth of her baby, the son of a building firm client for whom she had worked for a long time committed suicide. Some of her client's employees, desperate for their wages but unable to contact the father, came to see her in hospital and she ended up working out their wages:

> with a newborn baby that I was having to feed every two hours and I . . . literally had him beside me and I was working away doing the books. Then I would stop to feed the baby and change his nappy. It was very difficult.

The respondent illustrates the lack of resort to any kind of network of a significant kind. This is also where we would expect non-economic linkages to be activated but they were not. Her husband had his own career and as with male respondents she emphasised that it was *her* business and *her* responsibility for its success or failure.

One significant finding was the inability of respondents to recall incidents regarding contacts with their local authority. These connections could have been in relation to rates, building regulations or even the local authority as a client for the business. This non-response is particularly revealing for a major theme of this chapter, the analysis of localities and economic activities. This is consistent with a lack of reference to local authorities in other answers. Local authorities, when mentioned, were discussed mainly negatively in the context of regulations over planning permission and parking and so on but these criticisms were not accompanied by direct contacts with the authority very often.

Critical incident analysis of the above kind allows a greater understanding of the motivations for using links with others outside the business. The findings show that owner-managers tend to have relatively small and non-extensive networks with little resort to external contacts, with economic contacts such as accountants, solicitors and bank managers. The results also show that owner-managers rarely use non-economic contacts based on family, kinship or social groupings for business information or advice.

Three main reasons explain the low level external contacts by owner-managers. First, a plethora of research suggests a dominant psychological characteristic frequently displayed and emphasised by owner-managers is independence and autonomy (Bevan et al., 1989; Curran, 1986; Scase and

Goffee, 1982 and 1987; MacMillan et al., 1989). Running a business is an exemplification of these values and any resort to external advice or discussion may be interpreted by owner-managers as showing an over-dependence on others. This produces a 'fortress enterprise' mentality in articulating with the wider environment which suggests that levels of linkages with external economic contacts, as well as any embeddedness in the locality which has implications for their business activities, will be limited.

More pragmatic factors also explain this underdeveloped level of connecting with the external environment. Business owners are extremely busy and this restricts their ability to undertake extensive networking. Most were married or in stable personal relationships and a high proportion had children living at home. This restricted severely their ability to socialise in areas outside their economic activities even if they wanted to, or even if there was some chance that some contacts might prove beneficial for business. Most professional sources of advice were considered to be expensive and as a result were kept to an absolute minimum. Other sources such as enterprise agencies were not thought likely by the owner-managers to be able to help their business.

Overall, the results from the critical incidents study revealed that business owners' connections with their environments do not approximate to the closely integrated economy implicit in many models of the local economy. This was true not only of their involvement in economic activities but their involvement in non-economic areas of life outside the family. Indeed, business owners were found to display only a very low level of embeddedness in their locality. This finding renders the opportunity for the development of a local business environment akin to an industrial district, as depicted, for example, by Pyke (1992), remote.

CONCLUSIONS

This chapter has examined how small business and their owners articulate with their environments. Numerous models of business-to-business activities exist central to which is the notion of local economic linkages, often emphasising agglomeration economies, economies of scope and the potential of emerging 'industrial districts'. These models have achieved considerable credence in the literature. Large firm–small firm relations within the local economy are often seen as integral to these models. Other models of the economy suggest that small firms are in an uneven, dependent power relationship with large firms, acting as suppliers to specifications laid down by the principal firm.

Business owners are also epitomised as strong 'networkers' participating in and sustaining a web of economic and social links for information, customers and supplies. These connections are seen as indicators of the level of integration in the economy and of the embeddedness of small business owners, that is the participation of owners in local community groups, political parties, sports and social clubs. These latter connections are seen as underpinning a vibrant local economy and a prerequisite for a successful local economy of the 'industrial district' type.

Small firms in manufacturing have often been seen as linked particularly closely with local economies and much of the recent debate on the role of the small firm in economic restructuring has related it to the development of industrial districts or JIT networks within a spatially delimited area. Similarly, service sector businesses are often seen as central to local economy providing services that are not 'exportable' or transportable since consumption often takes place at the point of purchase or in that such businesses primarily serve the requirements of other local businesses.

The findings from the studies reported here throw into question the applicability and relevance of these conventional views on how small businesses articulate with their environments and especially how they connect to the local economy and community. They also question many of the accepted views of how larger businesses contribute to local economies, the topic examined closely in the next chapter.

Our evidence found that the trading patterns of the businesses varied greatly by sector and even within the same sectors. For many of the small businesses their core markets did not have a local focus. Business services such as advertising, marketing and design; employment, secretarial and training agencies; and computer services as well as electronics, for example, had high levels of sales outside their local economies. The greater the level of specialisation a business had, the wider the geographical sales area of that business.

Consumer service businesses were, as expected, more tied to local markets and will continue to be so. However, the notion of a 'local market' is far from straightforward because of inter- and intra-sector variability in geographical market 'shapes'. For example, a free house's local market in a suburban area may be confined to a few streets over a mile or less, whereas one in an inner city or rural area may capture a wider market geographically. Similar findings came from other consumer services such as video outlets and restaurants. In other words, even businesses in the same geographical area need not share the same market. Even those in the same sector may differ greatly. What the data revealed was the different ways in which small firms, though ostensibly offering the same service, created a niche through a combination of management strategies and market or sector circumstances.

The main finding reiterated in the data was the importance of business *sector* in understanding how firms articulate with their environment. A focus on the *substantive* relations of businesses revealed that these do not coincide with any 'local economy' as defined by local authority or administrative boundaries. Moreover, emerging newer sectors of the economy, computer services and electronics, for instance, are *less* locally based than older sectors and this suggests that the notion of a local economy is becoming even less tenable. Evidence from patterns of purchases in the printing and electronics sectors substantiated even further the weak local substantive relations of small business.

Most of the business undertaken by manufacturing small firms was with other small and medium sized firms, a finding which is not surprising given the extreme skewness in the size distribution of UK businesses. There was evidence of some large firm–small firm linkages in two local economies examined, Sheffield and Kingston upon Thames. However, a closer analysis reveals that many of these links were indirect and intermittent. Some of the small firms did work for large firms but this was sometimes a different branch of the organisation located elsewhere in the UK and not the large firm in the locality.

One explanation for this is the lack of enthusiasm on the part of small business owners for doing business with large organisations because of the belief that they were slow to pay. Another reason was the fear of over-dependence on large firms for a high proportion of sales. When dealing with other firms, small business owners attempted to personalise their connections and if their contact in a large firm left or was moved, they might lose the order. Business owners were also becoming aware of new trends in the purchasing criteria of corporate and public sector organisations, most notably BS 5750 and preferred supplier policies. Some perceived that this would further militate against the development of large firm connections.

In almost all cases in studying the various trading patterns, memberships and the levels of advice seeking, sector considerations swamped local differences. There were some local variations but often these were contingent on sector or intra-sector differences. For example, electronics businesses in Kingston were much less locally orientated than those in Sheffield. On closer inspection this appeared mainly a result of the types of high tech products, the maturity and the location of clients outside the locality, for example, on the M4 corridor. In short, the shape of the substantive relations of the sampled businesses bore little resemblance to any simple patterns based on locality and differed strongly from sector to sector.

The above results were reinforced by the evidence on the involvement of owner-managers in the local economy through institutions such as chambers of commerce and in the local community such as local political parties. The data reveal that most business owners are *not* joiners of local organisations except where there is a very direct economic benefit to the business as in the case of employment agencies. The overall level of embeddedness of the businesses owners in the local community was very low and showed a steep decline since that alleged in the Bolton Report (1971). It was revealing that national trade associations were overall more important than local institutions. This suggests that a level of local integration of the kind normally associated with 'industrial districts' and other local economic models of economic development was very unlikely.

The reasons for the poor level of local memberships, advice linkages and embeddedness were threefold. The opportunity costs of attending meetings and seeking advice is often regarded by small business owners as too high. Second, the psychological outlook of business owners, stressing autonomy and independence, is very important. Seeking advice and joining clubs does not correspond to this self view and may be interpreted by the owner-manager and outsiders as showing an overdependence on others. Even when close friends and relatives were informed of business views or problems, this was to allow them to act as stress relievers rather than as sources of advice and help. This finding of low level of embeddedness in the local community is also not surprising given the long hours business owners work and their personal circumstances.

Work and family commitments rendered extensive networking of the kind advocated elsewhere in the literature unlikely. Business owners also had strong views about the quality and cost of available advice. Professional services were seen as expensive and their use was, therefore, strictly limited. The public and quasi-public sector was often seen as providing advice that was too general or of poor quality. Even the newly formed and heavily promoted TECs were not attractive to these owners. Again one major determining factor here was the emphasis on sector knowledge rather than the importance of locality.

It is not surprising, therefore, that little or no evidence of a local integrated economy was found in any of the 7 areas. Instead, businesses' substantive relations were contingent on sector and market niche resulting in widely different spatial outcomes. Moreover, the substantive relations of the new expanding sectors studied were over a much wider geographical area than older sectors and emphasise the role of newer small businesses in a rapidly changing UK economy.

Notes

1. We use the term 'substantive' in exactly the same sense as Sayer (1992:88) uses the term 'substantial'. We prefer 'substantive' since we believe this conveys the intended meaning more clearly to most readers. Sayer is making a distinction between *formal* relations where although people are categorised as sharing certain characteristics such as 'male' or 'female', 'middle class' or 'the poor', there need be no interaction between those so categorised and *substantial* (substantive in our usage) relations where there are real connections and interaction.

2. Small businesses have a poor record of exporting as other wider studies have reported. For instance, Storey and Johnson (1987:221) found, even taking all sectors into consideration, only 6% of small firms exported any of their output.

3. The activities of these firms appear closely related to those of the advertising, marketing and design businesses interviewed in the present research programme (see Keeble et al., 1991 and 1993).

4. The definition of high technology firms in Gripaios et al. (1989) covered pharmaceutical products; telecommunications; aerospace; electronic data processing; instruments and research and development. This is broader than our coverage (see Chapter 3 for definitions) but the implications are similar.

5. Obviously there were some variations in the proportion of customer type within the 'Business' and 'Consumer' categories. For example, plant and equipment

hire relied on other businesses for 59.2% of their sales whilst advertising, marketing and design had a 92.3% business customer base.

6. See Chapter 2 for a fuller discussion of this literature. Thorburn and Takashima (1992) provide exceptions to this as does Rainnie (1989) but both studies are rooted in the manufacturing sector. Imrie and Morris (1988) for example, suggest that there has been a rise in 'preferred supplier status' relations and imply that this involves small firms. However, their evidence failed to take into account the recipients of the work 'put-out' and therefore could not discuss the size of the businesses receiving contract work.

7. This involved showing the respondents a card on which 10 large local private and public sector organisations were listed. Eight of these in each locality were among the large businesses and organisations interviewed in the research programme in Kingston and Sheffield and the results are reported in Chapter 5.

8. As is usual in rendering spoken English into a printed form, there are problems in punctuation and arranging the wording to ensure that the meaning of what the respondent said is expressed clearly and unchanged. The printed quotations try to ensure that these aims are met as fully as possible. Where text had to be added to aid understanding this is included in square brackets.

9. Although the printing and electronics sectors provided the bulk of the evidence on the varying relations between small firms and their large firm clients, evidence from the producer service sectors studied verified the diversity in relations likely to be found.

10. This symmetry of power between large customers and small suppliers parallels the findings from Bryson et al. (1993) who in their discussion of management consultancy and market research found suppliers to be in an even relationship with customers because of their specialist knowledge.

11. It must be stressed here that these are respondents' views and that they do not necessarily accurately describe the practices or behaviour of the firms named.

12. This point will be developed in Chapter 5 which reports a reluctance among large firms to do business with small firms.

13. In fact, despite all the attention being given to BS 5750, official statistics available in 1992 (British Standards Institute, 1992) indicated that only 20,000 businesses had implemented BS 5750, that is, less than 0.5% of the estimated 3 million businesses in the UK. This total also included firms which had acquired other quality standards such as the defence industry's Allied Quality Assurance Publications (AQAPs) standard now being superseded by BS 5750.

14. These variable centred approaches have introduced associated concepts to improve our understanding of networks. They include the level of *extensiveness*, the number of units or members which comprise the network; the *density* of the network, measured by the number of links between members measured by the total number of links recorded as a proportion of the total number which could exist if all members were linked to each other; *activity levels* measured by the frequency and length of contacts between members and who initiates contact; and *centrality* and *reachability* measured by the number of other members a given member can reach and the number of contacts which have to be made to reach other members. Unfortunately, researchers using counting approaches to study networks rarely integrate these measures into their analyses in any comprehensive fashion.

15. For example, even after the heavy promotion of the DTI's Enterprise Initiative on television and in the press, only 77,000 applications for support were received as of March 1991. This represents no more than 3% of the total number of businesses eligible for support (Stanworth and Gray, 1991:Ch.8).

16. For a fuller explanation of this technique see Curran et al. (1993b). The findings from this part of the research programme are also reported below.

17. Indeed, since this question asked have you *ever* sought advice from any of these bodies, then results often exaggerate the level of contact with these outside agencies.

18. Data was collected on the level of satisfaction of external advice from different sources for the service sector sample and is reported in more detail elsewhere (See Curran et al., 1991:40–55).

19. For example. it was reported that at November 1992 the high street banks had 4.4 million small business customers to whom they had lent £43.6 billion (Bank of England, 1993).

20. This question asked respondents if they had *ever* sought advice or help from their bank manager and this may therefore have been a single occasion which had occurred some time ago.

21. There are, unfortunately, deficiencies in surveys based on members of small business lobby groups. Relatively few small business owners are members of these groups as shown in our data and it may be that those who join differ significantly in their experiences, problems and political outlooks from the bulk of business owners who do not join. The two main lobby groups have approximately 21,000 (Forum for Private Business) and 50,000 (Federation for Small Business) subscribing members. Certainly, the memberships are biased in terms of size and sector. For example, a Forum of Private Business sample of over 6,000 businesses on their views on their relations with banks showed that business owners in manufacturing and retailing were over-represented and those in services were under-represented (Forum of Private Business, 1992:Table 1).

22. For example, it has been estimated that between 1979 and 1985, £1 billion was spent by government on support for small businesses (Edmonds, 1986).

23. The Small Firms Service was one of the more popular government initiatives, attracting 317,000 enquiries and providing 50,000 counselling sessions in 1989–1990 (Employment Department, 1991:20). Responsibility for the service was devolved to the TECs in 1990/1991.

24. The DTI has offered a variety of schemes for high-technology based manufacturing industries, such as Support for Innovation and SMART, an annual competition to encourage innovative technology firms with less than 50 employees. Seven (23.3%) of the electronics sector businesses had approached the DTI for assistance.

25. The city's involvement in the World Student Games was a particular issue at the time of the interviews and its cost was attracting critical attention from the media.

26. One of the main reasons for this is that small business policy is difficult to define. Support for small firms is dispersed, for example, among employment policy (eg Enterprise Allowance Scheme), industry policy (eg Support for Innovation) and taxation and financial policies (eg the Loan Guarantee Scheme). See May and McHugh (1991).

27. The 1992 results (Curran and Blackburn, 1992) covered 274 firms. The 1993 results (Woods, et al. 1993) covered 203 firms.

28. The Richardson et al. sample was based in manufacturing and, on average, the businesses were larger than the services sector business from which we draw results.

29. Reported in Curran (1993) using data provided by Local Economy Research Unit, University of North London. This TEC covers one of the localities, Islington, in our research programme.

30. None of the business owners interviewed in the surveys stated that they were members of a TEC board or involved in TEC activities.

31. This represents 28 manufacturing businesses (printing and electronics) and 148 service sector businesses.

32. As part of the research strategy, focus group discussions comprising business owners, accountants, solicitors, bankers and representatives of local public organisations (local authority, enterprise agencies) were undertaken in Nottingham and Islington.
33. These data on active membership do not cover the printing or electronics sectors but there is no reason to assume that their levels of activity were any higher than those in services.
34. The rationale for this approach is discussed in detail in Blackburn et al. (1990).
35. As a test of examining the representativeness of these sectors relative to the larger sample from the service sector as a whole, a check of their external contacts compared with the full 350 service sector firms was undertaken (Table 4.10). Overall, there were few substantial differences between the three selected types of enterprise and the main sample of 350 service sector businesses.
36. The wide range of critical incidents offered was broad enough for respondents to illuminate their links with others outside the firm. In practice, critical incidents related to the themes had been experienced by virtually all respondents.
37. Other incidents reported by the owner-managers included long-term illness in the family and an owner-manager's wife suffering severe post-natal depression.

5

LARGE FIRMS, LOCALITIES AND SMALL FIRMS

INTRODUCTION

Large firms receive an enormous amount of attention from the mass media and researchers. They are treated as the lords of economic creation to the extent that many see the 'real' economy as composed almost exclusively of large firms. As this book has demonstrated, the neglect of smaller enterprises and over-emphasis on larger firms amounts to a distorted picture of how the economies of advanced industrial societies function. Moreover, it neglects the complexities and a central paradox of contemporary economic restructuring. It is true that at one extreme globalisation is producing huge trans-national corporations with branch plants in many countries and weaker links with their country of origin. At the other extreme, small-scale enterprise is also expanding in many of the most advanced economies. In the UK by 1991 'over one-third of people in non-government employment (some seven million people) worked' in firms employing less than 20 people (McCann, 1993:12). This compares with only just over a quarter in 1979.

The links between large firms and localities are also often emphasised. The stories of Pilkington and its association with St Helens in Lancashire, Cadbury's with Bournville, Lever and Port Sunlight, Rowntree's New Earswick and ICI and Teesside are well known. Not only did these firms dominate[1] their local economies but often also the social and political communities as well (Lane and Roberts, 1971; Wagner, 1987; Beynon et al., 1989; Ackers and Black, 1991; Bennett and McCoshan, 1993:266–268), Indeed, in several instances the factory and firm were crucial factors in the growth of the locality itself as they created the conditions for urban growth and supplied key members of local political and social elites (Joyce, 1980).

In turn, the small firms in any locality are often seen as directly or indirectly dependent on the activities of the large firms. Through subcontracting or creating local supply chains or the more general multiplier effects resulting from injections of purchasing power, particularly through wages to employees, large firms are depicted as creating and sustaining local economic activities in myriad forms of small-scale enterprise. In some instances, these were seen as examples of the 'industrial districts' discussed in Chapter 1 but more often the result was a more generalised economic, political and social clustering around larger enterprises in the locality.

Widespread doubts already exist on the extent to which the above characterisation of the role of large firms in local economic activities remains at all accurate today. There are many reasons offered to support these doubts. First, many of the large firms which provided an economic, political and social focus to particular localities have gone, especially in the major recessions at the beginning and end of the 1980s,[2] or been transmuted into new forms of enterprise whose relations with localities are quite different. Lash and Urry (1987), for instance, offer a widely cited thesis on the emergence of what they term 'disorganised capitalism'. In this model new distinct forms of capitalist enterprise emerge with 'polycentric' structures and which:

> develop into the crucially important 'global corporations' as they take over other firms often producing quite different products and which themselves are operating multinationally, firms based on different industrial processes. The attachment to any single economy becomes more tentative, as capital expands (and contracts) on a global basis. A much more complex spatial division of labour develops in which different parts of different production processes are separated off and develop within different national economies.
>
> (Lash and Urry, 1987:90)

Of course, not every UK large firm has become one of these new global corporations but strong tendencies towards globalisation and detachment from their localities of origin have been manifested by many of the most famous businesses in the UK economy. ICI, for instance, has rationalised and reduced its operations in the UK so that by '1985, 60% of ICI's worldwide assets were located outside the UK' (Lash and Urry, 1987:90). On Teesside this went with a reduction in the number of jobs from 31,500 in 1965 to 14,500 by 1985 (Beynon et al., 1989:277). Similarly, Pilkington was the world's largest flat glass producer by 1983 'with 38,000 employees, a turnover of £900 million, and 200 subsidiary and associate companies in twenty-one countries' (Ackers and Black, 1991:34). Again, evidence of a weakening of the relations between company and local community was apparent with a halving of its St Helens workforce (Ackers and Black, 1991:51 and 53).

Another reason for the weakening of economic, political and social ties between large enterprise and localities stems from the increasing separation of ownership from locality. Not only have many major UK firms lessened their links with UK, many firms in the UK are now foreign-owned as are many of the newly established plants, particularly in electronics and car making. This inward investment is much more marked in the UK than in other advanced industrial societies because of low labour costs, a skilled labour force, government deregulation and encouragement, and the linguistic advantage of being an English-speaking country (Auerbach, 1989:272). Auerbach estimated that by 1989, one in seven workers in manufacturing in the UK was employed by a foreign-owned company. Coates (1991:71) estimated that 55% of car production in the UK is now foreign owned.[3]

Third, localities themselves have, in effect, detached themselves from large, local businesses. Local populations have become more mobile geographically. Skilled workers, particularly the increasing proportion with higher education qualifications, are much more mobile than other workers. Often this means managers running local large firms and plants are more likely to come from outside the locality. Economic restructuring and the collapse of training for manual and routine workers, especially by large firms, broke the links between the generations where son followed father or other close relative into 'the works' to go through the cycle of apprenticeship, skilled craft worker and, perhaps eventually, to supervisor or middle management for the most able and ambitious. Public sector industries (especially where privatisation took place) such as steel, coal and railway engineering, contributed to this detachment of the community through their restructuring and decline.

In other words, large firms and their relations to localities and local economic activities, including small firms, have become highly problematic. Many of the accepted assumptions about local economic integration, large firm–small firm relations and the role of the small enterprise in the economy rest upon loosely formulated models of Britain's economy of the past: the economy before 1979 or even 1970. One of the major aims of this book is to examine these assumptions afresh: in the last chapter the small firm was the focus of attention for this examination. In this chapter the empirical focus is on large firms' strategies and behaviour and their implications for local economic activities and small firms.

LARGE FIRMS AND PUBLIC SECTOR ORGANISATIONS IN TWO LOCALITIES

As explained in Chapter 3, because the data underpinning the arguments presented in this book are drawn from more than one study, the material on the large firms and public sector organisations is taken from two localities, namely Sheffield and Kingston upon Thames, and not from the full seven localities from which the small firms were recruited. It will be argued, however, that there is no reason to suppose that, had the second study recruited large firms and organisations also, the main results and interpretations would have differed significantly.

The firms and organisations were selected from lists of the largest employers in the two localities to include manufacturing, services and public sector organisations. The inclusion of public sector organisations in the sample to represent large enterprises in the local economy might seem odd at first glance but in a modern economy the contribution of large public sector organisations to local economic activities is impossible to dismiss. In Sheffield, for instance, the City Council is by far the most important local organisation in terms of direct employment, 30,000 at the time of the study, and over twice the size of the next largest, also in the public sector, with 12,800 employees. Public sector organisations are major providers of services but also need to buy in materials and services on a large scale. Their inclusion might also be favourable to the hypothesis of high levels of local economic integration since it might be expected that on ideological grounds if not on more mundane economic grounds, large public sector organisations would have a commitment to purchasing locally wherever possible.

Table 5.1 shows the distribution of the large firms and public sector organisations between the sectors in the two localities.[4] Between them the organisations employed around 50,000 people. In terms of recent data on the size distribution of businesses in the UK, measured by employment numbers, the private sector businesses were all within the top 1%. On average, the public sector organisations were considerably larger than the private sector businesses and, as noted in Chapter 4, the firms and organisations in Sheffield were, on average, much larger than those in Kingston upon Thames. The main reasons for this difference were that the private sector firms in Sheffield were mainly in older style manufacturing, steel and steel products, for example, or ex-public sector, while those in Kingston included newer, high tech sectors which are less labour intensive and where employment levels are typically lower. In Sheffield, also, the public sector organisations were larger in part due to a more interventionist and developed public sector emphasis in local life.

The economic importance of these firms and organisations can also be measured in turnover although this is not easy to calculate for the localities. As several private sector respondents pointed out, the accounting practices of private sector firms are often complex and it is sometimes difficult to apportion contributions to overall turnover from branch plants especially where the branch performs specialist services, such as R&D or marketing services, for the business as a whole. Where estimates were offered, they suggested that local turnover could be very substantial. For instance, the service sector firm in Kingston had a turnover of about £40 million resulting

Table 5.1   Large Firms and Public Sector Organisations in Two Localities

	Kingston upon Thames	Sheffield	All
Manufacturing	4	3	7
Construction	1	–	1
Services	1	2	3
Public Sector	2	3	5
	8	**8**	**16**

from its local operations and 3 of the manufacturing firms in Sheffield had a combined turnover of £45 million attributed to the activities of plants within the locality. The public sector organisations were easier to assess since they were generally what would be termed 'single plant' operations located exclusively in the locality being studied. All were substantial with the smallest having a turnover of £18 million and the largest £220 million. In short, the firms and organisations participating in the study have very substantial purchasing power with a potentially strong impact on economic activities in their respective localities.

PURCHASING AND LOCAL ECONOMIC LINKS

There are many ways in which large enterprises can interact with other businesses and organisations in their localities but a critically important link, in terms of assessing their contribution to levels of local integration, is through their purchasing. Most large employers in any locality also often proclaim their links with the local community through their support and sponsorship of various activities, membership of chambers of commerce and local economic development initiatives, participation in TEC boards, support of local charity, sport and cultural activities and so on. Yet their financial and economic contributions are arguably much the more important. Often also, the importance of their local economic behaviour for local, small businesses is stressed: for instance, Business in the Community's initiative, Springboard for Growth argued that 'local purchasing is a way of helping to sustain and stimulate growth for the smaller companies' (1990:3) and offered guidelines for local purchasing projects with the targeting of local large firms and organisations stressed.

However, assessing the extent to which such behaviour occurs in practice is difficult to measure in strict quantitative terms particularly where, as argued in Chapter 1, what might be designated the 'local economy' is so difficult to demarcate. Moreover, the majority of our respondents could not have supplied the necessary information to make such a calculation with any hope or precision without having to spend a great deal of time and effort – more than we felt we could ask for – and even then the information might still have been difficult to compare and analyse.

Instead, the interviews with respondents from the large firms and public sector organisations concentrated on purchasing policies and behaviour. The respondents were selected to have a specific knowledge of these either as the senior manager responsible for formulation and administering the policies, or as the local manager responsible for purchasing or ensuring that overall organisational policy was being followed. These respondents were, therefore, able not only to state what the policies in relation to purchasing were but what were the trends in the policies. To what extent, for example, are there trends towards more or less purchasing of materials and services from local suppliers in the selected localities?

Group Purchasing Department

Vision Statement:

To provide a *group wide* procurement service covering all products and services that are sourced on external suppliers. In so doing to ensure *total* conformance to agreed specifications, timely delivery, *minimum* overall cost and *maximum* protection from supplier failure, by the use of effective contractual arrangements.

To maintain the highest *professional* standards and absolute business integrity at all times, thereby enhancing _____'s image as the most professional _____.

Source: Major service sector business, Sheffield.

Notes: The original is in the form of a plastic laminated card (8.5cm × 11.5cm) issued to those responsible for purchasing. Emphases in the original. Blanked out words disguise name and activity of the business.

Figure 5.1

The majority of the large firms and public sector organisations had highly explicit purchasing policies, often summed up in a mission statement on purchasing, backed up with equally clearly formulated purchasing procedures which all departments were expected to follow. Some of the mission statements also mentioned other issues discussed later in the chapter, such as BS 5750, indicating either their relatively recent origin or that they were subject to fairly frequent revision.

Figure 5.1 reproduces one example of the kind of purchasing policy mission statement commonly found. As with the majority of such statements, the overwhelming stress is on economic considerations with phrases such as 'to maximise the value for money' and 'to buy goods and services at the right price and quality' recurring frequently. Nor is it simply naive to note this emphasis. There is a wide variety of other factors which might be mentioned in a mission statement, which is usually highly normative or prescriptive, that is, it asserts the ideals to which senior management would like to be thought to adhere and which they might admit may not be always reflected in practice. For example, a large firm or organisation might proclaim a commitment to supporting local economic activities or helping small businesses where possible, at least as an *ideal* in its purchasing strategies.

What is striking about the replies of respondents to questions on the firm or organisation's overall purchasing policy is the absence of references to locality or small firms or issues which were not easily subsumed under a fairly narrow economic rationality. The other strongly represented theme was the 'good economic management' practised by large enterprises or organisations who wish to be seen as operating successfully in the 'lean, fit economy' supposedly developed by UK business (with government encouragement and help) in the 1980s and 1990s:

we are actually trying to ensure the business nationally has got a common purchasing policy to follow and it's currently being revised.

> Basically the policy is that we will buy in all the goods and services that are required by operational managers to fill their objective of meeting customer demand first time, every time, at the right price, the right quality with a view to moving towards only using qualified suppliers in readiness for the single market.
>
> (Representative, public service organisation branch in Sheffield)

In this quote, two further common themes, also discussed below, are introduced, that is, the notion that suppliers will be restricted through some process of vetting and/or possessing some qualification or other indicating that they reach a minimum standard such as BS 5750, and the Single European Market (SEM).

Where, on the odd occasion, locality was mentioned in the initial statement on purchasing policy, it was usually qualified by stressing the overriding importance of economic criteria such as price:

> basically the prime objective is that anything of any reasonable value must be tendered. Now obviously when you tender something your main problem is, of course, finding people able to tender for the supply or service . . . Now that invariably means that obviously you start nearer home. You want people that work as close to the site as possible but it can extend right through to the other side of the country if somebody is capable of tendering for that facility or capable of providing you with the service you require . . . if he is capable of doing it, even from a distance, then obviously they have the ability to bid. Ultimately, it comes down to price at the end of the day. If a supplier who is based in the West Country tenders for something like the supply of electrical components and he is considerably cheaper than someone down the road and can still deliver within one working day, he'll get the business. There's no loyalty to somebody because they are based around the company if they can't produce the goods in terms of price. That's what the basic strategy is. We want to get the best value for money . . . because ultimately we report to shareholders.
>
> (Representative, large manufacturing firm, Kingston upon Thames)

One other reason for the lack of prominence of locality in purchasing decisions, was that in many instances the purchasing policy comes from outside the locality where the interviews took place. For example, the main source of purchasing policy decisions for the above Kingston manufacturer was in Lancashire while a Sheffield manufacturer respondent stated that main purchasing decisions were made in Rickmansworth, Hertfordshire. Where this kind of national approach is used, it is much less likely that locality will be stressed: consistency across the firm's operations regardless of there they happen to be geographically, is the main aim.

It might be expected that public sector organisations might offer rather less economistic statements in relation to purchasing policy. They have, after all, a public interest dimension to their activities and, in the case of local authorities, a community interest dimension. On the other hand, they have also been subject to intensive central government pressure to adopt business ideologies and practices over the last 15 years or so, particularly through the enforced introduction of privatisation or through compulsory competitive tendering (CCT) for an increasing range of local government services. Asked whether the organisation had a corporate purchasing policy, a respondent representing a public sector organisation in Sheffield said:

> The quick answer is 'yes' but we don't think these are very satisfactory. Circumstances change, new legislation by the government etc means that currently these [purchasing policies] are under review so they will be changing.

What is your basic policy then?

> To, I suppose, maximise value for money in procurement for goods and services for the Authority.

An educational organisation in Kingston had a more pluralistic approach since larger sub-units had considerable autonomy because of their differing special needs but, nevertheless:

> There are certain thresholds beyond which one is obliged to seek . . . quotations . . . There is a policy about seeking value for money in all our purchases. That translates itself into a threshold above which one is required to get . . . quotations. Other policies when it is concerned with not purchasing so much as letting out contracts for building works . . . there is a set tendering procedure to which we adhere quite rigidly and that's anything over 5,000 quid, be it building supplies or the central supply of work.

These examples of general purchasing polices tell us little about the specifics of purchasing activities and how these manifest themselves into links with businesses in the wider economy. For example, while neither locality nor size of firm might be mentioned in these statements, they might become more significant when attention shifts from mission statements to actual purchasing decisions and behaviour. In the interviews, therefore, the questions following the discussion of general policy probed the detail of purchasing links and the significance of locality and size of firm in these decisions.

LOCALITY AND SIZE OF FIRM IN LARGE FIRM, LARGE ORGANISATION PURCHASING

The inclusion of locality and size of firm in purchasing decisions and behaviour may be perfectly consistent with highly economistic overall policies. There is no *a priori* reason to assume that these criteria cannot go together and common sense assumptions might suggest that in some respects they could very well reinforce each other. Local firms have advantages in knowing the local market, being able to respond quickly and deliver quickly. These, after all, are key assumptions associated with the currently fashionable management emphasis on the superiority of 'just in time' (JIT) relations between suppliers and buying organisations discussed in Chapter 3. JIT models further stress the value of increasing close relations built up between firms over time to enhance supplier responsiveness and efficiency in meeting the purchasing organisation's needs.

Asked what role locality had in purchasing policy and decisions, the majority of large firm and public sector organisation respondents either gave it no significance or cast it as of only minor importance. For example, the large manufacturing firm's representative in Kingston quoted earlier was asked whether there was any policy on buying locally:

> Well no. As I explained to you before, it all basically comes down to price. I mean, we will invite local companies and any others which may not be so local to tender for something. Ultimately, if a local company is more expensive than something further away and the one further away can still provide you with the level of service you require, they'll get the business.

The same question was put to a respondent speaking for a Sheffield steel product manufacturer, Because of Sheffield's history as a steel-making 'industrial district', the heavy weight, the complexity of many bought-in products and services, and awkward transport problems of many steel products and materials, it would be expected that other local firms would be regarded as a natural supplier network. But the respondent's answer to the question, while favourable to local links, still emphasised cost and quality considerations as being of overriding importance. Was it policy to purchase locally?

> No, not particularly. Having said that . . . you work in conjunction with the production people, the engineers, service departments and company policy. Now there are a lot of local companies obviously in an industrial area of Sheffield, Rotherham and Doncaster and even into Derbyshire and there are a lot of people who are local who produce . . . products we use. Because they are local, the transport costs are low, the service, as far as getting stuff here, is good. If you have any queries or any requirement for technical support, they can be here very quickly. So we use that as a sort of nucleus of how we use people but because we are so keen to get a quality which is going to . . . produce the best quality steel we can or that the plant keeps on running and we don't have any down time, we are always searching for alternatives to what we are currently buying. So we go further afield both in this country and abroad. When we get details of competitive materials or components . . . [they] are analysed and perhaps trials done on them and we eventually go for the most cost effective . . . So there is no specific policy of buying locally but it obviously has advantages.

A service sector business in Sheffield, an example of the decentralisation of financial services activities which occurred in the UK in the 1980s, had less incentive to link to local economic activities and suppliers. The respondent for this business gave a flat, unqualified 'no' to the question on whether there was any policy to buy locally. This, in other words, showed no dent in the economistic emphasis on price, quality and reliability dictated by central buying policies despite any tendencies to localism in other kinds of economic activity in Sheffield.

Public sector organisations were just as detached from local economic relations. A Sheffield public sector organisation (not the City Council) representative gave the same flat, unequivocal 'no' as the service organisation representative had. A parallel organisation in Kingston gave the same reply. The local authority organisations would be expected to be more locally minded and, indeed, one did state that where possible the policy was to support local industry but the main aim remained value for money. The other had no policy to purchase locally.[5]

The significance of public sector organisations in local economic activities has often been neglected due to an over-concern with manufacturing activities. The findings on the service sector organisations, public and private, suggest that this neglect may very well be responsible in part for what is beginning to appear to be misleadingly high perceptions of levels of local economic integration in relation to what is conventionally characterised as a local economy.

ATTITUDES TO SMALL FIRMS

The other issue probed in the further questions on purchasing policies and behaviour of the large firms and public sector organisations was their relations with small firms. Where such relations exist, they might also be seen as likely to be local in that small firms are assumed to operate over restricted geographical areas.[6] Government has encouraged such links especially on the part of public sector organisations and, indeed, one of the aims of the introduction of CCT for the provision of local authority services was to create opportunities for small businesses (Employment Department, 1992:23).

Representatives of the large firms and public sector organisations were asked directly whether they had any general policies on buying from smaller businesses. The replies indicated a good deal of generalised goodwill towards smaller firms but almost invariably this was qualified or doubts were expressed.

> No general policies no. My feeling is if I can help a small business along then I wish to do so.

> It's not a policy as such?

> Not as such but it falls in line with the policy of the most cost effective way of doing it because if you go to a two or three man business the overheads are less than one with 3,000 employees so therefore . . . It depends on what it is . . . somebody producing a pen like this, a three man firm. He's probably hand-making them . . . it's going to be more

expensive than Bic or whoever who is turning out millions of the things but it is not as good a quality. That Bic will last you, say, 50 writing hours and the hand-made one 100 writing hours. On the other hand, it might be the other way round . . . You would have to test the thing out and see what is the most cost effective . . . You can't generalise on small or large companies on who is the most cost effective.

(Representative of a large steel engineering firm, Sheffield)

I can give you my view – we don't have a policy . . . My view is that it is a little bit, if I can use an expression, 'horses for courses'. We do have . . . the services of a lot of big companies . . . but also I have a lot of small people who work for me and I encourage it *if* they are cost effective and if they can provide me with something the big boys can't and it's identifying what they can provide that the big companies can't that makes me employ them . . . Just to given an example, when I moved into this job all the plumbing in the buildings were looked after by _____ _____ which are a big engineering concern . . . The problems we had with them led me to investigate why we were employing them . . . what the costs were and what alternatives there were . . . and would they be cost effective and would it be worth giving it a try? In actual fact, in the plumbing area we did change. We are currently with a very small business, for very good reasons and it has been very cost effective for us as a business to do that. So I don't have a policy except that I try and examine what both have got to offer because big firms have got things to offer which are different than what small firms have to offer . . . if it's better to go to a small firm, a small local firm, then I do so.

(Representative, large manufacturing firm, Kingston upon Thames)

A public sector organisation representative based in Sheffield also gave a very similar kind of answer to the question on whether there was any general policy on buying from smaller businesses:

No, there's no policy to buy from a small company for the sake of it but if the authority is giving some support to a local business then we as a department try to put them in a position where they can be competitive and help them in terms of tendering. But it would be unfair to say that we have a policy of supporting local firms again without bearing in mind value for money.

There were also some indications that small firms might find doing business with large businesses or organisations harder in the future. In electronics and electronics-related industries, such as defence equipment manufacturing, where there is a tradition of sub-contracting, and the sector where half the sample of small manufacturing businesses discussed in the previous chapter were located, several respondents mentioned considerations of these kinds:

we have over the last 6 months been under . . . a company directive or initiative to reduce the . . . or number of people that we do business with . . . A year ago we were finding that if you added up the number of people on our procurements corporate system . . . we had 15,000 suppliers who we were dealing with at one time or another which was basically too many people to have business going on with . . . The initiative that has . . . come from company board level . . . was to reduce the data base or the number of people we did business with so that we reduce in turn our costs in terms of, well, for instance, the number of bank accounts that you have to deal with, the number of orders you have to place on different suppliers. Basically, we have got the number from 15,000 odd down on the new procurement system . . . to some three and a half thousand . . . So it has been drastically reduced and what it has meant, of course, is that we are dealing with less people who deal with more services. We tend to place larger, more global orders with them to reduce the amount of paperwork needed or required of us and also of the suppliers in terms of the amount of paperwork they have to deal with. A hundred small orders rather than one large order dealing with a variety of items . . . By virtue of the fact that we are tending to go for bigger companies in that they have a wider variety of services and goods that they can offer us . . . smaller companies are . . . more specific in what they can offer to you. I would suggest that perhaps the greater part of the people we deal with now are bigger companies that can offer a wider range of services than a smaller one can.

(Large manufacturing company representative, Kingston upon Thames)

Another major privatised public service business representative in Sheffield stated that he liked to use local suppliers because they often gave better service than national suppliers. But he could see a problem emerging since there was a centralising trend occurring. National contracts emphasised price–volume advantages and local suppliers might not be able to handle large volumes:

The other bit we are having to be careful of now, as well, is that we make sure that the suppliers are actually on our 'qualified suppliers list' which nationally we are just setting up. We haven't got a national data base of who we will trade with but we are working on that right now with a view to having it established by the end of this calendar year so that we don't fall foul of the new EEC legislation the following year. In the process of setting up that qualified supplier list, I believe a large number of our one-off infrequent suppliers will fall by the wayside because, for whatever reason, they will not respond to the questionnaires we ask them to fill in.

Do you think that is going to disproportionately affect small businesses?

I think it probably will.

Small firms are, therefore, seen as often having advantages. But the large firm and large organisation representatives qualify their generally favourable attitudes by stressing that small firms can only be seen in context. They have to be able to compete on price and service and large firms may have other advantages which push the smaller business out of contention.

The last views cited mention supplier rationalisation trends among large firms and organisations which came to the fore in the late 1980s and early 1990s. They see this shift towards reducing numbers of suppliers and the adoption of 'preferred supplier' strategies involving the supplier demonstrating conformity to a standard of some kind, as likely to reduce the opportunities for small firms. To this might be added the more specific effects of the growing importance of BS 5750 which were also discussed in Chapter 4 and are again discussed later in this chapter. These will also be seen as narrowing the market opportunities of small firms at least in the short to medium term, that is, over the next 5 years.

'Tough but fair' was the theme that recurred in many of the respondents' accounts of their purchasing behaviour but other sources suggest that there are other factors which can affect small firm relations with larger firms and organisations adversely. Some of these our respondents might have been less likely to mention because it would not show them, or their organisation, in a good light. One which has received a good deal of attention recently is late payment particularly by large firms in their dealings with small firms. This it has been argued, increased sharply in the late 1980s and early 1990s to the extent that:

> The government is concerned that late payment by large companies of their debts is damaging Britain's small firm base.
>   (Department of Trade and Industry, 1993:5)

Whether this is a new long-term strategy adopted by large firms in their relations with small firms or simply a reflection of the recession is a matter of debate (Cork Gully/CBI, 1991; Nash, 1991; Midland Bank, 1993b) but to the extent it occurs, it reduces the likelihood of small firms seeking to do, or being able to do, business with larger firms and organisations.[7]

In an unusually frank in-house paper examining the purchasing policy of a major manufacturing company, the writer, a senior manager responsible for purchasing, admits that previous practices were unacceptable and inefficient. Suppliers were traditionally dealt with on a 'thrash and bash basis', that is, treated in a very aggressive way:

> Contrary to popular opinion, our suppliers do not exactly welcome business with open arms. We screw the price down, do not pay on time, change the design half way through the contract then argue about extras.

The solution proposed in the paper was one mentioned by several other respondents: fewer and better suppliers whose commitment to the company would be carefully nurtured:

> The logistics of managing a large supply base are difficult and costly. The more suppliers we have the less we are able to control them. The

cake is cut into smaller and smaller pieces and the incentive for a supplier to actually pursue our business becomes less attractive.

The new policy would be a much smaller number of preferred suppliers on a 'close co-operating partnership' basis to both firms' 'mutual benefit'. BS 5750 accreditation would be mandatory. The proposed new approach and its co-operative ideal were somewhat undermined, however, by the insistence that all suppliers would be expected to accept that:

> All contracts would be entered into with a fixed price with no variations. All deliveries would be subject to liquidated damages, contract terms and conditions would be back to back or better, standard terms of payment would be extended from 30 to a minimum of 60 days, all contracts must be self-financing, there will no stage payments and retentions and guarantees will become an intrinsic part of any purchase order as a standard means of control.

The inference which might be drawn from the above is that small firms, though not mentioned in the paper, will find it more difficult to do business with this firm in the future. The new conditions are much easily met by larger, or at least medium sized, firms which have more resources to invest in such changes to achieve 'preferred supplier' status.

Overall, the large firms and public sector organisations are clearly more favourable to small firms than local firms in terms of purchasing policies in that 'small firms' elicit more positive attitudes and behaviour than the notion of 'local firms'. As we have argued in Chapter 4, any idea that 'small firms' and 'local firms' are broadly the same populations under different labels is not tenable.

THE PURCHASING BEHAVIOUR OF LARGE FIRMS AND ORGANISATIONS

The above sections reported the declared mission statements and policies of the large firm–large organisations as articulated by their representatives. The implications of these, we have suggested, do not bode well for small firms or local firms. Mission statements and stated policies, however, may not accord with practice. A large public sector organisation may have a policy of ensuring that small and local firms are aware of its needs and of inviting any suitable business to bid to supply goods and services. If, on the other hand, the contracts offered never fall below a certain value to ensure efficient and cost effective administration, then, in practice, many small or local businesses will find themselves excluded.

Having discussed policy considerations with the large firm and public sector representatives, we then explored in detail how different kinds of goods and services were *actually* purchased. We explored on what basis they were purchased, that is, the extent to which the work was on long-term or regular contracts, as opposed to one-offs and non-repeated purchases, and whether the work was done by small or local firms in contrast to large, non-local suppliers.

We also subdivided the type of work and services the firms and organisations might buy in. There are potentially a wide range of outside purchases that can be made by businesses and organisations and different types of work might be purchased in very different ways. Manufactured components, for example, might be purchased on a long-term contract while professional services might be purchased only on a one-off basis or to deal with emergencies such as a temporary overload on the in-house department's capabilities. Different kinds of firms and public sector organisations could be expected to purchase different kinds of goods and services. For example, manufacturing firms would be more likely to buy in components or semi-finished work while service organisations, private and public, would be much less likely to engage in these kinds of exchanges instead buying equipment more on a one-off basis.

The three subdivisions adopted were:

i)   *Manufacturing.* The external sourcing of components and semi-finished goods either on one-off orders or contract as defined in Chapter 2, that is the supply of items on the basis of written agreements which specify the type and delivery of the items over some period of time but excluding one-off orders.

ii)   *Non-Professional Services.* Including a wide variety of items such as printing, catering, transport and dispatch, car leasing and servicing, travel services and office cleaning. There have been arguments that the external sourcing of services of this kind has been on the increase in recent years (Wood, 1991). To the extent this has happened it could have created more opportunities for local and small firms though such services, for example, transport and delivery, can also exploit economies of scale so that the new opportunities benefit larger businesses operating nationally or even internationally.

iii) *Professional Services.* These are the kind of services supplied traditionally by banks, accountants, solicitors, insurance companies together with newer services such as management consultants and employment and training agencies. Again, also, there have been arguments that the external sourcing of these kinds of services has been on the increase in recent years. For instance, employment and training services are now more commonly offered by the private sector as government has attempted to reduce the state's involvement in these activities.[8] Accountants have widened the range of services they offer. Most of the largest firms now have consultancy divisions and many smaller firms also offer consultancy services. The clearing banks have been increasing their range of products for business customers from payroll preparation to insurance and are keen to offer other services.

MANUFACTURING

These types of external purchases, of components and semi-finished goods, have been the subject of an enormous literature as the discussion in Chapter 2 demonstrated. 'Subcontracting', in particular, has been the focus of much theorising and research though, as Chapter 2 argued, this appears to slip easily into over-statement. The large firms and public sector organisations in this study had very differing needs for bought-in manufacturing sourcing: those in services, for instance, usually offered a much smaller potential market than firms themselves in manufacturing.

Sheffield's old industrial district characteristics were evident in the replies given by the representative of a major steel-making and steel products firm. A wide range of materials and products were externally sourced from scrap metal to feed the steel-making, to finished products such as bearings and couplings. In some instances, particular processes were externally sourced, such as heat treatments. A very high proportion of this work, about 60–70% overall, was carried out or sourced locally. In part, this was due to the presence of local specialist suppliers and, in part, to the weight of some of the materials used making transport costs a major factor. A high proportion of the external sourcing was on long-term contracts, for instance, the supply of scrap and special alloys. Some went to small firms but only because they could meet the need. There was no special preference for small firms.

The respondent noted, however, that 'local' could be misleading in this context. Since Sheffield was a major area of steel-making and steel products but the industry was increasingly global, many 'local' firms were branch outlets of national or multinational businesses. Other purchases of non-steel products and services, office and IT equipment, for instance, might be local and might go to a small firm but most would be sourced from outside the locality.[9]

An example of a potentially large-scale user of external sources of manufactured goods was in electronics in Kingston. During the previous 12–15 months the firm had externally sourced for wiring, loom assemblies, console assemblies and part-build contracting. Some of this was contracted work and was what the respondent called 'free issue contracts', that is, where the purchasing firm is still designing a final product and suppliers receive work in small lots as the design work proceeds.

The majority of this work over the previous 12 months had gone to 3 firms. Two were outside the locality and these had received about two-thirds of the work. None of the firms were small in the conventional sense, that is, they were all branch outlets of larger firms. The one local firm, for instance, had been bought out by a larger firm whose head office was not local.

Is any of the work you contract on a long-term or regular basis?

No. There's . . . we never put out any long-term contracts.

Outside suppliers were also used to deal with overflow or specialist work beyond the firm's own capabilities or capacity. The respondent went on to say that all the external sourcing firms dealt with had to have either AQAP[10] or BS 5750 accreditation, or both. While many small firms in electronics now have such accreditation, a firm has to be well established and reach a minimum standard of performance before it can be attained. Young, smaller businesses inevitably find this more difficult.

In contrast, a further major defence contractor in the same area bought in the great majority of the components that went into its final products. Much of this equipment was very specialised including radar equipment, weapon systems etc:

> We are basically glorified Lego builders in that we have a lot of expertise in the actual construction of the [main product] . . . but a good deal of the parts . . . are bought in assemblies that we spend a great deal of money on . . . It's very much like a car manufacturer in that way . . . we are really final assemblers.

Because of the very high proportion of bought-in components, the firm has a separate sub-contracts department with its own complex procedures. Much of the purchasing is based on long-term contracts especially where the bought-in components are dedicated parts of a long-term development programme.

Yet despite this very high proportion of external sourcing, the firm's representative stated that only 'a minimal amount' came from local firms. Their external suppliers were virtually all national or international companies, some very large indeed. Small firms would also be unlikely to be involved to any great extent since much of the kind of work small firms might do such as 'metal bashing', was carried out in-house because it was highly specialised and security sensitive.

Services firms and organisations offered a rather wider range of responses, many of them not of the kind discussed in the conventional subcontracting literature. A major retailing business with turnover in excess of £50 million purchased a huge range of manufactured goods from external sources, some made to the firm's own specification to be sold as 'own brand' goods. But the respondent could think of no branded goods produced by local firms though it was possible an 'own brand' good might sometimes be sourced locally but as a proportion of total bought-in goods, these would be 'minuscule'.

A major national financial services business in Sheffield needed to buy in a substantial amount of manufactured goods, particularly IT equipment as well as office furniture and other equipment. There were long-term (that is, 4-year) contracts for some kinds of office equipment, for example, photocopiers, and there were around 100 firms on a 'preferred supplier' list which had steadily expanded. One-off buying of special equipment, might go to any suitable firm. Very little of any of this purchasing, however, went to local businesses: 'a half to a quarter per cent' of total purchasing turnover.

Some of these would be small firms supplying office equipment usually on one-off orders.

Overall, therefore, only Sheffield showed much of an approximation to an integrated local economy and only in relation to its long established steel-making, steel products sector. In the other instances, the examples of large modern high tech manufacturing and services businesses, locality was not significant in the purchasing patterns of manufactured goods and processes, and small firms appeared to receive only crumbs at best.

NON-PROFESSIONAL SERVICES

The likelihood and patterns of purchasing non-professional services is likely to be more evenly spread across the types of large firms and organisations selected for study. Regardless of their core activities, most will need services such as office cleaning, transport and printing. They do not, however, necessarily have to buy them in: they may be provided in-house. However, as discussed earlier, one of the major management fashions of the 1980s was the notion that businesses should decide what their core activities were and concentrate on these, externally sourcing all other 'peripheral' activities.

Of course, not every large organisation followed this fashion for outsourcing of non-professional support services even if there was a general shift towards the external sourcing of some services. The large defence firm in Kingston shows how mixed the pattern can be even where, as this company's representative stated, there is a move away from in-house provision:

Printing. Mainly carried out in-house certainly for routine printing but externally sourced where the printing was specialised or high quality colour. The respondent did not say who provided this externally sourced printing but it is unlikely to have gone to a local jobbing printer.

Catering. The contract was held by Gardner Merchant, one of the largest UK contract caterers, who provided catering services for the firm nationally. This was an example of the firm's shift from internal to outside sourcing in recent years.

Dispatch and Goods Transport. Provided in-house using own vehicles. Some of the transport needs were very specialised and hence it was felt that external sourcing would not provide the kind of service needed.

Cars and Personal Transport. Provided in-house through the firm's links with another firm in the same group of companies.

Office Cleaning. Carried out by a national company. The respondent felt that it was unlikely a local firm could cope with their needs since the number of offices and other buildings on the site was so large.

Travel Services. This was provided partly in-house and partly externally sourced. The respondent did not know who provided the external service but it may have gone to a local firm or local branch of a national specialist in travel services.

Maintenance. There was an in-house maintenance department but in recent years this had been drastically reduced in size and more and more work had gone to outside firms. This shift had been helped by the weakening of the trade unions in this sector. The respondent estimated about half of this work now went to local firms and of these, about 80% were small firms. Sometimes a larger job, a painting contract, for example, might be given to several firms.

A similar mixed pattern was offered by another large manufacturing firm whose Kingston office was concerned with management services rather than manufacturing activities directly. Again printing was almost entirely in-house but two local small printing firms received any overflow work though it was stressed that this produced orders only infrequently. Dispatch and personal transport work went externally to several small local firms and some larger, national hire firms. Office and building cleaning was carried out mainly by a medium sized firm with about 100 employees, which operated in and outside the Kingston area. Maintenance of plumbing, decorating and similar needs had also been won by local small businesses, in one instance from a large national contractor. Catering was carried out entirely in-house. Overall, the respondent estimated that about 25% of non-professional services were provided by small firms and between 5 and 10% were provided by local firms.

In Sheffield there was a similar, mixed picture in non-professional services provision. A major public sector organisation was virtually self-sufficient for the whole range of such services. The only work put out was overflow work and specialist work which in-house sources could not provide. In other words, despite government exhortations to public sector organisations to source from 'the market' and the private sector, and the fashion for sourcing non-core needs externally, this organisation remained steadfastly traditional. If it could be provided in-house, then it should be.

In contrast, a large manufacturing firm offered a picture much closer to that advocated by management texts. Originally, virtually all non-professional services had been provided in-house but over the last decade or so there had been a major shift to external sourcing based on the view that non-core activities of these kinds were better provided by outside specialists.

Printing. This had been mainly carried out in-house until about six months before the interview for this study but was now entirely externally sourced. It was felt that equipment, particularly new technology in printing, was expensive and that the switch to using outside suppliers was now the right decision. Some – perhaps most – of the routine printing would be expected to go to local firms with specialised work being sourced further afield.

Catering. The original in-house service had been first of all switched to a new business set up by the former in-house manager who had successfully tendered for the contract. But later he decided to give up the contract and concentrate on other business interests. The contract was then won by Compass, a national industrial catering division of Grand Metropolitan. They had since expanded into other parts of the organisation on other sites.

Office and Amenity Cleaning. This was a major service requirement with over 200 offices on site and employees needing facilities to shower after working 3 shifts over 24 hours in a dirty work environment. This had been entirely in-house but it had been put out to tender. The in-house manager had won the contract and set up a new business to provide the service. Like the former catering manager, however, he had decided to let the contract go and it was won by a national company who now provided the service.

Transport and Car Leasing. Most was now on contract hire. At the start, external sourcing was from local outlets of national vehicle distributors though problems had been experienced in maintaining the level of service required. More recently a local firm had won the contract but one large enough to supply and maintain 300 cars. This firm had won on price and the quality of service since had been superior to previous suppliers.

The respondent stated that he preferred, where possible, to source from local and small firms but he emphasised that all work had to be tendered for and that he monitored closely the price and performance of all current contracts. He had no hesitation in inviting new tenders when contracts came up for renewal or where existing contract holders asked for price increases or their performance was unsatisfactory. Clearly, from his replies, he was very keen to ensure value for money and quality and, despite his expressed preference for local and small firms, had accepted bids from national suppliers over local and small firms on strict commercial criteria in a majority of instances.

A major financial services business in Sheffield was also involved in external sourcing in its approach to non-professional services. Virtually all such services were externally sourced though a small proportion of printing needs and maintenance was provided in-house. Office cleaning had been provided in-house but was now externally sourced from a national business with some work going to local small firms. But the purchasing executive stated that only about 10% of these services was provided by small and/or local firms. In printing, for instance, there were 4 'preferred suppliers' who were given the opportunity to quote for all colour print work. None were local. The firm also had a 'preferred supplier' list from which the external supplier of catering services was drawn and travel services were provided by another firm in the group. All work was on a contract basis and subject to review and renewal periodically.

The overall picture which emerges in relation to the supply of non-professional services confirms the suggestion in the literature that more of these services are now provided externally than in the past (Wood and Smith, 1988). The pattern is, however, mixed: in some firms and organisations a proportion of such services remain sourced in-house for various reasons. The externally sourced services and the trend towards their use are not related to local economic activities in any simple way. Much of the work generated is locally sourced but these are often outlets of national firms sometimes set up specifically to provide the service contracted out. This clearly provides jobs and an income flow to the locality but these might exist anyway (perhaps in greater numbers and for a larger income flow) if the service was provided in-house. Profits, however, flow outside the locality. Other work bypasses the local economy completely.

The amount of work carried out by small businesses and strictly local businesses was usually only a small proportion of the total and there were indications that they were losing ground in the long term. In some areas of non-professional services, such as catering, concentration was already very apparent with several national contract catering firms already well represented. The emphasis on price, quality and renewable contracts was as strong in the supply of non-professional services as in the external sourcing of manufacturing components and services discussed earlier. Trends in the rationalising of these suppliers, such as the emergence of 'preferred supplier' lists, were also apparent though perhaps less strongly than in manufacturing.

PROFESSIONAL SERVICES

The provision of professional services, namely legal and financial services, insurance, employment, marketing and advertising services for example, is rather more difficult to externally source completely. All businesses and organisations of any size, for instance, must have some in-house financial management and many will have at least a small in-house legal service. On the other hand, the use of external sources for of these kinds of services by large firms and organisations is a long-standing practice with virtually every firm and organisation having services of these kinds on tap from external sources.

Whether there have been trends towards more external sourcing of professional services is difficult to estimate. There has been a considerable expansion in independently provided management consultancy services in the UK in recent years (Bryson et al., 1993) but whether this represents a shift from in-house to external sourcing, is unclear. It might be, for example, that the concern with management strategies and organisational structures, upon which consultants offer specialist advice, are new phenomena arising out of an increasing awareness of the poor economic performance of UK businesses or the need to survive the restructuring and recessions of the UK economy over the last 15 years.[11]

All businesses and organisations studied used conventional banking, accounting/auditing services and insurance mainly supplied by large, national providers. Some of the firms and organisations were branches (albeit large ones) of national or multinational enterprises. Here the majority of professional services were handled by the head office of the businesses or organisations studied, either from in-house sources or head office responsibilities for the enterprise's external relations with professional services suppliers. Where this arrangement held, branches such as those in the study were usually required to use the head office provision. The one widespread exception was employment services where recruiting, particularly of temporary workers, secretaries and lower level white collar workers, was often locally sourced. These could be either small, local agencies or local branches of national chains or both to ensure a choice of suitable people. There was also some use of specialist professional services such as consulting engineers but the likelihood of local firms picking up this kind of work was not great. Even in Sheffield where there was more of a tendency to source locally, particularly for manufacturing components and services, professional services were firmly in the hands of non-local suppliers with few exceptions.

Professional services, in other words, were the least likely to be locally sourced in a strict sense, though local branches of national suppliers did reasonably well. Small firms and especially local small firms did worst of all in this third type of potentially externally sourced activity.

There are very large numbers of small providers of professional services who are ready to serve local markets including small accountancy firms, small legal partnerships and management consultants. But the large firms and large public sector organisations in the study clearly practised size homogamy in sourcing professional services: large opting for large, just as the small businesses in our studies satisfied their needs for most professional services from suppliers near to their own size.

Finally, in this section of the interview respondents were asked a general question about their experiences of working with small local businesses. Although as the detailed examination of the three kinds of potential external sourcing above showed, the use of local and small firms was extremely variable, virtually every firm and organisation had *some* dealings with local small firms. This might be only on a very intermittent basis and for a very limited range of activities but nevertheless all our respondents had views on this question.

The common theme in answers to the above question was the pro-small firm stance adopted. There was a great deal of generalised goodwill towards smaller businesses. Many of the positive views were what would be conventionally expected. These views stressed the widely accepted advantages of the small firm: speed of response, close attention to customer's wants and keen and competitive pricing due to low overheads. Asked his view on small local firms the representative of a Kingston service business said:

Very good.

Can you highlight any advantages and disadvantages?

Obviously, close proximity . . . able to deal with on a one-to-one basis
. . . people we deal with locally are probably cheaper.

Another Kingston respondent from the management services office of a
large manufacturer said:

I've had very good experiences with smaller people. They are more
flexible. They are more willing to discuss price because I basically think
their overheads are probably less . . . They are eager for the work. They
are more likely to do a little bit extra for the money you are paying them
than a big firm because, in general, a big firm . . . representative doesn't
particularly identify with his firm's relationship with my firm. It's just a
job to him whereas a smaller outfit, they tend to be more particularly
concerned with the item of business they are actually doing and the
relationship with me . . . I am [name of respondent firm] to them. They
work harder on that relationship.

But having extolled the virtues of the small local firm, the same respondent
was also clear on the drawbacks:

They might not be there tomorrow. They might have actually problems
of their own in terms of finance or whatever. The labour they provide
me with now might change . . . or because they haven't got the right
tools, because they are not as big a concern, they just can't go out and
buy a £200 item of equipment to help them here. They may be using
equipment that is not quite modern.

A major defence contractor's representative in Kingston said:

I think you get a better personal service . . . They are a lot more involved in the . . . level of service or performance they are actually
giving you . . . you will get, for instance, the director of a company
coming in and making sure that whatever is being done or provided [is]
to a satisfactory standard whereas if you are dealing with a huge company . . . as far as they are concerned, you are just another company on
the list . . . The smaller local companies that we deal with . . . you over
the years develop a bit of, a more of a [relationship with] . . . Although
we try to keep quite at arm's length with suppliers in general, you
develop a bit more of a personal relationship in that you know the, for
instance, managing director and if there's a problem you can ring him
up directly yourself and talk to him and . . . in general you will get a
better response.

On the disadvantages, the same respondent mentioned the limited scope
of the work small firms could handle and problems in meeting time dead-
lines when they were busy. An order from a large firm could easily over-
stretch a small firm's capacity. In dealing with small firms, a judgement
always had to be made on whether it was thought the small firm had the
capacity to handle the order even where it claimed it could.

In addition, for defence work, there was also security, quality and traceability issues. The MOD needed to be assured that all work for them met

their stringent demands on these issues. The Ministry, as noted earlier, usually insists that all firms, prime contractor and all secondary contractors, have quality accreditation. 'Traceability' refers to the need to be able to identify the original maker of any component often up to several years after it is supplied. Small firms were a risk because if they went out of business, traceability could not be met.

In Sheffield where local firms, though not necessarily small or completely local firms, received more of the business from the large firms and organisations in the study, respondents had similar views on the benefits and drawbacks of dealing with small firms. A financial services firm representative said:

> There are clearly advantages and disadvantages. A small local business, they are on your doorstep. They are likely to be more flexible . . . You can look at it both ways on their costings, they have low overheads and, therefore, should be more cost effective. But on the other hand, they are not buying . . . in bulk typically and therefore their input cost can be higher which can offset the other advantages . . . We are not going to buy a photocopier locally when we can get them direct from Rank Xerox at a Rank Xerox type price.

Interestingly, the steel makers and steel products firms in Sheffield were more likely to emphasise the disadvantages of dealing with small firms:

> Basically, it's a very difficult relationship, a large company–small business relationship. The small business is . . . you either get them who are very overawed by the thought of dealing with a big company or you go to the other extreme . . . You know, 'I've built this up myself lads and you are not going to tell me what to do' . . . It's a very big undertaking for a small company to deal with a major company.

Small firms undoubtedly received a lot of favourable comments in our respondents' replies but it is possible to suggest that some of these were ritualistic: a version of the 'small is beautiful' rhetoric which manifests itself in discussions of many areas of social and economic life from education to living in small communities. More important were the hard economic considerations which influence relations between businesses and large business purchasing behaviour. Price, quality, delivery, reliability and capacity were the criteria mentioned again and again in replies to questions dealing with inter-firm relations. On these criteria, small local firms were in direct competition with larger businesses or businesses outside the locality and too often they appeared to be viewed less favourably. Nor were the long-term trends in their favour. The trend towards reducing the number of suppliers and adopting 'preferred supplier' lists, which firms could only join by passing quality assessments and demonstrating their ability to meet a wide range of tasks, are not favourable to small, local firms.

The same criteria, price, quality, delivery, reliability and capacity, were mentioned when contract relations were discussed. Few of the large firms or public sector organisation representatives were willing to contemplate long-term contract relations with suppliers. The great majority of contracts for components and especially for services such as catering, were relatively short term, that is, up to 3 years but often for shorter periods. Automatic renewal was very unlikely and most reported instances of non-renewal. Although preferred suppliers meant closer relations, respondents were still very explicit that the continuation of preferred supplier status would depend on the same criteria continuing to be met.

THE IMPACT OF BS 5750 AND THE SHIFT TO PREFERRED SUPPLIERS

'Quality' has become one of the management mission words of the 1990s supported strongly by government in its drive towards improving the performance of UK businesses and the UK economy (Department of Trade and Industry, 1991). Although there are a wide variety of formal quality standards, many of them specific to particular kinds of economic activities, the key standard is BS 5750 and its European equivalent ISO 9000. Industry is now inundated with information and guides on BS 5750 and the more encompassing notion of total quality management (TQM) (Drummond, 1992). Many of the large firm-large organisation representatives mentioned BS 5750 and its impact on their relations with suppliers and small firms.[12] Often this was mentioned in conjunction with a reduction in the number of suppliers and the shift to 'preferred supplier' relations.

Nine of the 16 large firms and public sector organisations had undertaken more or less major restructuring of internal procedures and relations with suppliers in the previous 2 years. Several others were expecting a similar exercise in the near future. The public sector organisations were adopting private sector procedures in dealing with suppliers and, indeed, in some instances appeared ahead of private sector firms in terms of how few exceptions to the new procedures were allowed.

Sometimes the restructuring was integral to a takeover or amalgamation of businesses of which the respondent's firm was a part. One large firm representative outlined the common trend towards supplier rationalisation emphasising price and quality as well as readying the firm for SEM in his firm. Asked whether BS 5750 was part of these processes he replied:

> Yes. We're moving towards using suppliers that have got BS 5750 accreditation . . . Again depending on the type of work . . . [this] will dictate how far down the BS ladder we have to go. For example, if we want to buy a multi-million pound exchange that handles all the calls, they've got to have BSI registration. If we're just buying pens and pencils it doesn't really matter because the network we provide our customers is not going to fall over if a biro runs out. But if one of the fuses in that exchange isn't up to the job, you could end up with thousands of people without a telephone service.
>
> (Representative of a large manufacturing firm, Sheffield)

The move towards 'preferred supplier' lists, usually with BS 5750 accreditation emphasised, could reduce the number of suppliers a firm dealt with by up to 80%. In one of the large firms, as noted earlier, this had meant reducing the number of suppliers from 15,000 to 3,500. Another respondent said:

> there was no logic in having 2,000 suppliers . . . In the 1970s it was mandatory to . . . dual and even triple source. Industrial relations were tricky at that . . . time. Strikes and disputes were horrendous . . . as we hit the 1980s and people became leaner and fitter, we looked at the number of times our production had been affected by industrial disputes and the answer was 'none'. So when we started going around offering suppliers a larger share of the cake, we found financially we in turn benefited. Jaguar and Nissan operate such a policy now. Our intent is that our suppliers become totally responsible for their quality. We at present send out a . . . representative to check out the quality but this has got to stop. We have to have sufficient confidence of all our suppliers that what we get is going to be right.
>
> (Representative of a large manufacturing firm, Sheffield)

The implications of a shift to adopting BS 5750 and insisting that firms with whom they have dealings also have BS 5750 by large firms and organisations are that, on balance, neither is favourable to local economic relations or small firms. BS 5750 accreditation becomes another criteria added to the list of price, quality, delivery, reliability and capacity or, more accurately, it elaborates the quality criteria already stressed. This moves 'locality' further down the list. It might be argued that the adoption of BS 5750 by local large firms offers both a model and a message for the future to smaller firms. But as we saw in Chapter 4, small firms generally were not very enthusiastic about BS 5750 and what it could do for their business.

In the neglected area of non-manufacturing relations, the supply of non-professional services especially, BS 5750 is currently much less relevant. It has made less impact in services, where the great majority of small businesses are located, and there are considerable problems in developing suitable objective quality standards in services. In printing, for example, a service[13] used by virtually every business, specifying 'quality' in ways which customers can readily use to compare different kinds of work and different firms, is very difficult.

Where BS 5750 adoption and purchasing procedures insisting on supplier BS 5750 accreditation are integral to preferred supplier strategies, this again hardly favours local economic relations or small firms. First, preferred supplier strategies usually involve reductions, sometimes very large reductions as the examples cited earlier illustrated, in the number of firms from which goods and services are purchased. On a simple numerical basis, this reduces the opportunities for inter-firm relations to occur.

Second, where large firms and public sector organisations move to preferred supplier purchasing, they are likely to favour suppliers who can provide a wide range of goods or services. Setting up a preferred supplier list is time consuming and expensive and, where possible, the reduction in the number of businesses dealt with is very attractive as many of the large firm-large organisation respondents stressed. It is likely that larger rather than smaller businesses will be able to offer a range of goods and services as well as have the resources to jump the initial hurdles including vetting, inspection, proof of standards etc, to achieve listing. It is also less likely that businesses in the immediate locality will be selected where the purchasing firm or organisation is rationalising supplying nationally, since it depends on them not only meeting all the other requirements to achieve listing but often being able to supply outlets in a wide range of localities.

Third, as several large firm-large organisation representatives mentioned, the shifts towards BS 5750, preferred suppliers and the more general rationalisation of purchasing, are often coupled with restructuring for the SEM. These processes are only slowly developing but will accelerate as the Market establishes itself. The shifting focus from local to national and now to a Europe-wide market appears to be a slow but inexorable historical trend. It is a trend that makes 'locality', in the sense that most people would define 'a local economy', less and less important. While small firms will survive the historical change to the increased importance of the SEM, their relations with the largest firms and organisations are unlikely to be invigorated.

Neither BS 5750 accreditation nor preferred supplier strategies have penetrated the UK economy fully as yet. Despite the enormous media attention and management literature devoted to both, the reality is that both are being adopted relatively slowly. In part, this is due to the effects of recession. Although much of the discussion of BS 5750 and supplier rationalisation stresses that adopting both is a response to the need to survive the recession, businesses that are only just surviving may be cautious about embarking on major and costly reorganisations. It is more likely that their adoption will accelerate when economic recovery eases the costs and risks.

There is also a good deal more to learn about the problems and effective strategies required to make adopting BS 5750 and preferred supplier lists a success: experienced managers know that 'nothing is for nothing' in organisational change. Yet the long-term trend appears to favour the wider adoption of BS 5750 and 'preferred supplier' strategies and these will reduce levels of local economic integration and small firm-large firm interrelations. The longer term development of the SEM can be expected to reinforce these trends still further.

THE EMBEDDEDNESS OF LARGE FIRMS AND PUBLIC SECTOR ORGANISATIONS

The economic significance of large firms and organisations for their locality is often emphasised. For instance, the collection of studies edited by Cooke (1989a) based on Economic and Social Research Council research, shows this tendency very clearly. Almost without exception, the various authors highlight the major firms in the localities while other firms and economic activities in the areas are only superficially analysed. Where a major firm closes due to recession or restructuring, its impact on local economic activities is widely discussed with the assumption that the impact beyond its direct employment effects will often be devastating. Certainly, where several large firms in a locality close over a relatively short period, the impact will be great, even if other economic activities expand or enter the locality. But the assumption that the economic significance of large enterprises will be great in any local area also presupposes high levels of economic integration. A major theme of this book has been to question this presupposition as well as the assumptions stemming from it.

To be clear, it is not being argued that large businesses and public sector organisations are not economically important in any locality. We have shown in this and the previous chapter, that inter-firm links between large firms–public sector organisations and local businesses, particularly the large number of small businesses which constitute a high proportion of local economic activities, however defined, are not great. But this is not the whole story. Through the jobs created by large firms and public sector organisations, powerful injections of buying power can support local economic activities more generally. These contributions to local buying power produce secondary, indirect links between firms and even offer markets for some businesses. For example, the employees of large manufacturing plants or public sector organisations may offer a market for nearby small shops. However, these income multiplier effects should also not be over-stated. The incomes generated in many large organisations are often spent in other localities from which their employees, especially the better paid, commute. The number and size of local businesses which depend on a particular large business or public sector organisation for a substantial proportion of their business, say more than 20%, may not be very substantial.

A great deal will depend on how permeable local activities are, that is, the extent to which economic activities in any designated locality, 'Sheffield' or 'Kingston upon Thames', are mutually supporting.[14] The evidence from the studies which stimulated this book suggests that permeability in this sense is variable. Sheffield, for historical and other reasons, shows indications of being a much less permeable locality than Kingston upon Thames. As we noted in Chapter 3, such was the high level of permeability in the latter, we found it very difficult to draw a boundary around what could be designated 'the Kingston upon Thames local economy' and the data presented in this and the previous chapter have supported this point strongly.

But large businesses and public sector organisations are also embedded in localities in other ways. They can also be significant players in the social, political and cultural lives of localities. In the opening section of this chapter, for instance, the familiar stories of the role of Pilkington in St Helens and other 19th and early 20th century major businesses in their localities were cited.

What is, or was, important about these non-economic dimensions of business involvement in localities is that they are, or were, critically important in the promotion and maintenance of economic relations. This was not only due to the crude influence large employers could exert through the local political and social system to favour their own and businesses generally but in many other ways such as the increased efficiency of the labour market when information passes through social networks rather than solely through conventional labour market linkages. As Harrison (1992:476) has argued, the revival of the industrial district, as a vehicle for economic growth, rests on similar assumptions of embeddedness and the importance of the non-economic in the level and character of economic relations in any locality.

To what extent are the large firms and public sector organisations of the kinds taking part in this study embedded in the localities? We asked respondents how involved their firm or organisation was in local bodies and development initiatives. The replies showed local involvement, overall, to be variable but fairly superficial. As expected, the indications were that Sheffield's firms had greater involvement, though the public sector organisations such as universities and hospitals appeared less involved. The same was true of public sector organisations in Kingston upon Thames.

As other recent research has shown, the great majority of large businesses, particularly in manufacturing, and many public sector organisations are members of local chambers of commerce (Bennett et al., 1993:9–10) although 'membership' may mean different things. At one extreme, the firm or organisation pays its subscription each year because it is felt that a firm or organisation of its size or prominence should be a member in terms of image or the need to be seen as a good local corporate citizen, a kind of *noblesse oblige* attitude to membership. At the other extreme, a senior manager might be an active member of the chamber energetically promoting its activities. The great majority of the firms and organisations were closer to the former rather than the latter.[15]

Other institutions, enterprise agencies, educational institutions, local economic development initiatives and training and enterprise councils[16] had not elicited a great deal of participation from the respondent firms and organisations though again there were exceptions. Some respondents were themselves potentially important non-economic members of local networks, such as the institutions of higher education but their replies confirmed the general lack of linkages between the economic and non-economic.

Respondents both in Sheffield and Kingston were unsure about how developed the local economic network was but most were doubtful. In Sheffield, those in manufacturing were more confident that there was a local network and that it spilt over into the non-economic. Those in other sectors such as financial services or in the public sector thought there was a network but did not see themselves as part of it or of any social or political dimensions of the network. One Sheffield steel firm representative put the insider view colourfully when asked if he felt there was a developed local network:

No, there's a Sheffield Mafia . . . Most of the smaller companies around here have almost an incestuous relationship . . . We deal with two companies run by two brothers so they know exactly what work is going out from [name of respondent firm] sometimes before we actually do!

The same respondent went on to say that he felt that his firm played an important part in the network. He was not aware of any local business-to-business directory but said that if one was available he would use it.[17] This was, however, a minority view. The majority of respondents in both localities felt that such a directory would be only marginally useful, for example in an emergency when something was needed in a hurry, and would not change their firm's behaviour in relation to dealing with local firms in any real way. In other words, the old industrial distinct character of Sheffield still persisted within the steel making and steel products sector to an extent with economic and non-economic links between firms both showing themselves.[18] But outside this sector, the representative of the other newer kinds of businesses interviewed did not feel part of wider networks to any extent.

In Kingston, the lack of embeddedness of the large businesses and public sector organisations was very apparent with one exception, a large service organisation which had been in the locality since the 1860s. The firms from the electronics and defence-related sectors either did not involve themselves at all, focusing instead on a much wider non-local horizon, or participated in local activities because of the need to be on good terms with local people:

There is involvement by our directors and certainly higher managers, for instance, our works engineering manager, with local issues and local societies and all the rest of it. They do get involved with the educational authorities and bodies . . . we have open days once a year where the whole local community can come in and see what's built here and all the rest of it. By the nature of what we are, ie a manufacturing unit in a middle of a fairly high class residential area, we have to keep a good rapport or relationship going with the local community.
(Representative of defence industries manufacturer)

The exception in Kingston, the long established service firm, had a former chairman, now in his late 70s, who had led or served on a wide range of local bodies such as the scouts, sea cadets, RSPCA, local hospital and the local authority. Again, however, it was impossible to find a counterpart in any of the other large firms or organisations in the study and local residents could not suggest any other local business leader likely to take his place.

Local authorities have traditionally been seen as key integrating institutions in their localities bringing together people from different sections of the local population, including those representing local business, to develop local policies. In the 1990s doubts can be cast on whether this role continues for many reasons. Local populations hold local government in low esteem generally (Jowell et al., 1988:119). The reasons offered for this decline include the growth of central government control over local authorities and their spending, the loss of control by local authorities over key activities such as housing, education and health as well as media campaigns against 'wasteful' and 'inefficient' local government. The creation of alternative non-elected bodies, health trusts and TECs, for example, also reduces the importance of local authorities in local matters.

The representatives of the large firms and public sector organisations shared the general lack of confidence in local government. The majority said they did not believe that the local authority played an important part in promoting links between local businesses, and many of the comments, particularly in Sheffield, were hostile. As one Sheffield steel maker-steel products representative said:

> They [the City Council] make a lot of noise from time to time, that they do [promote local economic activities] but in the end they don't because they . . . their inability to do anything and their intransigence with industry in that they want to call the tune. They weren't there as a partner, they were there to try and lay down the law and, of course, private industry, they won't let them.

> Do you think it [the City Council] could do more? Do you want it to do more?

> I don't think it could do more . . . Industry and commerce and local authorities are in opposition, at loggerheads. The public image they like to give from time to time is that they are working together very amicably. I don't believe it.

Several Sheffield respondents were critical of the council's hosting of the World Student Games which took place during the period in which the interviews were conducted. They felt that this meant that resources which could be used to help the locality in other more important ways such as promoting an environment more favourable to industry and employment, were being used for something essentially ephemeral. The debt incurred would take many years to pay off and the permanent benefits, such as new swimming pools, were a poor return.

In Kingston, the local authority has been Conservative controlled for most of its life and in recent years has taken a strongly market-orientated view of economic activities. In other words, while ideologically it is very positive towards industry, it does not actively promote economic activities in the same way as, for instance, many Labour controlled authorities (such as in Sheffield) have attempted. For example, there is no economic development unit. Instead, the authority has spent much of its energy in encouraging the development of the town as a major retailing centre for South West London.

Despite the Kingston local authority's less proactive local economic role, in relation to manufacturing, however, the attitudes of the large firm representatives were, if anything, more favourable in Kingston than in Sheffield.

This might perhaps be ideological, that is, representatives of industry might well feel that a Conservative controlled authority will be more helpful to local industry than their counterparts in Sheffield where the local authority is a high profile, Labour controlled body.[19] But the difference should not be over-stated and needs to be kept in context. The large firms in Kingston were not very enthusiastic about the role of the local authority in promoting economic activities and, compared with Sheffield, it is economically prosperous therefore requiring less intervention.

One representative of a defence industry firm in Kingston felt very strongly about the part local authorities could play in promoting local prosperity:

> If the local authority wants the businesses within that local authority to do better or thrive or communicate more or trade more with each other, it's up to the local authority to do something about it.

What do you think the local authority could do?

> If there was to be a initiative or policy to try and get as much local trading done, it would be very much up to them to find out who can do what in their area, who can supply what and what do people want and mesh the two. If the two can integrate then obviously you've got . . . a starting block for trying to get some or increased local trade . . . . Find out what (a) people want from the local traders and (b) what the local traders are able to offer.

In your view does the local authority play an important part in promoting links between local businesses?

> I don't know. I'd have to say 'no', I don't think so . . . They spend too much time trying to get one up on each other instead of working together.

Even the representative of the long established large service organisation in Kingston whose chairman had close links with the local authority, was not very enthusiastic. He did believe that through the chamber of commerce and its links, the local authority was helping to promote economic activities but he believed it could do much more, particularly to help small businesses.

Overall, therefore, whatever the local authorities in the two localities do in terms of integrating economic and non-economic activities, clearly the respondents in this study were not aware of these efforts. Even in terms of economic activities themselves, respondents in both localities were generally unimpressed by what the respective local authorities were doing. This may, of course, be unfair to the local authorities concerned but local integration, economic, social and political, depends greatly on the perceptions of those substantively involved. Respondents who are highly involved in the external relations of their organisations by the character of their work responsibilities did not, however, perceive their local authorities as scoring highly in promoting economic and other local linkages.

THE MESSAGE FROM THE FUTURE: THE SEM AND LOCALITY

The respondents representing the large firms in the study, were, as might be expected, very aware of the advent of the SEM. They were asked whether their firms had carried out an assessment of the likely impact of the SEM on the firm's activities. Almost invariably they replied that the firm was well ahead of simply assessing the likely impact and already operating in several areas of the community as well as following active strategies to ensure the business benefited further. In replies to earlier questions on the organisation of supplier linkages, several respondents stated they were rationalising their supply chain with a main reason for this being anticipating the full impact of the legal and other requirements of the SEM.

In terms of the impact of the SEM on relations between the large firms and other local firms, most respondents thought this would only be very slight mainly because they had so few dealings with other local firms. The exception here might be thought to be Sheffield but, in fact, one steel firm's representative stated that the SEM in the form of existing European Community regulations already governed relations:

> It [the SEM] already has had effect on our business because we are restricted on what prices we can charge . . . What increases we can put on our steels . . . We already sell and buy a lot in Europe.
> (Steel-maker and steel-products firm representative)

In fact, this is an over-statement in the sense that the SEM's regulations will only fully come into play over a period which will continue long after these interviews were carried out. Yet he was correct in emphasising the Community's already well developed attempts at regulating steel production to deal with the massive over-capacity which existed, particularly in the 1980s.

Another respondent from a steel-making, steel-products firm offered another example of the way firms in this sector were anticipating the SEM. His firm already had:

> a joint understanding with a company in France called _____.
> And _____ has a very similar facility to our own. We would consider using _____ as an arm of our manufacturing.

Later he mentioned that his firm was considering a similar joint venture with a steel firm in Italy. In addition, this respondent also stressed that Eastern Europe was being seen as a promising market, one which would probably be more important than the European Community because the latter contained many very efficient steel firms already strongly situated in their areas of the SEM.

These respondents' firms, like the other large firms in the study, were, in other words, already 'thinking Europe', but this means that 'locality' in any conventional meaning is already decreasing further in importance as an area of significant business relations. Institutions such as Business in the Community (1990) may devote resources to encouraging local purchasing, through local purchasing initiatives, as a counter to what they accept are low levels currently but the coming of the SEM will make success all the more unlikely.

The defence-related firms in Kingston were much more obviously international in their outlook because their already existing markets stretched well beyond the European Community.[20] The SEM for them was simply another market with its own rules which they would need to take into account but this was normal for them since all their markets had their own special rules. Again, many of the defence firms in the Community had their local markets well secured, though joint ventures were possible and had occurred, and UK defence firms would continue to see other markets such as the Middle East, as having great potential.

Public sector organisations also recognised that the SEM would have an impact on them though they did not appear to be as far along the road as the private sector firms in preparing for its impact. They do not normally sell outside the UK and therefore did not need to be market-conscious in the same way as the private sector firms. They were mainly aware of its potential effects on purchasing particularly for larger works or higher value service contracts. European Community rules would require tendering to be open to businesses elsewhere in the SEM. It meant, therefore, that more potential suppliers would be available. Several mentioned, for example, that refuse collection contracts were already being won by companies from elsewhere in the Community.

Public sector organisations' links with their locality were not especially strong overall, as the information presented earlier demonstrated. The advent of the SEM will not make them any stronger and potentially could weaken them still further. These organisations, like the private sector firms, were being pushed towards seeing Europe, in the form of the SEM and its rules, as a source of suppliers for major works and services. The above does not, however, take into account any potential for UK firms, including local firms, to successfully resist new competition from elsewhere in the Community. In fact, few of our respondents mentioned this possibility: the implicit assumption in many of their answers to questions on the impact of the SEM was that UK businesses would not compete successfully. In their answers, they were concerned about how serious the negative effects of the SEM might be. Several of the private sector firms felt that their firms could at least counter any negative effects through their own efforts in Europe and in markets outside the Community. Other firms, however, might not do as well. Many of the private firms also welcomed more suppliers entering the market to serve their needs though they felt the advantages to be gained would not be dramatic.

CONCLUSIONS

In this chapter we have been examining the role of large firms and public sector organisations in local economic activities and their relations with local small firms. Conventionally, it is usually assumed that large firms are critical in local economic activities and that through their dealings with other firms, especially small firms, they are the kingpins around which local economic integration is constructed. In this and the last chapter, we have presented detailed findings to question these conventional views. In this chapter, for instance, it has been shown that many large firms and public sector organisations do very little business with local firms, small or large.

For large firms and public organisations, the over-riding logic of the situation which guides their dealings with suppliers is economistic. Four criteria guide their purchasing relations: price, quality, delivery and capacity. Other considerations such as locality and size of firm were of much less or minimal importance in sourcing goods and services. This economistic perspective may have been less strong in the past but is clearly paramount in the early 1990s. Nor should this be surprising. The belief that business relations should be determined strictly by market considerations has become powerful due to economic restructuring and recession effects, the increased professionalisation of management and almost a decade and a half of government determined to impose economism on the public sector and the labour market and to encourage and reward the private sector for behaving similarly.[21]

Small businesses are often disadvantaged by this economism because of their size. Purchasers prefer to negotiate a single large contract rather than several small contracts because of cost considerations. Larger contracts are almost invariably subject to tendering. But tendering is expensive for smaller firms. Nor is there any guarantee that the 'hit rate' of small firms in winning contracts, that is, the ratio of successful to non-successful tenders, will be high enough to justify the resources required. Larger suppliers will also, other things being equal, be able to offer a wider range of goods and services making them more economical to deal with.

Combined with the above economism are beliefs relating to size of business and the ability to provide appropriate goods and services. Here small firms did badly again. Most of those responsible for purchasing preferred to deal with larger enterprises for various reasons. For instance, doubts were frequently expressed about the capacity of small businesses to handle larger orders or to be reliable over time. In the defence industries 'traceability' was a special case of the latter consideration. Large firms, acting as prime contractors, were under pressure from the MOD to ensure that all components could be traced to their sources and small suppliers were thought to be less likely to be able to meet this requirement.

Locality varied in importance between the two areas studied, a finding which may be taken as illustrative of what happens in a wider range of local areas in the UK. Sheffield's larger firms had more local dealings than those in Kingston upon Thames. But in Sheffield this greater degree of localism was much more evident in steel-making and steel products than in other sectors. The reasons for this were twofold. First, the traditional industrial district, built up over more than a century of local steel making activities, still survives even if it is much reduced in size and scope. Second, much of the product handled by firms has high transport costs due to weight. The result is a considerable amount of inter-firm relations within the local area. However, the long-term trend in these relations is away from locality: globalisation in steel making and steel products is occurring so that more and more Sheffield steel firms are making links with firms outside the locality. Nevertheless, where older manufacturing industries remain important in an area, the level of local inter-firm relations is likely to be higher than in localities where other kinds of economic activities predominate. Even in Sheffield, inter-firm relations in the non-steel sectors were much lower.

In Kingston with a relatively smaller manufacturing sector based on high tech and defence-related activities, inter-firm relations were much lower overall. The large manufacturing firms did not source locally except for small purchases or emergencies, a finding confirmed in the previous chapter when the trading patterns of relevant small firms were examined. The non-manufacturing firms and public sector organisations were, like their Sheffield counterparts, even less likely to source locally. Because Kingston's economy is more permeable, that is, less easily defined in terms of boundaries within which economic relations are patterned, the level of localism was even lower among these non-manufacturing firms and organisations than in Sheffield.

As a result, of the two localities, it might be argued that Kingston is closer to Britain's future economy or at least the kind of economy that many would see as the route to economic salvation. An economy based on a relatively small manufacturing sector with a high proportion of high tech firms and a wider economy based on services and knowledge-based white collar activities is often seen as offering a more competitive and prosperous future than one based on older manufacturing industries and low tech services. The key characteristic of economics of the Kingston variety is that they are less localised: the whole range of economic activities in which they are engaged belong to emerging wider, national and cross-national economies.

The longer term outlook for smaller businesses, including local smaller businesses, is also clouded by the current trend to adopt formal quality standards and the rationalisation of supply sources by large firms and organisations. The evidence on the commonest formal quality standard, BS 5750, is that, so far, small businesses have been much more reluctant to seek accreditation than large businesses. Where larger businesses and organisations have adopted BS 5750, they are also more likely to insist on or prefer suppliers who are also BS 5750 qualified. The disadvantages of small firms may not be long term however. Should BS 5750 become widely adopted more small firms will be forced to seek accreditation and they may be helped by current efforts to make BS 5750 procedures more suited to the needs and resources of small firms.

More serious for the long-term chances of small, local firms having closer contacts with large firms is the rationalisation of supplier sources and the adoption of preferred supplier lists. This typically involves larger suppliers who have passed some kind of assessment to achieve 'approved' status. The suppliers are likely to be larger rather than smaller businesses because purchasing firms prefer to source as much as possible from each approved firm, otherwise the exercise of constructing the preferred lists produces fewer savings. Existing suppliers who, as the evidence in this chapter indicates, are already likely to be larger rather than smaller businesses, are in a more favourable position to achieve approved status than other firms. But many of these will inevitably also fail to remain suppliers where the reduction in suppliers is substantial.

The analysis in this and Chapter 4 concerned itself with embeddedness, that is, the extent to which the economic and the non-economic are integrated with each other in the localities studied. In Sheffield, the impact of the old industrial district connected with the steel sector had embeddedness effects but more generally embeddedness was much less evident in Sheffield or Kingston upon Thames. Large firms and large public sector organisations generally do join economic and non-economic bodies but the extent of any penetration into social and political relations in the localities appears slight.

Sponsorship of local activities such as sports, artistic and charity activities, was common but whether this indicates real embeddedness is doubtful. Many of these sponsored activities are evanescent rather than permanent aspects of local life. Many of those responsible for the decisions to be involved are not members of the local population but managers, part of whose current role is 'community relations'. These executives may not themselves live in the locality and will often move to other localities as they are promoted. Some are responsible for these relations in branch plant areas where they do not live or work and have no other links with the area. There was a *noblesse oblige* element in the involvement of these firms and organisations as well as corporate public relations element but none of the in-depth involvement or intense community commitment reported to have been characteristic of many 19th century large firms in their localities.

The large firms and organisations were involved in bodies such as chambers of commerce and some were involved in what has been termed more generally as 'boosterism',[22] that is, *ad hoc* committees whose task it is to promote local communities and their economic activities. Enterprise agencies were an early common example of this kind of activity, as is their parent body Business in the Community, though their focus was narrowly economic. But there are also special bodies to promote industry in a locality as well as specific projects such as bids to be host city for the next Olympic Games. Again, the extent to which these activities impact on local economic activities generally is debatable. The weakness of chambers of commerce in the UK has often been stressed, for example. Activities which are business inspired for mainly business interests, whatever other claims are made for them, may not have much impact beyond the economic in the long term or may promote cynicism in many sections of the wider population.

Even where such bodies have their successes, it might be argued that they are only off-setting the decline of the local authority as a local force to integrate the economic and the non-economic. Central government emasculation of local authority powers to influence their locality's future through well resourced proactive policies has been partly responsible for the emergence of 'boosterism' according to Colenutt and Ellis (1993). Our respondents' opinions of local authorities as significant actors in the localities were generally low, even in Sheffield where the City Council retains remnants of a strong interventionist strategy.

In the opening chapter we discussed the notion of the 'industrial district' and the thesis that the UK economy might be revived by the regeneration or creation of such districts. Large firms and public sector organisations would presumably have a key role to play in such a regeneration process even if the industrial district proper is much more closely focused on a network of small businesses in a locality. The evidence here indicates that the large firms and public sector organisations were unlikely to offer much of a contribution to these processes either economic or non-economic involvement.

What is more, the developing SEM seems likely to cause large firms to orientate their attention more and more to extra-locality issues and problems. Indeed, almost every one of the large firm respondents stated that their firms were already involved positively in the SEM, adjusting their procedures and developing or consolidating existing trading relations with other parts of the SEM. Several also stressed that the European Community and its market was only one area outside the UK in which they were operating and they would be increasing their non-local activities. These trends were much less apparent in the large public sector organisations but even these were conscious that large-scale procurement now had an increasingly important SEM dimension. These developments to answer the call to 'think Europe' made by successive recent UK governments or to respond to world market developments, do not contain much to strengthen local economic ties.

The data in this chapter, taken from the interviews and background material on the large firms and public sector organisations in two of the localities, add powerfully to the overall thesis we seek to present. In terms of any notion of 'local economy' the overall thrust is to support an argument that there are low levels of economic integration and under-developed networks, as measured by inter-firm relations between large firms/large organisations, on one hand, and small and/or local businesses, on the other. What is more we have identified several trends ranging from supplier rationalisation policies to the SEM which will push levels of local economic integration still lower.

There were significant differences between the localities with Sheffield offering a less good fit to our overall argument and Kingston a much better fit. In Sheffield the decline of the locality as an economic whole is slowed by the remains of a once all-dominant industrial district based on steel products. The chances of a revival of this district, or the building of a new district based on other kinds of activities, appear negligible. Kingston is a locality with characteristics which will become increasingly common in Britain, with a permeability of economic relations and their detachment from other social and political dimensions of local living. This high level of permeability will be a characteristic of the locality of the future if the UK economy is successful in its attempt to rejoin the ranks of the prosperous industrial societies in the 1990s and beyond.

Notes

1. 'Dominate' is something of an over-statement in a literal sense. Despite their economic importance and the close association of company name and place, in strict fact in several of these instances the named business (eg Pilkington) was one among several businesses creating the economic locality (Lane and Roberts, 1971:25–31).
2. Analyses of the 1979–1982 recession stress the way in which manufacturing declined massively (Wells, 1989; Coates, 1991:63–69) and one result was the failure of many long established manufacturing firms who had developed as key parts of 19th century urban industrial localities. Others survived in name only or as branch plants of foreign-owned enterprises employing many fewer people and ceasing to have the close relations with their localities built up previously.
3. A proportion which now is almost certainly an understatement. Not only has the only large-scale UK car maker, Rover, been taken over by BMW but both Honda and Toyota have opened their own new plants since 1991. These, like Nissan's longer established plant in Sunderland, have been greenfield start-ups, involving a major foreign-owned, foreign-managed large enterprise entering local economic relations in their respective areas.
4. In what follows, there is some lack of detail because of the need to preserve the confidentiality of respondents, particularly those in the private sector. It is not easy to be sure that we have achieved this since it is possible that knowledgeable local readers, or those with a special knowledge of the industries in which the firms are operating, will be able to make an informed guess at the name of the enterprise. Public sector organisations are more difficult to disguise but are, in any event, much more part of the public domain.
5. One of the local authority respondents later sent information that it estimated that it dealt with 44 firms based in the *county*, that is, an area much larger than what might be seen by most people as 'the local economy' and the total value of the dealings with these businesses was under 1% of total turnover (£20 million) of the commercial services division, the main department responsible for dealing with external purchasing. At the time of writing, the authors with Brian Abbott are conducting a study of the opportunities for small firms (including local small firms) resulting from the advent of CCT for local government services. The preliminary results indicate that neither local nor small firms have gained greatly from CCT.
6. Although, as Chapter 4 showed, this assumption is questionable. However, small specialist firms who operate over wide geographical areas might still have business relations with larger firms and public sector organisations.
7. As the discussion in Chapter 4 showed, late or slow payment practices were mentioned by small business owners as a reason for not seeking to do business with large firms or organisations.

8. Although not always successfully, as the collapse of Astra Training Services, a privatised skill centre and training network, with debts of over £10 million in July 1993, demonstrated.

9. This respondent offered some interesting comments on the increase in sub-contracting and flexible production methods in his industry in recent years. He pointed out that demand had become more uneven due to increased third world competition, globalisation and the recession. This had initially led to external sourcing to cope with the problems of predicting demand. But, more recently, there was a tendency to take some of this work back in, however, due to problems of maintaining quality, assured supplies and increased prices. Other researchers have reported similar findings about other industries (see, for example, Penn et al., 1992).

10. AQAP is a quality standard widely used in the defence industries and usually insisted upon by the MOD for any work for which it is the customer. Where a prime contractor puts out some of the work to other businesses, the MOD usually insists that these other businesses also meet the same standards.

11. In the public sector, the demand for externally sourced professional services has increased due to government insistence on the adoption of business methods in areas such as the National Health Service and the use of open tendering to invite the private sector to compete with in-house providers of such services. For local authorities, the government has legislated to ensure CCT is extended to professional services in the future although this has still to develop.

12. TQM was much less frequently mentioned. This might have been because the TQM idea had not taken root very extensively when the interviews were conducted (1991) or it had not become a key issue in relations with other firms as yet.

13. Although printing, as noted earlier, is classified by the official SIC as a manufacturing sector, in another sense, it is a service used by other businesses.

14. Another way of making this point is to suggest that the permeability of any designated local economy might be measured by the extent to which the output and inputs of businesses ('business' here includes all organisations producing goods and services) in the local economy are exchanges between these same businesses as opposed to exchanges with businesses outside the designated local economy. In addition, income generated by the economic activities of businesses in the form of profits and wages may also stay in the local economy or be exported. In Sheffield, for example, there was more business-to-business relations than in Kingston upon Thames but many of the businesses were branches of nationals or multinationals to whom any profits would be remitted.

15. As Bennett et al., (1993) report, many chambers of commerce are now providing an increasing range of services to members from advice on exporting to offering arbitration to resolve disputes between businesses. They argue that this tendency could help chambers of commerce become a more important nucleus for local economic networks but, equally, it could be argued that this might result in the chamber being treated as simply another supplier of various business services to be used as needed.

16. Since TECs only came into being in 1990–1991, the lack of connections with the respondent organisations could have been the result of their newness. It has emerged that the majority of representatives on the 82 TEC boards in England are drawn from medium and large businesses (Emmerich and Peck, 1992:14). However, since many TECs cover large areas the number of businesses from a particular locality directly represented may be quite small.

17. All respondents were asked whether they were aware of a local business-to-business directory and whether they felt such a directory would be useful. Most did not know of one and were doubtful about whether it would be useful.

18. One of the steel firm respondents stated that he expected the firm's managing director to become the Master Cutler sometime in the next few years. This local body, the Cutlers Company, is important economically, socially and politically in Sheffield and is almost an ideal type example of an integrating institution in an old style local economy based on a traditional industry such as steel (Cutlers Company, 1993).

19. For how high profile Sheffield City Council was in the early 1980s in terms of its Labour-based economic policy, see the account offered in Duncan and Goodwin (1988:83–86). At this time the council was led by the nationally known David Blunkett, who later became a Labour party front bench spokesman frequently seen on television and interviewed on radio and in newspapers.

20. A recent review of relevant research (The Scottish Office, 1993:14–16) suggests that firms in high tech related industrial activities are much more likely to be involved in inter-firm linkages across the European Community and between the European Community and other areas of the globe than firms in other sectors. It also suggested the trend had been strongly increasing in recent years.

21. 'Rewards' in this context range from the allocation of honours to business leaders who epitomise the practice of economistic management, to being appointed as advisers to government or to help run public sector bodies such as National Health Service Trusts and TECs, to reaping the rewards from the market opportunities resulting from privatisation.

22. The term 'boosterism' is explained with examples in Colenutt and Ellis (1993: 20). They define it as committees of the great and the good drawn mainly from business promoting local areas. The aims are to attract private and public investment. Their message:

> is articulated as stimulating that long lost Victorian value, 'civic pride'. A basic relationship is to pour resources into competitive city marketing of myth-making and literary invention . . . to pull in huge amounts of public-sector funding needed to 'lever in' private investment.

(p.20)

Colenutt and Ellis argue that these committees are claiming to be the legitimate voices of their cities or localities pushing aside the traditional claim to this role of elected local authorities.

---— 6 ---—

ENTERPRISE AND LOCALITY IN THE 1990s

INTRODUCTION

This book is about the interrelations between economic activities and localities in the 1990s. More specifically, its focus is on small businesses and their involvement in local economic activities, on the one hand, and small business–large business/public sector relations and locality, on the other. These two sets of relations are, of course, connected and, considered together, they can tell us a great deal about how small firms articulate with their wider economic and non-economic environments.

The idea of the 'local economy' has been an influential, integral part of much of the wide range of social, economic and, especially, policy thinking for over half a century. In much of this thinking, particularly since 1980, the small enterprise has been given an increasingly central role in sustaining and reviving local economies (Cooke and Imrie, 1989). Large enterprises and the public sector, in contrast, have had their contributions downgraded considerably but their importance in local economies is still acknowledged.

How local economic relations are structured in real localities has not been the subject of much systematic research. Much of the theorising which has dominated academic contributions in economics, economic geography, regional studies and sociology has tended to be macro-based. The concern has been with the economy as a whole and, within the economy, with changes seen from a strongly top-down macro perspective. Where these theories descend to lower levels – the region, urban areas, rural economies etc – the top-down perspective has remained or, at best, been supported by random, piecemeal, mainly quantitative assessments of this or that part of a region, urban area or similar entity. This has resulted in local economic patterns being seen only in a crude and incomplete way, which has allowed speculation and over-general theorising to be unfettered by much in the way of empirical constraints.

The alternative approach, which has been the foundation of the thesis offered in this book, is a *ground-level* one which focuses closely on substantive relations between people and businesses in real localities. The ground-level data on how owner-managers of small firms run their businesses and articulate with the wider economy and how large businesses and public sector organisations structure their relations with other businesses, especially local and small businesses, is drawn from a wide range of contrasting localities. Moreover, this data is recent, showing what is happening to these phenomena in the 1990s.

Not surprisingly, the results offer a much more detailed, empirically secure characterisation than is possible with macro-level analysis based on aggregate data. But more than this, they also offer a challenge to much of the general theorising on, for example, industrial districts, JIT relations, subcontracting, local economic networking, local economic initiatives and local relations between businesses, which currently dominate the literature. In turn, the alternative picture of economic relations and localities offered has clear implications for policy-making.

LOCAL ECONOMIES, LOCALITY AND SMALL BUSINESSES

In the first chapter we questioned the utility of the notion of the 'local economy' as a clear, definable set of substantive relations with specific geographical boundaries. The reasoning behind this questioning was the difficulties in practical terms of determining any particular 'local economy' as a bounded set of substantive relations between businesses which marked these off clearly from some set of wider relations such as the regional or national economy. The much used alternatives in economic geography, regional studies and other approaches to spatial economic issues – 'region', 'travel-to-work area', 'local labour market area' and the like – often have little or no demonstrated foundation in real economic and social relations in the areas to which they claim to refer but are essentially arbitrarily, imposed mainly for administrative or policy purposes.[1]

A further major weakness of conventional approaches to the analysis of local economic activities is the neglect of the non-economic, the ways in which economic relations are embedded in other kinds of social, cultural and political relations. People do not live by economic activities alone. If economic activities are 'local' in some sense then they are local in ways which link them to the non-economic, that is, these activities will impinge on local social culture and political relations and, in turn, the latter will have an impact on economic activities. The current neglect of the non-economic dimension of local economic activities is relatively recent. As Chapter 1 demonstrated, the literature on local economic relations in the UK before, say, 1970, is full of examples of detailed and clearly analysed assessments of the mutual relations between the economic and the non-economic in a wide variety of UK localities.

We do not offer a solution to the problem of conceptualising 'local economies' posed in the above form. This is not simply because we wish to avoid what is clearly a difficult problem but rather because we believe it is an issue that is losing its salience, as the rest of the chapter will argue. Instead, the phrase 'local economic activities' will be used to refer to relations between businesses within specific geographical or administrative boundaries and the links between such activities and social, cultural and political activities in the same areas. In other words, there is no presupposition of an integrated local economy clearly demarcated from any wider economy, or of an integrated community in which the economic and the non-economic are sufficiently mutually supporting to produce some whole, experienced and realised by those living and working in the area. This lack of such presuppositions allows the issues of the links between economic activities and locality to be addressed afresh, free from the conceptual and theoretical baggage of the past. It might be argued that this is particularly appropriate in considering such issues in the UK economy of the 1990s following the massive restructuring of the 1970s and 1980s, with the huge decline in manufacturing and expansion in services and the reorientation of the economy away from internal concerns towards the European Community and the SEM.

In any locality, however defined, and clearly in the 7 contrasting localities studied in the research upon which this book is based, the great majority of businesses will be small. It could hardly be otherwise given the extreme size distribution of businesses in the UK economy in which, in 1991 according to the most recent estimate, 'Only one-tenth of 1% of firms employed over 500 people' (McCann, 1993:12). While the issue of what constitutes a 'small' firm is not easily resolved, the 'grounded' definitions used in the studies in our research would probably more than meet any knowledgeable person's criteria of the sector. Nor is it questioned that for most small businesses a high proportion of the transactions in which they engage will be with other businesses and consumers within the locality defined in conventional administrative terms. The data on trading patterns in Chapter 4 clearly demonstrated this point.

However, the above is not by any means the whole story and neither does it say anything about trends in small business activities in relation to their host localities. A major aspect highlighted by the findings on trading patterns was the large variation in the 'shapes' of the markets within the locality in which the businesses operated. The small services businesses showed this variation very clearly. There were very marked differences both between and within the different sectors studied. The 'local market' served by small advertising, marketing and design agencies, for example, was very different to that served by small video hire outlets. The latter's geographical coverage was often confined to private consumers in a few streets in any direction from the outlet, while the advertising, marketing and design agency would not only cover a wider local area but, more importantly, its local business-to-business transactions often provided only a minority of its turnover. In other words, its spatial focus would be very much less concentrated than that of the video hire outlet.[2]

As Chapter 4 noted, even within sectors, local market 'shapes' could differ very sharply. The conventional local public house, for example, often resembles the video hire outlet in the restricted geographical area from which custom is drawn but as Chapter 4 noted, some free houses in city centres such as Nottingham or in rural areas, regularly drew customers from right across the locality and often from outside its boundaries. Similarly, small garages and vehicle repairers might offer a general servicing and repair service or might specialise in a particular make of vehicle or kind of service. The latter would generally have a much wider market geographically than the former.

The point to be made here is that such a wide variety of small business market 'shapes' divided between private consumers and business customers means that any notions of local 'economic integration' or 'integrated local economy' must be treated with considerable caution despite the ease with which such phrases are tossed into discussions of economic activities. As economies generally become more complex, that is, the types and range of economic activities increase, this fragmentation of local economic activities will increase, rendering notions of integration even less persuasive or achievable.

A further finding which has considerable importance for any estimate of trends in relation between localities and economic activities and which lends further weight to the above point, is the extent of extra-locality trading. As Chapter 4 reported, there were large differences in the extent to which firms were involved in exporting goods and services beyond the boundaries of the locality defined in administrative terms. For example, the advertising, marketing and design businesses and computer services reported they sold over 60% of their services outside the locality.

What is significant about the above findings is that both of these businesses, advertising, marketing and design and computer services, are examples of newer kinds of small-scale enterprise in sectors of the economy which have, in the recent past, and which can be expected in the future, to grow at above average rates. If the UK economy is to maintain, let alone improve, its performance relative to its competitors, many would argue that it will only do so if the economy moves towards a much greater emphasis on knowledge-based and high tech activities. This process has already started at least as evidenced by the high rates of expansion in small firms in these sectors since 1980 (see also Keeble et al., 1992:11).

Conversely, sectors with slower rates of growth are those most closely tied to locality in terms of markets served. The clearest example of this point is the stereotypical small enterprise in many discussions – the corner shop – which has been one of the few examples of small-scale enterprise showing an absolute decline since 1980. The corner shop is tied closely to locality for its market but is being squeezed out by large retailers who are now increasingly dominating through large outlets. The non-high-tech manufacturing sector, with the small, backstreet engineering firm is another favourite stereotype in discussions, and has been seen, on average, to be more reliant overall on local markets. These also showed a lower rate of expansion than the high tech and knowledge-based service areas.

In other words, the kinds of small enterprise which have been expanding most since 1980 and are most closely linked to areas of the economy which can be expected to grow, are those likely to be least reliant on local markets. To the extent that locally based businesses increasingly export their goods and services outside the locality, they contribute to a decline in local economic integration. Clearly, many small businesses will continue to find most of their custom locally but the trend is away from such local ties.

Two further points can be added to the above to suggest that local economic integration is, overall, on the decline where small-scale economic activities are the measure of integration. First, within manufacturing, small firms need to specialise to ensure competitive advantage. 'Generalists', those that will take on any business on the grounds that all business is good business, tend to be newer, smaller businesses or have poorer strategies in relation to their environment. It was noticeable in the interviews with manufacturing firms – particularly in electronics – that older, more established firms had often specialised in particular kinds of products. Their aim, overall, was to gain turnover with higher value mark-up products and niche market security. Strategies of this kind also reduce dependence on any particular customers, including large businesses.

In printing, 'generalists' were still by far the commonest type of small producer in the study and they were the second most likely, after video hire and small leisure businesses, out of the 9 types of economic activity covered to be selling to other business in the locality. But even in printing there are tendencies towards greater specialisations due to the capital costs of investment in new technology and the increasing sophistication of final products such as packaging printing.

Specialisation therefore has an inverse relationship with locality in terms of market relations. To the extent that larger, more established and more successful small businesses adopt niche strategies, they will tend to trade over increasingly wider geographical areas. In Kingston upon Thames, for example, almost two-thirds of the electronics firms sold less than a quarter of their output in the locality. Put another way, the most successful small firms generally and those in the leading edge sectors of the economy, knowledged-based and high tech activities, are the least likely to contribute to local economic integration.

The second point which might be added to the above analysis concerns the opposite link all businesses need to maintain with their environments, relations with suppliers. The studies of the small firms upon which this book is based collected data on small firm–supplier relations for the printing and electronics firms only. However, it is possible to suggest that for the other kinds of firms studied a high proportion of such transactions were also with businesses outside the locality. Several would find it difficult to purchase any of their key inputs locally. Computer services firms, for instance, purchase computing equipment and software to combine into packages for clients but these inputs would be locally sourced in only a few instances. Even where sourcing is local, the ultimate supplier is often outside the locality. For instance, many of the printing firms reported obtaining paper and ink suppliers locally but, in reality, these came from the local distribution outlets of the major paper-makers or ink suppliers.[3]

The broad conclusions to be drawn from the above are threefold. First, economic relations between small firms and other businesses in all the localities were common. But 'locality', defined as the local market in which the firms reported they were engaged in business transactions, varied enormously between the 9 kinds of enterprise studied. It is difficult or even impossible to see these varying local patterns of economic transactions as adding up to multi-sector integrated local economy. Second, the level of small firm relations with other businesses in the locality should not be overstated. In 3 of the 9 sectors studied, a significant proportion, that is, over 40% or more of output, was sold outside the locality and in one of the remaining sectors this proportion was higher than 20%. Third, and most significant for the overall argument being presented here, it was the sectors and firms which were engaged in the activities expected to dominate the UK economy of the future and the growth firms which were the most detached from their localities and local business-to-business relations.

LOCAL ECONOMIC NETWORKS AND NETWORKING ACTIVITIES

The idea of local economic networks composed of mainly small businesses, though with much larger businesses adding their activities and resources to promote a more effective local network, has become a fashionable conceptual vehicle for theorising local business-to-business links. Such networks are seen as having two components. First, business-to-business links based on the exchange of goods and services discussed in the previous section. Second, the links which arise when businesses in a locality interact with each other *across* sectoral boundaries, often through intermediate institutions such as chambers of commerce, enterprise agencies and, more recently, TECs and so-called 'growth coalitions'. Mediating relations of these kinds may also be promoted by others such as accountants and the local rotary club or round table, that is, business-based social and charitable organisations.

The first component above, that is, business-to-business relations, which basically comprise straightforward economic transactions based on market principles, are one possible basis of local economic integration. Where such transactions are common they may spill over into the second component, promoting activities and links which cross sectoral boundaries and even contribute to the promotion of non-economic activities in important ways. In the past, as the quotations from the Bolton Report (1971) in Chapter 4 illustrated, this could result in local authorities, the local bench and other local cultural and social institutions being dominated by those drawn from the local *petit bourgeoisie* and local large firms' senior executives.

As reported above, and in detail in Chapter 4, business-to-business relations in all the localities were common. But whether these functioned at a superficial level to promote strong local networks of the second kind, those crossing sectoral boundaries which might be seen as giving a locality a nucleus around which identification with the locality in a wider sense is promoted, is doubtful. We analysed the meaning and beliefs in the small business owner replies to questions on trading relations and found little evidence of local consciousness.

Local relations were largely defined as trading relations, that is, as functional exchanges between buyers and sellers with locality *qua* locality having little relevance. Many small business owners do seek to personalise their trading relations with others, especially customers, but this is a strategy to secure customer loyalty not a recognition of shared locality. In other words, personal linkages are promoted but only to bolster functional exchanges and not for any more generalised reasons such as shared awareness of locality or membership of a local business community. When a customer ceased to be a customer, personal links usually dissolved as well.[4]

One other indication of the restricted character of business-to-business relations is given by the common research finding that small business owners are unlikely to be aggressive, proactive marketers. Their marketing skills are often limited and they are often comfortable with a steady-state customer base. Our research indicates that the single most important way in which customers were gained was 'word of mouth', that is, the customer came to the small business rather than being actively recruited through some positive marketing strategy.[5]

Of course, if a customer is lost, particularly one who takes a significant amount of the firm's output, then a replacement may have to be sought. Similarly, in a recession as severe as that at the beginning of the 1990s, where customers were lost as they went out of business and continuing customers often ordered less, a more positive marketing approach might be adopted but the research indicates that this was a reluctantly adopted strategy.

The other main link small businesses have with other businesses is with suppliers. Many of these will be large firms while others will be firms of broadly the same size as the buying firm. Transactions with suppliers, particularly with large suppliers, were mainly transactions where the small firm, a small customer almost by definition, was one customer among many. Where the small firm was dependent on the supplier, for example, because the supplier was the only source or there were few alternatives, then the small firm was careful to honour credit restrictions and pay its bills.

Frequently, there would be a careful cultivation of the person(s) at the supplier with whom the small firm dealt in making orders, obtaining advice and any special treatment needed. But most of the small business owners carefully distinguished these relations which would have to be rebuilt from time to time as the key person with whom they dealt changed, from their relations with the supplier firm itself. Many owners reported that they felt there was a trend towards more impersonal, strictly economistic relations as suppliers rationalised their customer dealings, particularly in the recent recession.

The data collected on the second component of any possible local economic network covered the links with intermediary institutions, chambers of commerce, enterprise agencies, accountants, local educational institutions and TECs, for example, which can, given favourable circumstances, promote cross-sectoral links and higher levels of local economic integration. The institutions varied considerably in their potential for promoting local economic integration. For instance, chambers of commerce are widely recognised as potentially powerful integrators while others, such as trade associations, almost certainly have an extra-local and often narrowly sectoral focus. Links with some institutions are almost mandatory since without them it would be difficult to carry on the business at all. Virtually every business, for instance, has an account with a high street bank and an accountant. Relations with both of these, of course, may be much closer where they provide detailed advice and help to the business but the basic links arise out of the essential needs of the business to operate effectively. Other potentially important integrating institutions, on the other hand, such as chambers of commerce, local rotary clubs, round tables or TECs, are based on real choices: the small business owners may choose to join or use the services of the institution or not.

In the case of the less voluntary external links, high street banks and accountants, for instance, we found that even though they were almost universal, the small business owners had reservations about using more than their basic services. For instance, only a third of the small service sector firms had *ever* used their bank as a source of advice. Among the small manufacturing firm owners the level was significantly higher but still only just over half had used their bank for this purpose. Almost a quarter of this sub-sample reported that they had not had a discussion with their bank about their business for over a year. What emerged very clearly was that even where relations with the bank went beyond the latter providing routine cash transaction and overdraft services, they remained strictly one to one. In other words, the local bank very rarely contributed to generating links between local businesses and, hence, made little or no contribution to local economic integration or networks.

Accountants were used much more extensively than banks as sources of advice, particularly by the small service sector business owners but, again, the data does not show that accountants functioned as links in any potential local economic network. One reason for this was that owner-managers did not see accountants as especially knowledgeable about business, particularly their kind of business, and therefore did not expect accountants to function as knowledgeable intermediaries between businesses. A second reason was that owner-managers frequently viewed accountants' fees as high relative to the services they provided and were very conscious that contacts cost money: speculative contacts were therefore kept to a minimum reducing the opportunities for accountants to act as cross-sectoral promoters of local economic networks.[6]

However, it was the more voluntary institutions which offered arguably the best indications of the strengths of local economic networks and levels of economic integration. For many, the chamber of commerce would be the single most important potential vehicle for bringing local businesses together and creating a sense of belonging to a local economic community. Overall, only just over a quarter of the small firm owners belonged to their local chamber of commerce. In some sectors, garages and vehicle repairers for example, it was less than one in ten. It was highest among the printing firms and employment agencies but even among these it had failed to recruit more than half. Some localities evidently had stronger chambers of commerce than others but Guildford was the only one among the 5 localities in the services sector study where more than a third of the firms were members.[7]

'Membership' in this context could mean a wide variety of levels of participation from sending off a membership subscription once a year but attending no meetings and using none of the services provided by the chamber, to something much more active or even being an officer. In practice, however, respondents were much more likely to be nominal members. Nor are these findings particularly surprising. The weakness of the chamber of commerce movement in Britain has often been remarked upon. But what is especially interesting in the findings is that the highest membership levels were found among the two kinds of businesses most likely to benefit from making cross-sectoral links with other local businesses – printing and employment agencies. What the absence of other kinds of businesses in the study indicates, therefore, is a *lack* of importance of such links in the minds of other small business owners since only just over 20% of the remainder were even nominal members of their local chamber of commerce.

The other kinds of voluntary local linking about which data was gathered all functioned less well than chambers of commerce, as Chapter 4 reported. All had managed to have contacts with less than a fifth of the firms in the samples. 'Contact' in this context meant ever having a single contact which may have been some time ago. As Chapter 4 also showed, TECs, the most recent institution which might be expected to facilitate links between businesses and contribute to local economic integration, had not made a great deal of progress on this level in their first 2 years or so of existence though they may do better in future.

The data on local intermediary institutions which could function to bring businesses together to help create and sustain local economic networks can be contrasted with that on memberships of extra-local business-related bodies. Two in particular are interesting for the overall argument being presented here. First, the national bodies which act as pressure groups claiming to speak on behalf of the UK's small businesses, such as the Federation of Small Businesses and the Forum of Private Business. Between them these and similar bodies had managed to recruit less than 10% of the 410 small business owners. Second, trade associations had recruited more than local chambers of commerce and more than any other single body about which data was collected.

From the above, two inferences might be drawn. First, that cross-sectoral links between small businesses do not have a strong appeal compared with intra-sector identifications. Trade associations are based upon a common awareness of being part of a particular sector, the motor trade, the public house or restaurant sectors, the construction industry etc. National small business pressure groups claim to represent a national 'small business community' but manage to recruit only a tiny fraction of the potential 3 million people operating various kinds of small-scale enterprise and have only very small total memberships compared to the combined memberships of trade associations in Britain.

The second inference which can be drawn from the above, and which again has considerable importance for our overall argument, is that as national sectoral bodies such as trade associations recruit more strongly than any locally based institutions, this does not indicate either powerful and active local economic networks or high levels of local economic integration. This inference is in line with the data on trading patterns discussed earlier both within localities (the highly variable market 'shapes' found) and the significant proportion of small businesses, particularly those in the newer and expanding sectors of the economy, whose main trading links were outside the locality.

EMBEDDEDNESS AND LOCAL ECONOMIC ACTIVITIES

At the beginning of the chapter, we mentioned the importance of embeddedness in discussing the extent to which economic activities in a locality might be said to cohere into a whole, that is, integrate to a level where both trading patterns and the awareness of those involved, indicated the presence of a distinct local economy. 'Embeddedness', it will be remembered, refers to the ways in which economic activities are inter-connected with non-economic activities. In the kind of highly cohesive economic, social, cultural and political relations of the 19th century cotton town in Lancashire or the contemporary industrial district reported in Northern Italy, levels of embeddedness are high allowing the economic and non-economic to mutually support each other.

We collected data on memberships of both 'half-way' institutions such as rotary clubs and round tables which straddle the divide between the economic and non-economic and the extent to which small business owners used family and friends to bolster their business activities or vice versa, as well as their participation in other spheres such as local politics. As Chapter 4 showed, across the board, there were very few indications of embeddedness in any of the localities studied.

Halfway institutions such as rotary clubs and round tables which can function as 'bridges' between the economic and the non-economic, attracted few small business owners, less than 4%. Membership of local political parties was also very low, in line with the below average levels of political participation recorded for the *petit bourgeoisie* in recent national studies such as Parry et al. (1992). Not a single small business owner reported being a local councillor or magistrate. In the critical incident study reported in Chapter 4, it was clear that spouses and partners, family and friends were not seen as ways of linking the business with other areas of life outside the economic sphere or as a means of reaching other areas of the economy. In other words, there was very little evidence of owner-managers networking via non-economic social relations such as those based on family and kinship or friendship groupings or through leisure activities.

There were two clear reasons for this lack of embeddedness relations among the small business owners: one mundane and one motivational. The mundane was connected to time constraints. As Chapter 4 reported, the small business owners worked long hours compared with the typical employee in the UK even when overtime working by the latter is taken into consideration. Moreover, the age distribution of small business owners is heavily concentrated in the 35–45 age groups, the age groups where partner-spouse and immediate family demands on the owner-manager are likely to be high (Meager, 1991; Campbell and Daly, 1992). A high proportion of the owner-managers, for example, had school age children.

In short, small business owners are people who need to consider the opportunity costs of particular kinds of activities very carefully and especially activities which are not central to their businesses, in terms of a clear and immediate return, or which make demands on the very limited time they have for leisure and social activities outside partner-spouse and family commitments. Research reported in annual surveys such as the Social Trends (1993) shows that, overall, the UK population are not 'joiners', they take little active part in leisure or sports or cultural activities. Given the heavy commitments to their businesses and limited time for activities beyond the immediate family circle or partner relations, small business owners are even less likely to be 'joiners'.

The second and much more important reason for owner-managers not to create and sustain any kind of extensive networks based on economic and/ or non-economic linkages is motivational. The self-definitions of many small business owners stress the importance of independence and freedom from control by others. Indeed, as many studies have shown, these motivations are often central to entering small business ownership in the first place. Their businesses, in other words, are the most tangible expressions of their achievement of personal independence. The results of motivational emphases of these kinds have been labelled a 'fortress enterprise mentality', that is, an extreme reluctance to engage in any behaviour which might lead to a dependence on others or even be seen as showing a need for others' help and support, whether others with whom they engage in economic relations or people in their non-economic lives. Of course, not all small business owners display these motivational characteristics in an extreme form but their presence even in weaker forms in the psychological make-up of owner-managers, is common. They militate against networking activities beyond those clearly demanded by the needs of the business and those which can be controlled by the owner-manager or threaten personal autonomy as little as possible.

In other words small business owners are less than ideal for the role of integrating the economic and the non-economic in their localities. They contribute little to embeddedness and, hence, little to the build up of mutually supporting economic and non-economic activities. These need to reach a sufficient critical mass to become a self-sustaining local economic community, recognised as such both by its participants and outsiders as economically and culturally distinct from any wider economy.

This conclusion contrasts sharply with historical characterisations of the close links between the economic and the non-economic in many localities in the past and the role the small business owner is said to have played in creating and sustaining a close reciprocity between economic, social, political, religious and cultural activities. The Bolton Report's (1971) picture of small business owners' central role in local non-economic activities, for example, which alleged that they had 'in many instances effectively replaced the squire as the local benefactor and leader' (Bolton Report, 1971:26) might have been true of the Britain of the 1960s, though it seems an overly romantic view even of most localities in the 1960s, but there were no parallels in the 7 localities in the present studies as indicated by the activities of the 410 small business owners interviewed.

LARGE FIRMS, PUBLIC SECTOR ORGANISATIONS AND LOCALITIES

While economic activities in any locality may be mainly comprised of the myriad small transactions of the large number of small enterprises operating in the locality, the most visible business will be a handful of large private businesses, those that employ over 500 people or so. To these should be added local public sector organisations whose activities are comparable in scope and impact to the large private sector business. Like the private sector businesses who may be businesses exclusive to the locality or simply large branch outlets of nationals or multinationals, the public sector organisations may also be firmly locally based such as a local authority or branches of larger central government or quasi-government organisations.

It is often accepted almost without question that large private sector businesses and to a lesser extent large public sector organisations will dominate local economic activities. By 'dominate' here will be meant that large enterprises of these kinds will be responsible for injecting large amounts of purchasing power into the locality through the employment they generate directly and indirectly, as well as their relationships with other local, often small and medium sized, businesses. The latter are often seen as very dependent on the orders they receive from these larger enterprises. In short, these large private firms and public sector organisations are assumed to be critical contributors to local economic activities and their integration.

The research we conducted in two of the localities examined the extent of large firm-large public sector organisations' involvement in local economic activities and especially their relations with small firms, local and non-local. There were clear differences between the two localities in the extent to which large firms and public sector organisations had a strong local presence. Sheffield's large private sector firms in the steel industry demonstrated links with other businesses in the locality as manifestations of the old industrial district based on steel-making and steel products, now much depleted due to the decline in these kinds of activities. Kingston's large businesses, with one exception, showed relatively few links with other businesses in the locality.

In Sheffield, the local links between steel-makers and steel products firms and the old industrial district were on the decline. The UK steel industry is now part of an increasingly integrated European Community steel industry subject to community-wide rules governing its operations. This is generating incentives for UK firms to make links with other producers in the Community. There are also more and more global links as UK firms develop relations with steel producers in other parts of the world. These forces pushing toward spatial disarticulation seem unlikely to be reversed in the foreseeable future.

In turn, producers and specialist firms from elsewhere in the European Community and from other major steel centres, may be tempted to set up branch outlets, particularly for technological exchanges, in Sheffield. In short, some of the 'local' firms in the industrial district will be industrial and technological 'cuckoos' rather than businesses which have grown out of the internal development processes of the district. Other large firms in Sheffield, such as the large branch of the national financial services business which took part in the study, are fairly recent arrivals to the locality. They have no good reason to become integrated closely with other kinds of local economic activities: their orientation is firmly to the national market the business serves.

The purchasing strategies of large firms generally were based on 5 key criteria: price, quality, delivery, reliability and capacity. Whatever the objective merits of small and local firms in meeting these criteria, the actual purchasing behaviour of large firms operated to rule out both. Locality was not a consideration – the ease of communication and transport in the UK gives local firms very little advantage. Small firms were viewed favourably in principle, but in practice they won relatively little business. The increasing emphasis on greater rationalisation in purchasing by large firms and the move towards preferred supplier lists, often combined with insistence on BS 5750 accreditation, is likely to reduce further opportunities for small and local firms.

Large firms' involvement in local non-economic activities was not high compared to the level depicted in earlier times when a Pilkington or an ICI exerted a high level of influence in local politics, cultural activities and social life. Large businesses are involved in community relations, senior managers, for instance, frequently sit on educational institutions' boards of governors, sponsor or part sponsor local sports events or community activities such as tidying up derelict sites or local charity events. But these involvements in the non-economic are not deep and do not contribute a great deal to embeddedness.[8]

Where the large firm is a local branch of a national business, community relations policies and budgets may be centrally determined. Frequently, the senior managers of the local branch will be in post locally for relatively short periods and may well live outside the locality while holding the post. In only one of the large private firms was there a long established pattern of local involvement and this was, uncharacteristically for contemporary large firms, still part managed by members of the local founding family. This firm had large branch outlets in other parts of the UK where it also presumably felt a need to have a community presence. More typical, it can be argued, are the professional community relations strategies of most of the large firms which are unlikely to achieve any deep penetration into the non-economic lives of localities or produce effects in the non-economic areas of local life sufficient to boost local economic integration.

What was more surprising was the relations between local economic activities and public sector organisations. Some of the public sector organisations were long established bodies set up to serve local needs. Local authorities, for instance, as the discussion in the opening chapter showed, have long been regarded by economic geographers and political theorists as central to a locality's economic and political activities as well as to its social and cultural activities helping weld all these into an integrated local community. Sheffield City Council, in particular, has often been cited as a leading example of a local authority adopting a highly proactive economic policy aimed at promoting local economic activities and employment. The development of a large shopping complex, Meadowhall, for example, provided an estimated 7,000 jobs as well as helping diversify the area's industrial base (DEED, 1989b). While the present study was being conducted, the City Council's sponsoring of the World Student Games was a further example of its style of positively promoting the city and locality.

Kingston's local authority and those in nearby areas have never had a reputation for high profile interventionist economic policies. Mainly Conservative controlled, their localities sharing the economic success of the South East Region over the last three or four decades, they have had neither the ideological taste for, nor the incentives from high unemployment among local voters, to adopt highly interventionist policies. Kingston's local authority has sought to attract more industry into the area mainly in the form of retailing, encouraging national retailers and property developers to make Kingston into a major shopping centre for the South West London/Northern Surrey area. The emphasis, however, has been on market led development with the Authority providing positive encouragement and infrastructural support.

Despite the central role claimed for local authorities in previous theorising and research, the findings from the present study do not show strong, positive local authority–local business relations. Paradoxically, as Chapter 5 pointed out, it was the Sheffield business respondents – small business owners and large firm representatives – who were most negative about their local authority's contribution to promoting local economic activities and business-to-business relations. Where they were not actually negative, respondents were very rarely positive or enthusiastic in their views on the local authority's support for the local economy. Their counterparts in Kingston were not so negative though they also showed little positive enthusiasm or regard for the local authority's contributions to local economic life.

Much has already been written about the 'crisis of local government' in the UK of the 1990s. This crisis has arisen largely out of the collision between the ideological stance and policies of central government since 1979, and local authorities, particularly those controlled by Labour. Four successive governments dominated by radical right thinking have produced a long unbroken period in which local authorities have lost resources, the discretion to generate and implement local policies (including local economic policies) and lost responsibility for local affairs in areas such as housing, health and education. These trends occurred against a background of sustained media criticism of alleged local authority over-spending and the policies of authorities controlled by Labour. The result has been a loss on the part of local authorities of their abilities to intervene and to make positive links with business and other institutions as the locality's first 'institutional citizen'.[9]

What the results show, therefore, is that local authorities as local forces for economic integration and for bridging the economic and the non-economic activities of the locality were not very effective in the opinions of respondents. The wider discussion of likely trends in the role of local authorities in Britain in the 1990s, particularly if the Conservatives are returned to power again at the next General Election, suggests that local authorities are not likely to be able to transform the views of respondents of the kinds we interviewed through their abilities to intervene in local life. In short, local authorities as key forces for local economic integration have declined considerably in the 1990s compared with a decade ago and look likely to decline further.

Local authorities are not just political institutions in their locality, they are, like all other kinds of public sector organisations, generators of economic activities also. They employ people whose buying power adds to local demand but more importantly, they are purchasers and producers. The revenue and capital expenditure of Sheffield City Council and Kingston Borough Council, for example, added up to over £800 million in 1990–1991. The other kinds of large local public sector organisations whose representatives we interviewed, also had substantial multi-million pound budgets. Yet relatively little of their purchasing appeared to end up in the locality other than through employee wages and salaries or to result in business for local and especially local small firms.

The main reason for this lack of impact on local economic activities by local authorities and other public sector organisations lay in the purchasing strategies they have adopted. Almost without exception, they used strict tendering procedures for most of their purchasing and, more significant, tended to adopt high minimum values for contracts even where it was possible to subdivide orders. The reason for the latter strategy was mainly administrative – larger contracts are easier to manage. But this tended to rule out small firms and very often local firms also. Larger orders and contracts tended to go to large specialist suppliers who were likely to be national or at least regional rather than local. These strategies have been reinforced by the government's insistence on CCT by local authorities, which has covered an increasingly wide range of purchases and activities since the early 1980s.

Other public sector organisations, although not bound by CCT, have become very conscious of the need to have well documented, rational purchasing procedures able to withstand government scrutiny. As for the local authorities, the other large public sector organisations generated surprisingly little business for local firms through their purchases, given the size of their budgets and very little business indeed for local small firms.[10]

It has been argued recently (see, for instance, the discussion in Shaw, 1993) that the decline in local authorities as key local economic instigators is being offset by the emergence of local 'growth coalitions', that is, groups of individuals and other non-local authority, non-elected local institutions who come together to promote local economic activities. The research instruments used in the studies upon which this book is based were not designed to explore whether growth coalitions of these kinds had emerged in any of the 7 localities but there were no mentions of their presence by respondents. However, even if they were present, they would be unlikely to be able to replace the local authority's previous potential to be able to link the economic and non-economic activities to promote embeddedness.

INDUSTRIAL DISTRICTS, SUBCONTRACTING AND JIT

In the opening chapters there was an extended examination of some of the main contributions to theorising and research on economic activities and locality and business-to-business relations. The industrial district thesis, for example, has generated a large literature with one of its central themes emerging as an assessment of the extent to which it is, or could become, a model for promoting local economic activities in the UK. In the earlier discussion, the existence of industrial districts in the UK particularly in many localities in which 19th century manufacturing developed, was noted. But equally, the discussion stressed the ways in which the decline in manufacturing, economic restructuring and recession over the last two decades had destroyed or much reduced these old industrial districts.

In the 7 localities studied here, only Sheffield showed indications of the presence of an industrial district. This was based on steel-making and steel products which, as pointed out earlier, has not only declined greatly from its former importance but continues to decline. Doncaster, one of the other localities in the study, showed indications of its links with older industries, coal, railway manufacturing, which like steel (Doncaster is geographically adjacent to former steel-making activities also) was the basis of a mixed industrial district of the past. But these fading industrial districts were not matched by indications of new districts emerging in any of the localities. Not only were there no indications of the economic networks through which industrial districts might be generated, there were also no indications of the political, social and cultural infrastructures which the full blown industrial district requires according to influential theorists such as Pyke (1992). In fact, as the earlier discussion in the chapter argued, the trends are very clearly away from both the economic and non-economic conditions required for the thesis to be fulfilled.

In Chapter 2, it was argued that the large literature and theoretical concentration on subcontracting in the discussion of business-to-business relations, grossly over-stated the importance of such relations in the UK economy of the 1990s. One reason for this exaggeration is the over-emphasis on manufacturing now only a small part of the UK economy and, within manufacturing, on industries which show high levels of subcontracting.

It is necessary to be clear what is meant by 'sub-contracting' as a type of relationship between businesses. Here it has been taken to refer to relations between businesses where both understand clearly, with the support of written agreements, that they are engaged in a set of transactions continuing over time which both are confident will continue. In other words, subcontracting does not refer to one-off market transactions or to infrequent transactions where one or other party has no clear expectation that the transaction will ever be repeated. If one business, the purchasing firm, for example, believes it is 'sub-contracting' to another firm in the way defined above, the supplier must share this belief. It is not enough for the purchasing firm to declare it is engaged in sub-contracting for the relationship to be said to exist.

The findings from the studies upon which this book is based suggest that sub-contracting in the above sense is unusual particularly where the relations are between small and large firms or between firms in the same locality. There were a number of reasons for this absence of sub-contracting as a common business-to-business relationship. First, a high proportion of the small businesses in the study, like businesses overall in the UK economy, were in services. A substantial proportion of services firms meet the needs of individual consumers only or serve both individual consumers and other businesses. Subcontracting for these businesses is simply statistically less likely.

Second, where the services businesses did meet the needs of other businesses, a high proportion of their transactions were either one-offs or what might be termed 'regular-irregular intermittent', that is, there were repeated transactions between the firms but there was no clear understanding, particularly on the part of the supplier, that orders would be repeated. For instance, an employment agency having supplied a temporary or permanent employee to a client business might hope that the latter would be satisfied enough to come back again when other employees were needed but could have no certainty that this would happen. Printing firms offer an even better example of this pattern. They normally work hard to retain a core of customers who will use them for supplying their needs for letterheads, invoices, promotional materials etc and most general printers are successful in this strategy. However, few orders will be 'sub-contracting' in the sense defined above. Purchasing firms can and do switch printers or use more than one printer. The frequency and size of orders will depend on the purchasing business's level of activity. Recession, for example, will reduce the flow of orders from customers while expansion may lead to more.

The other manufacturing industry covered in the research programme, electronics, does have a tradition of high levels of business-to-business relations and of separate businesses carrying out part of the work only in the production of goods. Several of the large electronics or defence-related firms in the study in Kingston were involved in sub-contracting relations which fitted the above definition closely. What was notable about these relations, however, was that few small firms were involved and, equally, few local firms. The type of relations between small electronics firms and their customers, large or small, varied from being routine work to very specialised tasks. Moreover, the nature of the relationship varied according to the balance in the level of technological know-how between supplier and customer.

Overall, the absolute level of sub-contracting was low and most business-to-business relations were 'regular-irregular intermittent'. Small firms had low levels of *any* kinds of relations with large businesses and, similarly, relations between firms in the locality were low with the exception of those involved in steel-making and steel products in Sheffield.

It needs to be repeated that the small firms in the study with mainly business customers were not necessarily hungry for subcontracting or more links with large firms. Large firms were seen as difficult to deal with by many small business owners. They were unpredictable, could produce large orders which were difficult for a small business to digest or could lead to becoming too reliant on a single customer. They often paid late and the links with the business depended greatly on personal relations with the large firm's representative who might move on or be promoted. Again, the small business owners' common need for autonomy and independence is relevant: too close a dependence on a single large customer might threaten that independence. Many of the small business owner respondents were very conscious of the connotations of dependence which are built into conventional notions of and the very term, 'sub-contracting'. These in themselves were very often sufficient to make them begin their answers to questions on their business-to-business relations by stating that they avoided such relations and to demonstrate that while their business was small, its independence was safeguarded carefully in relations with other businesses.

It could be argued that the absence of sub-contracting relations in the form they have been defined for this study results simply from the kinds of economic activities, firms and localities in the studies. Certainly, the samples did not include the kinds of industries and firms which appear in so many studies of subcontracting such as motor car and clothing manufacture and, doubtlessly, had these been included the findings would be different. But the types of economic sectors chosen for the present study are more representative of the UK economy of the 1990s: mainly services sectors whose activities now provide the bulk of jobs and output in the economy and areas of manufacturing which included substantial representation of high tech businesses in the form of electronics and electronics-related activities. In other words, the arguments being presented do not deny the importance of subcontracting relations in some, much studied, sectors of the economy but instead assert that a more balanced picture of the UK economy of the 1990s, reduces the significance of sub-contracting as a form of business-to-business relations.

The above considerations also bring out the implications for the significance of another fashionable, much discussed notion in developments in business-to-business relations: JIT relations. The findings did not produce a single example of a small or large firm involved in JIT relations with other businesses. Again, the argument might be made that this is unsurprising since the sectors covered are not those in which JIT relations have developed such as, again, motor car manufacture. However, the point to be made from the findings is precisely that this absence indicates that the importance of JIT relations as a form of business-to-business relations needs to be kept in perspective. To date, it appears to be relevant to only a very small part of the UK economy, that is, mainly parts of the car making industry, and even here there is some debate on its extent as the discussion in Chapter 2 showed. It is not significant as a type of business-to-business relation elsewhere in the economy.[11]

SMALL FIRMS, LARGE FIRMS, LOCALITIES AND POLICIES

Local economic development and accompanying policies to promote and enhance economic activities in localities have been a central concern of UK governments since at least the 1930s. For much of the period it was accepted that responsibility for these activities was firmly in the public sector, particularly where they were aimed at arresting regional and local economic decline. In the 1980s the emphasis shifted as it became widely believed that previous public policies had failed. In tune with the ideological preferences of central administrations since 1979, there has been a shift away from mainly public sector sponsored policies towards a mixed public, private, voluntary sectors approach with the public sector supposed to be the pump primer and co-ordinator rather than the prime mover as in past decades. Government has still produced new initiatives, such as TECs and various inner city programmes but these were designed to allow government to have only a minor role. Whatever the changes, however, the belief in the importance of *locality* as the unit of policy delivery has largely remained.

The findings from the present research have important implications for these policy assumptions. The main finding has been of the *lack* of importance of locality in relations between businesses in the sense of an integrated local economy, that is, local business-to-business relations and the latter's articulation with non-economic relations where those involved and outsiders would accept they form a coherent whole. Small businesses are frequently local in their business and customer relations though the 'shapes' of their 'local' relations vary enormously. As we found, people were still prepared to discuss the locality in which their businesses were situated and to see a local economy in some symbolic sense but when it came to describing local relations at the practical level it was found these were often severely attenuated or even non-existent in some instances. Large firms and public sector organisations were often *in* the locality in a physical sense but not *of* the locality in economic or non-economic terms. Large firms and public sector organisations have fewer and fewer relations in which the locality from which they operate are significant.

The decline in non-economic relations in the localities, the local authorities' loss of a central role and the lack of, or only superficial involvement of, business representatives such as small business owners and large enterprise managers, in intermediary institutions such as chambers of commerce, means that economic coherence cannot easily be bolstered by local action. More recent alternatives such as 'growth coalitions' are not genuinely local in the sense of arising out of the real concerns of a wide range of local population members acting through well established local institutional means. Instead, they are often narrowly business-led, though frequently with the co-operation of the local authority if only because it cannot afford to be left out, with the support of external funding. While these initiatives have had some successes they have also been shown to have clear limitations, particularly where the main aims were property and land development.

The above approaches rely heavily on the notions of a local economy and community able to respond to the initiatives when locality, in both the economic and non-economic senses, is declining. Local economic networks in any real sense are largely absent or only poorly developed in the localities we have researched except in a sectoral sense in Sheffield for one kind of activity, steel-making and steel products.[12]

If any locality's economic activities are largely comprised of the activities of small firms while the handful of large firms and organisations are relatively detached from the locality, more attention needs to be paid to how small firms operate. As was seen earlier, what distinguishes small business links with the wider economy is their 'market shape' and this is largely sectorally determined. It is formed by their relations with suppliers whose character depends on the kind of activity and who are commonly located outside the local area and, even more important, their relations with customers. As the data indicated, the small business owners were very sectorally conscious. They were involved closely in particular kinds of economic activity and defined themselves in this way, that is, as printers, computer specialists, restauranteurs etc, and not as members of some wider 'small business community', 'local economy' or 'local community'. In the kinds of activities where small businesses have been increasing most since 1980, this lack of local consciousness is greatest. This ground-level view of the external involvements of small business owners, and larger enterprises, reduces locality's importance very considerably.

Given the higher levels of sectoral consciousness and lack of concern about and even decline of, locality, the clear implication for policy is that it should become more sectorally focused. The model here might be along the lines of the Japanese approach where there is said to be a much greater consciousness of sectoral importance. The Ministry of International Trade and Industry (MITI) regularly assesses sectoral significance and the required policies to promote sectors likely to be important over the foreseeable future, say a ten-year period. In assessing sectors, however, the focus is on small *and* large firms. Japan's small firm sector is seen, by MITI and more generally, to be critical in the country's economic success since World War Two. The role small firms can play with large enterprise in their sector overall is the focus of attention. In other words, sector is important and small firms are important but they are seen as part of the larger picture of the sector in producing a coherent policy.

A shift in focus of the above kind, which argues for sectorally-based policies of economic support, would still have connections with localities. In some localities, there are strong established sectoral patterns, as in Sheffield, so that policy delivery could retain, in part, a local dimension. More generally, policies need an implementation network if they are to be nationally effective which, ideally, should bring policy and sector closer together. At ground level this requires a network of delivery points. These might take several forms from those specially tailored to the needs and distribution of businesses in the sector using, for example, trade associations and the industrial training organisations, which are sector-based, augmented by other newer delivery vehicles. Alternatively, given a shift in emphasis to sectorally-based policies, other existing institutions could be used by changing their missions. The TECs, for instance, are still finding themselves in terms of their policies and mechanisms for delivering help and support to small firms. Their approach could be converted into one which emphasises sector rather than locality. That they are geographically spread across the country could even be an advantage once the assumption that they are involved in cohesive local economies is put to one side.

Sector-based economic development policies have been tried before in Britain in several industries with some success but the idea that they might replace policies based on notions of 'locality' such as regions or urban areas is relatively new. The failure of regional policies and local economic development initiatives in recent decades suggests alternatives are needed. If the suggestions for sector-based approaches which have been argued here to arise out of the findings from our research are accepted, one paradoxical result might well be that because sectors (especially those that are expanding) cut across locality, the regional economic inequalities so persistent under previous approaches over the last half a century and more might be substantially reduced.

CONCLUDING REMARKS AND A SUMMARY OF THE ARGUMENT

The research programmes which stimulated this book have led to a focus on relations between 3 areas of phenomena: small-scale enterprise, large firms and organisations, and localities. The experiences of the 410 small enterprises in the 7 localities and the large private sector firms and public sector organisations in two of the localities, were argued to indicate trends in the UK which weaken the importance of locality as a link between businesses.

In all probability, this link has been growing weaker for some time but has not been clearly recognised because, first, so much of the research on spatial aspects of the economy has been based on top-down, aggregate data analysis rather than on the closely observed activities of real people in real businesses in real places. Second, the concern (over-concern) with the economic to the exclusion of the impact and importance of non-economic activities, has not taken into account how the latter have changed in ways which no longer contribute strongly to supporting links between locality and economic activities. The decline, for example, in participation in local political parties and the loss of power by local authorities to intervene in local non-economic as well as economic matters are other instances of these trends. Notions such as 'local economic networks', in other words, have become fashionable in examining relations between industry and locality precisely when we begin to see that these relations are in decline.

Arguments under headings such as 'the globalisation of the economy' and the decline of links between large trans-national enterprises and their localities of origin, are now widely accepted. The need for large businesses (as well as medium sized and smaller businesses) to look outward and focus on the SEM is a commonplace in government and media exhortations. Small businesses do not behave like large business and their relations with locality, seen at ground level, show two distinct characteristics. First, different kinds of small businesses display their sectoral character by having their own 'localities' where their markets, though not usually their suppliers, are often spatially proximate. This local variation has been understated in the past because the full extent of the heterogeneity within the small business population has not been recognised: it has been too easy for academics and policy-makers to see small businesses as much of a kind in terms of their operations and markets.

Second, and more significant for assessing trends, newer and the most rapidly expanding kinds of small businesses, are much less likely to be tied to 'locality' in any conventional sense. Using modern communications they deliver their 'products', often intangibles involving knowledge manipulation rather than tangible objects, and maintain contacts with other businesses quickly and effectively, increasingly regardless of spatial considerations.

The conclusion which can be drawn from the above is that the 'local economy', defined in conventional arbitrary terms (travel-to-work areas, local labour markets, local authority areas etc) is less and less an integrated set of economic linkages and activities. If this is so, then certainly for academics but also, as the previous section argued, for policy-makers, the notion of the local economy ceases to be of key relevance in discussing and analysing economic activities and especially the role of the small business and its articulation with the wider economy.

The overall argument we have presented is depicted in simplified form in Figure 6.1. The figure concentrates on small and large firms and public organisations and the trends we have identified from the data from our own and other related research. It ignores, because of the difficulties in including them in a two dimensional figure, the changes we have alluded to in non-economic areas of social, political and cultural life but which, in our view, have strong embeddedness effects on economic relations. The ways in which the trends in embeddedness relations are reinforcing the decline in links between businesses and locality should be kept firmly in mind in assessing the overall thesis.

Neither does the figure more than very indirectly suggest some of the other implications from the analysis. For example, one implication is that

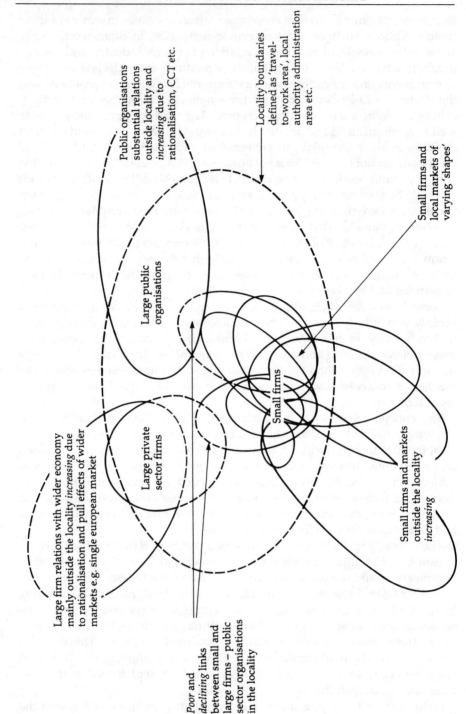

Figure 6.1 Small Firms, Large Firms/Organisations and Localities

size homogamy in business-to-business links appears to be on the increase in Britain, that is, a trend towards businesses to increasingly have transactions with businesses roughly of their own size. This holds for public sector organisations also. The trend is uneven, of course, but results mainly from greater rationalisation in market relations. There are attempts to counter this trend such as government campaigns from time to time to persuade its own departments to do more business with smaller firms. Similar campaigns by bodies such as the CBI have also been mounted. These efforts do not appear to be notably successful in practice. Similarly, the introduction of CCT for the supply of local authority services was intended to create more opportunities for small firms – including *local* small firms but appears to have failed in this aim so far: if anything, the trend has been towards larger businesses winning more CCT contracts over time.

Another implication of our arguments is that relations between small firms and the wider economy are much less ordered and small firms are much more independent, than many have argued in the past. Many previous arguments have seen the small firm as heavily dependent on customers and suppliers mainly larger than itself. There are sectors of the economy where such relations may be common – clothing manufacture is the example usually cited – but the thesis we put forward suggests that, typically, such relations are not common. Small firms in many sectors of the economy maintain their independence very successfully through the strategies of their owner-managers in handling their relations with other businesses, as the interviews with owner-managers in our research showed. Small firms are also heavily represented in service sectors meeting the needs of private consumers so that relations with other businesses are only a small part of their relations with the wider economy.

In many of the new, expanding areas of the economy based on knowledge and its manipulation and creativity, small firms are able to build their independence on their specialist skills. Nor, given their economic performance over the last 20 years or so, should the dominance and power of large firms in the economy be accepted without question.[13] In a period when the UK economy has been restructuring so fundamentally, business-to-business relations have become more atomistic in the sense of firms having fewer permanent relations with other businesses or participating in well defined, stable economic linkages.

The thesis presented in this book is based on the results from two research programmes on the small firm and small firm–large firm relations. The coverage of these programmes while extensive by the standards of UK small business research was not, of course, comprehensive. But the conclusions drawn are consistent with a wide range of other research and analysis. Arguments about economic globalisation, Post-Fordism, the growth of larger markets extending beyond nation-state boundaries, the emergence of world businesses, the decline of local communities, the perplexing failures of local economic development policies and the increase in the numbers of small enterprises all abound in the literatures of the relevant disciplines and in policy discussions. Many of those contributing to these arguments offer views which parallel, at least in part, those offered here.

Others, of course, will disagree but what we offer is a contribution to these ongoing debates from a ground-level view. This is based on the experiences offered in their own words, of real small business owners, large business and organisation representatives and others who share the experiences of our respondents and whose views have also been taken into account in our analysis. These real people are at the sharp end of the unprecedented economic and other changes which are re-shaping the UK economy in the 1990s and re-ordering the relations between businesses and localities.

Notes

1. It is worth emphasising again the points made earlier on the relationship between notions such as 'regions' and substantive relations. Some of these administratively determined areas have *some* relationship with real relations in particular geographical areas. Many, for instance, are labelled to echo what was, and still are, the areas with which people in the area more or less identify themselves culturally. There is, for instance, a 'Sheffield' local economy defined as the area covered by the City Council's administrative boundaries or some similar administrative boundaries and there is a 'Sheffield' with which people who live in and around the city often see themselves as part of culturally. But, clearly, the ways in which these two are related to each other are problematic and we cannot simply assume that they are equivalents. Neither do these two notions necessarily imply any particular patterns of real relations between businesses or people.
2. It might be argued that it is absurd to contrast two such very different kinds of business to make this point about small business market 'shapes' but both are legitimate forms of enterprise and it would be easy to cite a large number of equally 'absurd' contrasts in a highly developed, complex economy such as that of the UK in the 1990s.
3. It emerged also that 'local' in this instance was often interpreted by respondents to mean not the immediate area but a much wider area to encompass the nearest branch outlet of the supplier. A paper supplier's 'local' distribution source might actually be 20 or 30 miles from the user firm.
4. There were, of course, some links between firms not based on simple economic transactions. For example, colleagues who conducted a study of the impact of technological innovation on a sub-sample of the small service sector firms, did find co-operation between some firms in the localities. This appeared most common among the small garages and vehicle repairers in the sample. It resulted, in part, from the character of the sector itself. Motor vehicles are highly complex and technological innovation has been rapid. It was common for repairers to find they could not carry out all kinds of repairs and needed some of the work done by another repairer with the right equipment and expertise. One result of these needs was a good deal of reciprocity between businesses in putting work out to each other. For a further account see Dickson et al. (1994).
5. At best, therefore, this indicates possible 'latent networks' which function in a haphazard way to bring new customers to the firm from time to time but which call for little positive contribution from the owner-manager to keep them going.

This, however, is hardly the kind of local proactive economic network keen proponents of the small business network concept have in mind.

6. There is also the issue of potential conflict of interest to be kept in mind here. Accountants may be reluctant to bring different clients together to promote business between them for fear that complications could arise which might lead to accusations of failing to serve one or other client's interests.

7. In the two localities from which the manufacturing firms were drawn, the highest proportion belonging to the local chamber of commerce was in Sheffield (36.7%) but this is based on data for only two kinds of enterprise, both in manufacturing where the level of membership was significantly higher overall than among the small services firms.

8. One of the large defence contractor firms, for example, estimated that it spent just over £40,000 on local involvement in the year 1990–1991, of which just over half was on links with education. Relative to the size of the firm's turnover at the local plant and the size of the locality's population, this expenditure could not be seen as generous or likely to have a significant impact on local activities.

9. As Parry et al. (1992:403–411) demonstrate, people's relations with their local authorities are complex and reactions to how well the local political process functions vary widely. However, they report that, overall, almost half (45.3%) of their sample felt unable to given an opinion on how well local politics worked in the areas in which they lived. The fieldwork in Parry et al.'s research was carried out in 1984–1985, that is, halfway through the full 12 year period from 1979 to the fieldwork for the present studies. The positive impact of local authorities on the views of local populations may well have declined further since 1984–1985.

10. It is possible that for some kinds of externally sourced activities, local authorities and other large public sector organisations might change their policies of favouring single contract sourcing from large private sector suppliers. One reason for this might be experiencing poor service or even total failures to meet contractual obligations by suppliers. This can be very disruptive and cause the local authority or other public sector organisation considerable problems. It could result in services or the purchase of goods being spread across a number of smaller contracts with different suppliers so that failure of any one contract would be less harmful. Such a shift might be more favourable to small and/or local firms.

11. This is not to say that this form of business-to-business relation will not become more important in the future. The Japanese car makers, for instance, Nissan, Honda and Toyota, allegedly the pioneers and keenest enthusiasts for JIT supplier relations, have not so far developed large scale JIT relations with local suppliers around their plants in Sunderland, Swindon and Burnaston respectively (eg NEDO, 1991b). But none of these plants have been in existence for more than 7 years or reached full capacity. However, the deep-seated motivational concern with independence so commonly found among small business owners makes it unlikely they will rush to become JIT suppliers. Far more likely, is that other medium to large firms will become involved in joint developments to provide parts and services on a JIT basis or, as in Nissan's case already, separate but main producer-owned plants will be set up to provide JIT supplies.

12. We would have also found local sectoral networks in Nottingham based on textiles and clothing manufacture had our study in that locality focused on these industries. But again it should be noted that this arises out of old manufacturing industries not out of the new kinds of economic activities dominating the UK economy of the 1990s. Supporting and maintaining this network in Nottingham has not been without problems however, as Roberts et al. (1990) show.

13. Probably the best example of this point in recent years has been the history of IBM. From dominating the computing industry for a long period up to the 1980s, this huge multinational has turned in poor results, lost markets and had to make large numbers of employees redundant despite considerable efforts and investment to retain its dominance. What is more, as many observers have pointed out, this dominance has been challenged to a great extent by small firms.

REFERENCES

Abbott, B. (1993) Patterns of Privatisation and the Provision of Local Authority Services, Kingston Business School Working Paper, Kingston University.

Ackers, P. and Black, J. (1991) Paternalist Capitalism: An Organisation culture in Transition in M. Cross and M. Payne (eds.) *Work and the Enterprise Culture*, The Falmer Press, London.

Action for Cities (1987) *Action for Cities: Building on Initiative*, Department of the Environment and Department of Employment, London.

Aglietta, M. (1979) *A Theory of Capitalist Regulation: The US Experience*, New Left Books, London.

Aldrich, H. and Zimmer, C. (1986) Entrepreneurship Through Social Networks, in D. Sexton and R. Smilor (eds.) *The Art and Science of Entrepreneurship*, Ballinger, New York.

Allen, J. (1988) The Geographies of Service in D. Massey and J. Allen (eds.) *Uneven Redevelopment, Cities and Regions in Transition*, Hodder and Stoughton/Open University Press, London.

Allen, J. and Massey, D. (eds.) (1988) *The Economy in Question, Restructuring Britain*, Sage/The Open University, London.

Amin, A. and Robins, K. (1990) *Not Marshallian Times*, Centre for Urban and Regional Development Studies, University of Newcastle upon Tyne.

Atkinson, J. and Meager, N. (1986) *Changing Working Patterns. How Companies Achieve Flexibility to Meet New Needs*, National Economic Development Office, London.

Atkinson, J. and Meager, N. (1992) Running to Stand Still: The Small Business in the Labour Market, paper presented to a seminar for the ESRC Small Business Initiative, Warwick University, September.

Audit Commission (1989) *Urban Regeneration and Economic Development: The Local Government Dimension*, HMSO, London.

Auerbach, P. (1989) Multinationals and the British Economy, in F. Green (ed.) *The Restructuring of the UK Economy*, Harvester Wheatsheaf, Hemel Hempstead.

Aydalot, P. and Keeble, D. (eds.) (1988) *High Technology Industry and Innovative Environments: The European Experience*, Routledge and Kegan Paul, London.

AZTEC (1993) *Labour Market Assessment for British Aerospace.* AZTEC Training and Enterprise Council, Kingston upon Thames.

Balchin, P. N. (1990) *Regional Policy in Britain: The North-South Divide*, Paul Chapman, London.

Ball, M., Gray, F. and McDowell, L. (1989) *The Transformation of Britain, Contemporary Social and Economic Change*, Fontana Press, London.

Ballandi, M. (1989) The Industrial District in Marshall, in E. Goodman, J. Bamford and P. Gaynor (eds.) *Small Firms and Industrial Districts in Italy*, Routledge, London.

Bank of England (1993) *Bank Lending To Smaller Businesses*. Bank of England, London.

Bannock, G. (1991a) An Economic Survey 1971–1991 in J. Stanworth and C. Gray (eds.) *Bolton 20 Years On: The Small Firm in the 1990s*, Paul Chapman, London.

Bannock, G. (1991b) Opinion – BS 5750: No Rush to Register, *Small Business Perspective*, Jan–Feb, 15–16.

Bannock, G. and Albach, H. (1992) in *Small Business Policy in Europe: Britain, Germany and Europe*, Anglo-German Foundation, London.

Batstone, S. (1991) *Entrepreneurial Reputation and Social Capital*, Working Paper No 3, Warwick Business School Small and Medium Sized Enterprise Centre, Warwick.

Becattini, G. (1989) Sectors and/or Districts: Some Remarks on the Conceptual Foundations of Industrial Economics, in E. Goodman, J. Bamford and P. Gaynor (eds.) *Small Firms and Industrial Districts in Italy*, Routledge, London.

Bennett, R. J., Krebs, G. and Zimmermann, H. (1993) (eds.) *Chambers of Commerce in Britain and Germany and the Single European Market*, Anglo-German Foundation, London.

Bennett, R. J. and McCoshan, A. (1993) *Enterprise and Human Resource Development*, Paul Chapman, London.

Bevan, J., Clark, G., Banjeri, N. and Hakim, C. (1989) *Barriers to Business Start-Up, A Study of the Flow Into and Out of Self-Employment*, Department of Employment Research Paper No. 71, Department of Employment, London.

Beynon, H., Hudson, R., Lewis, J., Sadler, D. and Townsend, A. (1989) It's All Falling Apart Here: Coming to Terms With the Future in Teesside in P. Cooke, (ed.) *Localities, The Changing Face of Urban Britain*, Unwin Hyman, London.

Birley, S., Myers, A., and Cromie, S. (1989) Entrepreneurial Networks: Some Concepts and Empirical Evidence, Paper presented to the 12th National Small Firms Policy and Research Conference, The Barbican, London.

Bishop, P. (1988) Academic–Industry Links and Firm Size in South West England, *Regional Studies*, 22, 2, 160–162.

Blackburn, R. A. (1990) Job Quality In Small Business: Electrical and Electronic Engineering firms in Dorset, *Environment and Planning A*, 22, 875–892.

Blackburn, R. A. (1992) Small Firms and Subcontracting: What is It and Where?, in P. Leighton and A. Felstead (eds.) *The New Entrepreneurs*, Kogan Page, London.

Blackburn, R. A., Curran, J. and Jarvis, R. (1990) Small Firms and Local Networks: Some Theoretical and Conceptual Explorations, Paper presented to the 13th National Small Firms Policy and Research Conference, Harrogate, November.

Blackburn, R. A., Curran, J. and Woods, A. (1991) *Exploring Enterprise Cultures: Small Service Sector Enterprise Owners and Their Views*, ESRC Centre for Research on Small Service Sector Businesses, Kingston Business School, Kingston upon Thames.

Blunkett, D. and Jackson, K. (1987) *Democracy in Crisis: The Town Halls Respond*, Hogarth, London.

Boddy, M. and Fudge, C. (eds.) (1984) *Local Socialism?*, Macmillan, London.

Bolton Report (The) (1971) *Small Firms: Report of the Committee of Inquiry on Small Firms*, HMSO, cmnd 4811, London.

BPIF (British Printing Industries Federation) (1991) *Notes on the Printing Industry*, BPIF, May, London.

British Standards Institute (1992) Information provided by BSI Directory to the Small Business Research Centre, Kingston University.

Brownill, S. (1993) *Developing London's Docklands: Another Great Planning Disaster?*, Paul Chapman, London.

Brusco, S. (1982) The Emilian Model: Productive Decentralization and Social Integration, *Cambridge Journal of Economics*, 6, 167–184.

Brusco, S. (1992) Small Firms and the Provision of Real Services in F. Pyke, G. Becattini and W. Sengenberger (eds.) *Industrial Districts and Local Economic Regeneration*, International Labour Office, Geneva.

Bryson, J., Wood, P. and Keeble, D. (1993) Business Networks, Small Firm Flexibility and Regional Development in UK Business Services, *Entrepreneurship and Regional Development*, 5, 265–277.

Burrows, R. and Curran, J. (1989) Sociological Research in Service Sector Small Businesses: Some Conceptual Considerations *Work, Employment and Society*, 3, 4, 527–539.

Business in the Community (1990) *Springboard for Growth – Guidelines on Local Purchasing Initiatives for Business Support Organisations*, Business in the Community, London.

Business Monitor (1992) *Size Analysis of United Kingdom Businesses*, PA 1003, CSO HMSO, London.

Campbell, M. and Daly, M. (1992) Self-Employment in the 1990s, *Employment Gazette*, June, 269–292.

Census of Employment, (1987), Department of Employment and HMSO, London.

Champion, A. G. and Green, A. E. (1987) The Booming Towns of Britain: The Geography of Economic Performance in the 1980s, *Geography*, 72, 97–108.

Champion, T. and Green, A. (1988) *Local Prosperity and the North South Divide: Winners and Losers in 1990s Britain*, Department of Town Planning, University College of Cardiff, Wales.

Coakley, J. and Harris, L. (1992) Financial Globalisation and Deregulation, in J. Mitchie (ed.) *The Economic Legacy, 1979–1992*, Academic Press, London.

Coates, D. (1991) *Running the Country*, Hodder and Stoughton, London.

Cochrane, A. (1983) Local Economic Policies: Trying to Drain the Ocean with a Teaspoon, in J. Anderson (ed.) *Redundant Spaces in Cities and Regions? Studies in Industrial Decline and Social Change*, Academic Press, London.

Cochrane, A. (ed.) (1987) *Developing Local Economic Strategies*, Open University Press, Milton Keynes.

Cochrane, A. (1989) Restructuring the State: The Case of Local Government, in A. Cochrane and J. Anderson (eds.) *Politics in Transition*, Sage/Open University Press, London.

Cockburn, C. (1978) *The Local State, Management of Cities and People*, Pluto Press, London.

Cohen, A. P. (1983) *Belonging*, Manchester University Press, Manchester.

Cohen, H., Livingstone, I., McNab, A., Harrison, S., Howes, L. and Jerrard, B. (1989) 'Cheltenham: Affluence Amid Recession' in P. Cooke (ed.) *Localities, The Changing Face of Urban Britain*, Unwin Hyman, London.

Coleman, T. (1965) *The Railway Navvies*, Hutchinson, London.

Colenutt, B. and Ellis, G. (1993) Boosting the Tories, *New Statesman and Society*, p.20, 30 July.

Cooke, P. (1988) Flexible Integration, Scope Economies and Strategic Alliances, *Environment and Planning D*, 6, 3, 281–300.

Cooke, P. (1989a) (ed.) *Localities, The Changing Face of Urban Britain*, Unwin Hyman, London.

Cooke, P. (1989b) The Local Question – Revival or Survival in P. Cooke (ed.) *Localities, The Changing Face of Urban Britain*, Unwin Hyman, London.

Cooke, P. and Imrie, R. (1989) Little Victories: Local Economic Development in European Regions, *Entrepreneurship and Regional Development*, 1, 4, 313–327.

Coombes, M., Openshaw, S., Wong, C. and Raybould, S. (1993) Community Boundary Definition: A GIS Design Specification, *Regional Studies*, 27, 3, 280–286.

Cork Gully/CBI (1991) *Late Payment of Trade Debts*, Confederation of British Industry, London.

Coutes, K. and Godley, W. (1992) Does Britain's Balance of Payments Matter Any More?, in J. Mitchie (ed.) *The Economic Legacy, 1979–1992*, Academic Press, London.

Crompton, R. (1993) *Class and Stratification, An Introduction to Current Debates*, Polity Press, Oxford.

Cross, M. (1983) The United Kingdom, in D. Storey (ed.) *The Small Firm, An International Survey*, Croom Helm, London.

CSO Bulletin 58/91 (1991) *Size Analysis of UK Businesses (1991)*, Newport, Gwent, Central Statistical Office, September.

Curran, J. (1986) *Bolton Fifteen Years On: A Review and Analysis of Small Business Research in Britain 1971–1986*, Small Business Research Trust, London.

Curran, J. (1987) *Small Firms and Their Environments: A Report*, Small Business Research Centre, Kingston University, Kingston upon Thames.

Curran, J. (1990) Rethinking Economic Structure: Exploring the Role of the Small Firm and Self-Employment in the British Economy, *Work, Employment and Society*, Special Issue, May, pp 125–146.

Curran, J. (1993) TECs and Small Firms: Can TECs Reach The Small Firms Other Strategies Have Failed To Reach?, Paper presented to the All Party Social Science and Policy Group, House of Commons, April.

Curran, J. and Blackburn, R. A. (1992) *Small Firms and Local Economic Networks: Relations Between Small and Large Firms in Two Localities*, Small Business Research Centre, Kingston Business School Occasional Paper Series, Kingston upon Thames.

Curran, J. and Burrows R. (1988) *Enterprise in Britain: A National Profile of Small Business Owners and the Self-Employed*, The Small Business Research Trust/Open University, London/Milton Keynes.

Curran, J. and Stanworth, J. (1983) Franchising in the Modern Economy – Towards a Theoretical Understanding, *International Small Business Journal*, 2, 1, 8–26, Autumn.

Curran, J. and Stanworth, J. (1986) Small Firms, Large Firms: Theoretical and Research Strategies for the Comparative Analysis of Small and Large Firms, in M. Scott, A. A. Gibbs, J. Lewis and T. Faulkner (eds.) *Small Firms: Researching Their Growth and Development*, Gower, Aldershot.

Curran, J., Blackburn, R. A. and Woods, A. (1991) *Profiles of the Small Enterprise In The Service Sector*, ESRC Centre for Research on Small Service Sector Enterprises, Kingston University.

Curran, J., Kitching, J., Abbott, B. and Mills, V. (1993a) *Employment and Employment Relations in The Small Service Sector Enterprise – A Report*, ESRC Centre on Small Service Sector Enterprises, Kingston Business School, Kingston University, Kingston upon Thames.

Curran, J., Jarvis, R., Blackburn, R. A. and Black, S. (1993b) Networks and Small firms: Constructs, Methodological Strategies and Some Findings, *International Small Business Journal*, 11, 2, 13–25.

Cutlers Company (1993) *Company of Cutlers in Hallamshire in the County of York*, Company of Cutlers, Sheffield.

Dabinett, G. and Ramsden, P. (1993) An urban policy for people: lessons from Sheffield, in R. Imrie and H. Thomas (eds.) *British Urban Policy and the Urban Development Corporations*, Paul Chapman, London.

Daly, M. (1990) The 1980s – A Decade of Growth and Enterprise, Data on VAT Registrations and Deregistrations, *Employment Gazette*, November, 553–565.

Daly, M. (1991) VAT Registrations and Deregistrations in 1990, *Employment Gazette*, November, 579–588.

Daly, M. and McCann, A. (1992) How Many Small Firms? *Employment Gazette*, February, 47–51.

Daly, M., Campbell, M., Robson, G. and Gallagher, C. (1991) Job Creation 1987–89: The Contributions of Small and Large Firms, *Employment Gazette*, November, 589–596.

Daniels, P. (1988) Producer Services and the Post Industrial Space Economy, in D. Massey and J. Allen (eds.) *Uneven Re-Development, Cities and Regions in Transition*, Hodder and Stoughton, London.

Deakin, N. and Edwards, J. (1993) *The Enterprise Culture and the Inner City*, Routledge, London.

DEED (1989a) *Sheffield Into the 1990s: Emerging Themes for the Economy, Labour Market and Training'* Department of Employment and Economic Development, Sheffield City Council, November.

DEED (1989b) *Manufacturing in Sheffield: A Future for Engineering*, Department of Employment and Economic Development Engineering Working Party, Sheffield City Council, August.

Dennis, N., Henriques, F. and Slaughter, C. (1956) *Coal is Our Life*, Eyre and Spottiswoode, London.

Department of Employment (1987) *Census of Employment, NOMIS*, London.

Department of Trade and Industry (1991) *BS 5750/ISO 9000 A Positive Contribution to Better Business*, Department of Trade and Industry, London.

Department of Trade and Industry (1993) *Late Payment of Bills, A Consultative Document*, Department of Trade and Industry, London.

Dickens, P. (1988) *One Nation? Social Change and the Politics of Locality*, Pluto Press, London.

Dickson, K., Smith, S. and Woods, A. (1994) *Technological Innovation and Co-operation in Selected Service Sectors*, ESRC Centre for Research on Small Service Sector Enterprises, Kingston University, Kingston upon Thames.

Doncaster Metropolitan Council/NOMIS, 1989 Fact Sheet, Issue 3:10/89, Doncaster Metropolitan Council, Doncaster.

Drummond, H. (1992) *The Quality Movement*, McGraw Hill, London.

Duncan, S. S. and Goodwin, M. (1985) Local Economic Policies: Local Regeneration or Political Mobilisation, *Local Government Studies*, 11, 75–96.

Duncan, S. S. and Goodwin, M. (1988) *The Local State and Uneven Development*, Basil Blackwell, Oxford.

Eccles, R. G. (1981) The Quasifirm in the Construction Industry, *Journal of Economic Behaviour and Organization*, 2, 4, 335–357.

Edmonds, T. (1986) *Small Firms, Background Paper*, House of Commons Library, Research Division, June, London.

Emmerich, M. and Peck, J. (1992) *Reforming the TECs, Towards a New Training Strategy*, Centre for Local Economic Strategies, Manchester.

Employment Department (1989) *Small Firms in Britain 1989*, Employment Department, London.

Employment Department (1991) *Small Firms in Britain 1991*, Employment Department, London.

Employment Department (1992) *Small Firms in Britain Report 1992*, Employment Department/HMSO, London.

Employment Gazette (1991) Unemployment Area Statistics, Table 2.4, May, Department of Employment, London.

Eurostat (1992) *Enterprises in Europe*, Second Report, European Commission, Luxembourg.

Felstead, A. (1991) Facing up to the Fragility of 'Minding Your Own Business' as a Franchisee, in J. Curran, and R. A. Blackburn (eds.) *Paths of Enterprise, the Future of the Small Business*, Routledge, London.

Forum of Private Business (1992) *Small Businesses and Their Banks*, Forum of Private Business, Knutsford, Cheshire.

Frankenberg, R. (1957) *Village on the Border*, Cohen and West, London.

Friedman, A. L. (1977) *Industry and Labour, Class Struggle at Work and Monopoly Capitalism*, Macmillan Press, London.

Friedman, D. (1988) *The Misunderstood Miracle: Industrial Development and Political Change in Japan*, Cornell University Press, Ithaca, New York.

Gabriel, Y. (1988) *Working Lives in Catering*, Routledge, London.

Garraghan, P. and Stewart, P. (1992) *The Nissan Enigma*, Mansell, London.

Goddard, J. and Coombes, R. (1987) *The North–South Divide: Local Perspectives*, Centre for Urban and Regional Studies, University of Newcastle upon Tyne.

Goodman, E., Bamford, J. and Gaynor, P. (1989) *Small Firms and Industrial Districts in Italy*, Routledge, London.

Goodwin, M. (1989) The Policies of Locality, in A. Cochrane and J. Anderson (eds.) *Politics in Transition'*, Sage, London.

Goss, D. (1991) *Small Business and Society*, Routledge, London.

Graham, N., Beatson, M. and Wells, W. (1989) 1977 to 1987: A Decade of Service, *Employment Gazette*, January, 45–54.

Granovetter, M. (1985) Economic Action and Social Structure: The Problem of Embeddedness, *American Journal of Sociology*, 91, 3, 481–510.

Greater London Council Economic Policy Group (1983) *Smaller Firms and the London Industrial Strategy*, Greater London Council, London.

Greater London Council (1985) *The London Industrial Strategy*, Greater London Council, London.

Gripaios, P., Bishop, P., Gripaios, R. and Herbert, C. (1989) High Technology Industry in a Peripheral Area: The Case of Plymouth, *Regional Studies*, 23, 2, 151–159.

Guildford Borough Council (1993) Information Provided by Policy and Design Department, Guildford Borough Council, Surrey.

Hall, P. (1992) *Urban and Regional Planning*, 2nd Edition, Routledge, London.

Hankinson, A. (1985) *Pricing Behaviour*, Monograph, Department of Business Management, Dorset Institute, Poole, Dorset.

Hankinson, A. (1986) *Output Determination. A Study of Output Determination of Dorset-Hampshire Small Engineering Firms 1983–1986*, Department of Business Management, Dorset Institute, Poole, Dorset.

Hardman, H. (1973) *The Dispersal of Government Work From London*. HMSO, London.

Harloe, M., Pickvance, C. G. and Urry, J. (eds.) (1990) *Place, Policy and Politics, Do Localities Matter*, Unwin Hyman, London.

Harrison, B. (1992) Industrial Districts: Old Wine in New Bottles? *Regional Studies*, 26, 5, 469–483.

Hausner, V. (ed.) (1986) *Urban Economic Change*, Oxford University Press, Oxford.

Henderson, J. (1991) *The Globalisation of High Technology Production*, Routledge, London.

Hirst, P. and Zeitlin, J. (1989) *Reversing Industrial Decline? Industrial Structure and Policy in Britain and Her Competitors*, Berg, Oxford.

Holliday, R. (1993) Small firms and the Organisation of Production, unpublished PhD thesis, Business School, Staffordshire University.

Holmes, J. (1986) The Organization and Locational Structure of Production Subcontracting in A. J. Scott and M. Storper (eds.) *Production, Work, Territory, The Geographical Anatomy of Industrial Capitalism*, Allen and Unwin, Boston.

Holton, R. J. (1992) *Economy and Society*, Routledge, London.

Howe, W. S. (ed.) (1991) *Retailing Management*, Macmillan, London.

Hughes, A. (1992) Big Business, Small Business and the Enterprise Culture in J. Mitchie (ed.) *The Economic Legacy 1979–1992'*, Academic Press, London.

Hughes, J. (1990) *The Philosophy of Social Research*, second edition, Longman, London.

Imrie, R. F. (1986) Work Decentralisation From Large to Small Firms: A Preliminary Analysis of Subcontracting, *Environment and Planning A*, 18, 949–965.

Imrie, R. and Morris, J. L. (1988) Large Firm–Small Firm Links: The changing Nature of Sub-Contracting in Wales', Paper Presented to 11th National Small Firms Policy and Research Conference, University College Cardiff, Wales.

Imrie, R. and Thomas, H. (eds.) (1993) *British Urban Policy and the Urban Development Corporations*, Paul Chapman, London.

Islington Borough Council (1993) Information provided by Planning Department, Islington Borough Council, London.

Jennings, K. (1991) How to Make Your Start-Up Stay Up, *The Observer*, 17 March.

Jowell, R., Witherspoon, S. and Brook, L. (1988) *British Social Attitudes, The 5th Report*, Gower, Aldershot.

Joyce, P. (1980) *Work, Society and Politics: the Culture of the Factory in Late Victorian England*, Harvester, Brighton.

Keeble, D., Bryson, J., and Wood, P. (1991) Entrepreneurship and Flexibility in Business Services: The Rise of Small Management Consultancy Firms in the United Kingdom, Paper Presented at the National Small Firms Policy and Research Conference, Blackpool, November.

Keeble, D., Bryson, J. and Wood, P. (1993) The Rise and Fall of Small Service Firms in the United Kingdom, *International Small Business Journal*, 11, 1, 11–22.

Keeble, D., Tyler, P., Broom, G. and Lewis, J. (1992) *Business Success in the Countryside, The Performance of Rural Enterprise*, HMSO, London.

Keeble, D. and Wever, E. (1986) (eds.) *New Firms and Regional Development in Europe*, Croom Helm, Beckenham.

Kingston Borough Council (1993) Data provided by the Planning Department, July.

Kirby D. (1986) The Small Retailer, in J. Curran, J. Stanworth and D. Watkins (1986) (eds.) *The Survival of The Small Firm, Volume 1*, Gower, Aldershot.

Labour Force Survey (1993) *Quarterly Bulletin No 4*, June, Employment Department, London.

Labour Market and Skills Assessment 1990/1991 Barnsley and Doncaster (nd) Leeds, Training Agency.

Labour Research (1993) Transfer Rights Victory for Unions, *Labour Research*, 82, 6, 23.

Lane, T. and Roberts, K. (1971) *Strike at Pilkingtons*, Fontana, London.

Lash, S. and Urry, J. (1987) *The End of Organized Capitalism*, Polity Press, Cambridge.

Lazonick, W. (1981) Competition, Specialization and Industrial Decline, *The Journal of Economic History*, XLI, 3, 31–38.

Lee, D. and Newby, H. (1983) *The Problem of Sociology, An Introduction to the Discipline*, Hutchinson, London.

Lloyd, M. and Newlands, D. (1988) The Growth Coalition and Urban Economic Development, *Local Economy*, 3, 31–9.

Lloyd, T. (1986) *Dinosaur and Co., Studies in Corporate Evolution*, Penguin Books, Harmondsworth.

Lyons, B. R. (1991a) Contractability and Underinvestment by Subcontractors: A Transactions Cost Approach, mimeo, University of East Anglia, Norwich.

Lyons, B. R. (1991b) Specialised Technology, Economies of Scale and the Make-Buy Decision: Evidence from UK Engineering, mimeo, University of East Anglia, Norwich.

Lyons, B. R. and Bailey, S. (1991) Small Subcontractors in UK Engineering: Competitiveness, Dependence and Problems, mimeo, University of East Anglia, Norwich.

MacMillan, K., Curran, J., Downing, S. J. and Turner, I. D. (1989) *Consultation With Small Business*, Department of Employment Research Paper No. 66, Department of Employment, London.

Mair, A.(1993) New Growth Poles? Just-in-time Manufacturing and Local Economic Development Strategy, *Regional Studies*, 27, 3, 207–222.

Mair, A., Florida, R. and Kenney, M. (1988) The New Geography of Automobile Production: Japanese in North America, *Economic Geography*, 64, 353–373.

Malecki, E. J. and Bradbury, S. L. (1992) R & D Facilities and Professional Labour: Labour Force Dynamics in High Technology, *Regional Studies*, 26, 2, 123–126.

Marsh, D. (1992) *The New Politics of Trade Unionism*, Macmillan, London.

Marshall, A. (1920) *Principles of Economics* (8th edition), Macmillan, London.

Marshall, A. (1932) *Industry and Labour*, Macmillan, London

Marshall, J. (1989) Corporate Reorganisation and the Geography of Services: Evidence from the Motor Vehicle Aftermarket in the West Midlands Region of the UK, *Regional Studies*, 23, 2, 139–150.

Marshall, M. (1987) *Long Waves of Regional Development*, Macmillan, London.

Martin, R. (1988) The Political Economy of Britain's North South Divide, *Transactions of the Institute of British Geographers*, 13, 389–418.

Martin, R. and Tyler, P. (1992) The Regional Legacy in J. Mitchie (ed.) *The Economic Legacy 1979–1992*, Academic Press, London.

Marx, T. G. (1980) Distribution Efficiency in Franchising, *MSU Business Topics*, 28, 1, 5–14.

Massey, D. (1984) *Spatial Divisions of Labour: Social Structures and the Geography of Production*, Macmillan, London.

Massey, D. and Allen, J. (eds.) (1988) *Uneven Re-Development, Cities and Region in Transition*, Hodder and Stoughton, Denton Green, Kent.

Massey, D., Quintas, P. and Wield, D. (1992) *High Tech Fantasies, Science Parks in Society, Science and Space*, Routledge, London.

Mawson, J. and Miller, D. (1986) Interventionist Approaches in Local Employment and Economic Development: The Experiences of Labour Local Authorities, in V. Hausner (ed.) *Critical Issues in Urban Development*, Vol 1, Clarendon Press, Oxford.

May, T. and McHugh, J. (1991) Government and Small Business in Britain, paper presented to ESRC Small Business Initiative, Warwick, April.

McCann, A. (1993) The UK Enterprise Population 1979–1991, *The NatWest Review of Small Business Trends*, 3, 1, 5–13.

McDowell, L. (1989) Out of Work in M. Bale, F. Gray and L. McDowell (eds.) *The Transformation of Britain, Contemporary Social and Economic Change*, Fontana, London.

Meager, N. (1991) *Self-Employment in the UK'*, IMS Report No 205, Institute of Manpower Studies, University of Sussex, Brighton.

Midland Bank (1993a) Information Provided by Midland Bank to the Small Business Research Centre.

Midland Bank (1993b) Enterprise Monitor – Quarter 1, *Midland Bank Research and Analysis Unit*, Marketing Department, May, Sheffield.

Milne, S. (1991) The UK Whiteware Industry: Fordism, Flexibility or Somewhere in Between?, *Regional Studies*, 25, 3, 239–254.

Mitchell, J. C. (1973) Networks, Norms and Institutions, in J. Boissevain and J. Mitchell, *Network Analysis: Studies in Human Interaction*, Mouton, The Hague.

Mitsui, I. (1992) The Importance of the Subcontracting Relationship: the Development of Subcontracting Management in Japan and its Future, mimeo, Kamazawa University, Tokyo.

Mogey, J. M. (1956) *Family and Neighbourhood*, Oxford University Press, Oxford.

Moore, B. (1992) Taking on the Inner Cities, in J. Mitchie (ed.) *The Economic Legacy 1979–1992*, Academic Press, London.

Murray, R. (1985) Beneath Britain, *Marxism Today*, October.

Murray, R. (1989) Fordism and Post Fordism, in S. Hall and M. Jaques (eds.) *New Times, The Changing Face of Politics in the 1990s*, Lawrence and Wishart, London.

Nash, T. (1991) Late Payers, the End of the Line?, *The Director*, April, 39–44.

National Economic Development Office (1991a) *Electronics: Strengthening the United Kingdom's Technological Base*, NEDO, London.

National Economic Development Office (1991b) *The Experience of Nissan Suppliers: Lessons for the UK Engineering Industry*, NEDO, London.

Newby, H. (1977) *The Deferential Worker*, Allen Lane, London.

Newby, H. (1979) *Green and Pleasant Land?*, Hutchinson, London.

Newby, H. (1988) *The Countryside in Question*, Hutchinson, London.

Newby, H., Bell, C., Rose, D. and Saunders, P. (1978) *Property, Paternalism and Power*, Hutchinson, London.

Nolan, P. and O'Donnell, K. (1990) Restructuring the Politics of Industrial Renewal, in A. Pollert (ed.) *A Farewell to Flexibility*, Routledge, London.

Norris, K. (1984) Small Building Firms – Their Origins, Characteristics and Development Need, Paper Presented to the 7th Small Firms Policy and Research Conference, Trent Polytechnic, Nottingham, September.

North, J., Curran, J. and Blackburn, R. A. (1993) *Quality Standards and Small Firms: A Position Paper*, Kingston University Business School, Working Paper Series, Kingston upon Thames.

Oakey, R. (1984) *High Technology Small Firms*, Frances Pinter, London.

Oakey, R. (1991) Government Policy Towards High Technology, Small Firms Beyond the Year 2000, in J. Curran and R. A. Blackburn (eds.) *Paths of Enterprise, The Future of Small Business*, Routledge, London.

Oakey, R. and Rothwell, R. (1986) The Contribution of High Technology Small Firms to regional Employment Growth in A. Amin and J. B. Goddard (eds.) *Regional Industrial Change*, Unwin Hyman, London.

Oakey, R. P. and Cooper, S. Y .(1989) High Technology Industry, Agglomeration and the Potential for Peripherally Sited Small Firms, *Regional Studies*, 23, 4, 347–360.

Oakey, R., Rothwell, R. and Cooper, S. (1988) *The Management of Innovation in High Technology Small Firms*, Frances Pinter, London.

O'Farrell, P. N. and Hitchens, D. M. W. N. (1990) Producer Services and Regional Development. A Review of Some Major Conceptual Policy and Research Issues, *Environment and Planning*, A, 22, 1141–1154.

O'Reilly, J. (1992) Subcontracting in Banking: Some Evidence from Britain and France, Paper Presented to the Autonomy and Independent Workshop University of Nijmegen, November/December.

P A Cambridge Economic Consultants (1987) *An Evaluation of the Enterprise Zone Experiment*, Department of the Environment, London.

Parry, G., Moyser, G. and Day, N. (1992) *Political Participation and Democracy in Britain*, Cambridge University Press, Cambridge.

Penn, R. (1992) Contemporary Relationships Between Firms in a Classic Industrial Locality: Evidence from the Social Change and Economic Life Initiative, *Work, Employment and Society*, 6, 2, 209–227.

Penn, R. and Francis, B. (1992) Contemporary Subcontracting Relations Between Firms: Evidence from the Social Change and Economic Life Initiative in Britain, Paper Presented to the Autonomy and Independent Work Workshop, University of Nijmegen, November/December.

Penn, R., Scattergood, H. and Lilja, K. (1992) Flexibility and Employment Patterns in the Contemporary Paper Industry: a Comparative Analysis of Mills in Britain and Finland, *Industrial Relations Journal*, 23, 3, 214–223.

Pickvance, C. G. (1990) Introduction: the Institutional Context of Local Economic Development: Central Controls, Spatial Policies and Local Economic Policies, in M. Harloe, C. G. Pickvance and J. Urry (eds.) *Place, Policy and Politics, Do Localities Matter?*, Unwin Hyman, London.

Piore, M. and Sabel, C. (1984) *The Second Industrial Divide: Possibilities for Prosperity*, Basic Books, New York.

Pollert, A. (1988a) Dismantling Flexibility, *Capital and Class*, 24, Spring, 43–75.

Pollert, A. (1988b) The 'Flexible Firm': Fixation or Fact, *Work, Employment and Society*, 2, 3, 281–316.

Porter M. (1990) *The Competitive Advantage of Nations*, Macmillan, London.

Pyke, F. (1992) *Industrial Development Through Small-Firm Cooperation*, International Labour Office, Geneva.

Pyke, F., Becattini, G. and Sengenberger, W. (eds.) (1990) *Industrial Districts and Inter-firm Co-operation in Italy*, International Institute for Labour Studies, Geneva.

Rainnie, A. (1989) *Industrial Relations in Small Firms, Small Isn't Beautiful*, Routledge, London.

Rainnie, A. (1991) *Flexibility and Small Firms, Prospects for the 1990s*, Hatfield Polytechnic Business School Working Paper Series, Hertford.

Rainnie, A. (1992) Flexibility and Small Firms: Prospects for the 1990s, in P. Leighton and A. Felstead (eds.) *The New Entrepreneurs*, Kogan Page, London.

Richardson, B., Montanheiro, L., Ashcroft, J. and Nwanko, S. (1992) Marketing the TECs: Making the Connection, Paper presented to the 14th National Small Firms Policy and Research Conference, Southampton, November.

Richardson, H. W. (1976) *Regional and Urban Economics*, Pitman, London.

Roberts, P., Collis, C. and Noon, D. (1990) Local Economic Development in England and Wales: Successful Adaptation of Old Industrial Areas in Sedgefield, Nottingham and Swansea in W. B. Stöhr (ed.) *Global Challenge and Local Response*, Mansell, London.

Rogers, P. B. and Smith, C. R. (1977) The Local Authority's Role in Economic Development: the Tyne and Wear Act 1976, *Regional Studies*, 11, 153–163.

Rothwell, R. (1986) The Role of Small Firms in Technological Innovation, in J. Curran, J. Stanworth and D. Watkins (eds.) *The Survival of the Small Firm, Employment, Growth, Technology and Politics*, Vol 2, Gower, Aldershot.

Rural Development Commission (1988) *Suffolk Rural Development Area*, Rural Development Programme 1989–1990, Rural Development Commission, Ipswich.

Saunders, P. (1979) *Urban Politics, A Sociological Interpretation*, Penguin Books, Harmondsworth.

Savage, M. (1989) Spatial Differences in Modern Britain, in C. Hamnett, L. McDowell and P. Sarre (eds.) *The Changing Social Structure*, Sage, London.

Saxenian, A. (1985) Silicon Valley and Route 128: Regional Prototypes or Historic Exceptions, in M. Castells (ed.) *High Technology, Space and Society*, Sage, Beverley Hills.

Saxenian, A. (1990) Regional Networks and the resurgence of Silicon Valley, *Californian Management Review*, 33, 1, 89–112.

Sayer, A. (1992) *Method in Social Science*, 2nd edition, Routledge, London.

Scase, R. and Goffee, R. (1982) *The Entrepreneurial Middle Class*, Croom Helm, London.

Scase, R. and Goffee, R. (1987) *The Real World of the Small Business Owner*, 2nd edition, Croom Helm, London.

Scott, A. J. (1983) Industrial Organization and the Logic of Intra-Metropolitan Location II: A Case Study of the Printed Circuits Industry in the Greater Los Angeles Region, *Economic Geography*, 59, 4, 343–367.

Scott, A. J. and Kwok, E. C. (1989) Inter-Firm Subcontracting and Locational Agglomeration: A Case Study of the Printed Circuits Industry in California, *Regional Studies*, 23, 5, 405–416.

Scott, A. J. and Storper, M. (eds.) (1986) *Production, Work, Territory: The Geographical Anatomy of Industrial Capitalism*, Allen and Unwin, Boston.

Scott, M., Roberts, I., Holroyd, G. and Shawbridge, D. (1989) *Management and Industrial Relations in Small Firms*, Department of Employment Research Paper No 70, Department of Employment, London.

Scottish Office (The) (1993) *European Inter-Regional Economic Links: Conceptual Analysis and Literature Review*, The Scottish Office Industry Department and European Policies Research Centre, University of Strathclyde, November, Edinburgh.

Segal Quince and Partners (1985) *The Cambridge Phenomenon*, Segal Quince and Partners, Cambridge.

Shaw, K. (1993) The Development of a New Urban Corporatism: The Politics of Urban Regeneration in the North East of England, *Regional Studies*, 27, 3, 251–286.

Sheffield City Council (1990) *Sheffield Economic Bulletin*, December, No 1, Sheffield City Council, Department of Employment and Economic Development.

Sheffield City Council (1991) Sheffield Unemployment Bulletin, Department of Employment and Economic Development, Sheffield City Council, March.

Shutt, J. and Whittington, R. (1984) Large Firms and the Rise of Small Units, Paper Presented to the 7th National Small Firms Policy and Research Conference, Trent Polytechnic, Nottingham, September.

Skills and Enterprise Network (1993) *Skills and Training In Small Firms*, Skills and Enterprise Briefing, Employment Department, Nottingham.

Small Business Research Centre (1992) *The State of British Enterprise: Growth, Innovation and Competitive Advantage in Small and Medium-Sized Firms*, Small Business Research Centre, University of Cambridge, Cambridge.

Small Business Research Trust (1992) Quality Procedures: BS 5750, *NatWest Quarterly Survey of Small Business*, 8, 3, 18–22.

Smallbone, D., North, D. and Leigh, R. (1993) The Use of External Assistance by Mature SMEs in the UK: Some Policy Implications, *Entrepreneurship and Regional Development*, 5, 279–295.

Social Trends (1993) *Social Trends*, CSO, London.

Stacey, M. (1960) *Tradition and Change: A Study of Banbury*, Oxford University Press, Oxford.

Stacey, M. (1969) The Myth of Community Studies, *British Journal of Sociology*, XX, 2, 134–147.

Stacey, M., Batstone, E., Bell, C. and Murcott, A. (1975) *Power, Resistance and Change, A Second Study of Banbury*, Routledge and Kegan Paul, London.

Stanworth, J. and Curran, J. (1973) *Management Motivation in the Smaller Business*, Gower, Epping.

Stanworth, J. and Curran, J. (1986) Trends in Small Firm Industrial Relations and Their Implications for the Role of the Small Firm in Economic Restructuring in A. Amin and J. B. Goddard (eds.), *Technological Change, Industrial Restructuring and Regional Development*, Allen and Unwin, London.

Stanworth, J. and Gray, C. (1991) (eds.) *Bolton Twenty Years On*, Paul Chapman, London.

Storey D. J. (1994 Forthcoming) *Understanding The Small Business Sector*, Routledge, London.

Storey, D. J. and Johnson, S. (1987) *Job Generation and Labour Market Change*, Macmillan, Basingstoke.

Storey, D., Watson, R. and Wynarczyk, P. (1989) *Fast Growth Small Businesses, Case Studies of 40 Small Firms in North East England*, Department of Employment Research Paper No. 67, Department of Employment, London.

Szarka, J. (1990) Networking and Small Firms, *International Small Business Journal*, Volume 8, Number 2, 10–22.

Taylor, M. J. and Thrift, N. J. (1982) Industrial Linkage and the Segmented Economy: 1. Some Theoretical Proposals, *Environment and Planning A*, 14, 12, 1601–1613.

Thorburn, J. T. and Takashima, M. (1992) *Industrial Subcontracting in the UK and Japan*, Avebury, Aldershot.

Thorburn, J. T. and Takashima, M. (1993) Improving British Industrial Performance: Lessons from Japanese Subcontracting, *National Westminster Bank Quarterly Review*, February, 2–18.

Times 1000 (1992) *The Times 1000 1992–1993*, Times Books, London.

Training Agency (1989) *Training and Enterprise: Priorities for Action 1990/91 Labour Market Supplement, Yorkshire and Humberside*, Training Agency, Leeds.

Turner, G. (1964) *The Car Makers*, Penguin Books, Harmondsworth.

Turok, I. (1993) Inward Investment and Local Linkages: How Deeply Embedded is 'Silicon Glen'?, *Regional Studies*, 27, 5, 401–418.

Tym, R. and Partners (1984) *Monitoring Enterprise Zones Year Three Report*, Roger Tym and Partners and HMSO, London.

Wagner, C. (1987) *The Chocolate Conscience*, Chatto and Windus, London.

Wagstyl, S. (1993) Indians Key Into Market for Software, *Financial Times*, 17 February.

Wells, J. (1989) Uneven Development and De-Industrialisation in the UK Since 1979, in F. Green (ed.) *The Restructuring of the UK Economy*, Harvester Wheatsheaf, Hemel Hempstead.

West Midlands Economic Development Committee (1984) Combatting Economic Decline, *Economic Review No 1*, Birmingham.

Williamson, O. (1975) *Markets and Hierarchies: Analysis and Antitrust Implications*, The Free Press, New York.

Williamson, O. (1979) Transaction Cost Economics: The Government of Contractual Relations, *Journal of Law and Economics*, 22, 233–261.

Wilson, H. (1979) *The Financing of Small Firms*, Report of the Committee to Review the Functioning of Financial Institutions, HMSO, Cmnd 7503, London.

Winterton, R. and Winterton, J. (1990) Enterprise Culture and the Restructuring of the UK Clothing Industry, Paper presented to Employment Relations in the Enterprise Culture Conference, Cardiff Business School, September.

Wood, D. and Smith, P. (1988) *Employers' Labour Use Strategies, First Report on the 1987 Survey*, Department of Employment Research Paper No 63, Department of Employment, London.

Wood, P. A. (1991) Flexible Accumulation and the Rise of Business Services, *Transactions, Institute of British Geographers*, NS, 16, 160–172.

Woods A., Blackburn, R. A. and Curran, J. (1993) *A Longitudinal Study of Small Enterprises in the Service Sector, 1993 Survey Report*, ESRC Centre for Research on Small Service Sector Enterprises, Kingston University.

APPENDIX

Table A1 Year of Start-up, Employment and Turnover of the Small Businesses Surveyed

	Year of Start-Up				
	Pre 1970	1970–1979	1980–1984	1985 and after	Total
			%		
Printing	30.0	10.0	20.0	40.0	30
Electronics	6.7	26.7	33.3	33.3	30
Advertising Marketing and Design	3.8	17.3	30.8	48.1	52
Computer Services	2.0	5.9	29.4	62.7	51
Employment Secretarial & Training	4.1	16.3	10.2	69.4	49
Free Houses Wine Bars & Restaurants	6.4	17.0	21.3	55.3	47
Garages & Vehicle Repairers	26.0	26.0	26.0	22.0	50
Plant and Equipment Hire	40.8	22.4	12.2	24.5	49
Video and Leisure	6.1	10.2	36.7	46.9	49
All	12.7	16.4	23.9	47.0	407

Notes: Percentages may not add to 100 due to rounding. Full information is not available for three firms.

Table A2 Employment Size of Surveyed Small Businesses

	Number of Employees				
	Less than 5	5–9	10–19 %	20 or more	All
Printing	53.3	23.3	23.3	6.7	30
Electronics	40.0	20.0	20.0	20.0	30
Advertising Marketing and Design	47.1	21.6	25.5	5.9	51
Computer Services	51.0	19.6	23.5	5.9	51
Employment Secretarial & Training	60.4	22.9	12.5	4.2	48
Free Houses Wine Bars & Restaurants	22.0	48.0	18.0	12.0	50
Garages & Vehicle Repairers	61.2	24.8	10.2	4.1	49
Plant and Equipment Hire	33.3	29.2	18.8	18.8	48
Video and Leisure	67.4	19.6	13.0	–	46
All	48.7	26.5	17.5	7.3	403

Notes: Percentages may not add to 100 due to rounding. Full information is not available for seven firms. Figures exclude owner-managers or directors.

Table A3 Turnover of Surveyed Businesses

	Up to £49,999	£50,000–£99,999	£100,000–£499,999 %	£500,000 and over	Total
Printing	10.3	27.6	44.8	17.2	29
Electronics	6.7	16.7	50.0	26.7	30
Advertising Marketing and Design	6.0	8.0	48.0	38.0	50
Computer Services	12.0	10.0	50.0	28.0	' 50
Employment Secretarial & Training	22.2	20.0	44.5	13.3	45
Free Houses Wine Bars & Restaurants	8.7	19.6	58.7	13.0	46
Garages & Vehicle Repairers	17.0	25.8	36.3	21.3	47
Plant and Equipment Hire	10.9	15.2	41.3	32.6	46
Video and Leisure	22.2	46.7	22.2	8.9	45
All	13.1	20.6	43.8	22.2	388

Notes: 22 respondents were unable to answer the question because their firm was too new or the information was classified as confidential. Figures in Advertising, Marketing and Design require careful interpretation because of the inclusion of 'billings' in the calculation of turnover (See Curran et al., 1991: Table 5).

Table A4 Year of Start-Up of the Small Enterprise in Electronics and Printing in Sheffield and Kingston

| | Kingston | | Sheffield | | |
	Printing %	Electronics %	Printing %	Electronics %	All %
Pre-1970	40.0	6.7	20.0	6.7	18.3
1970–1979	6.7	46.7	13.3	6.7	18.3
1980–1984	20.0	13.3	20.0	53.5	26.7
1985 and after	33.3	33.3	46.7	33.3	36.7
Total	**15**	**15**	**15**	**15**	**100**

SUBJECT INDEX

AUTHOR INDEX